Constructing Gender

Multicultural Perspectives in Working With Women

MARIA JULIA

Editor
Ohio State University

Brooks/Cole
Thomson Learning™

Australia • Canada • Mexico • Singapore • Spain
United Kingdom • United States

Senior Acquisitions Editor: *Lisa Gebo*
Assistant Editor: *Susan Wilson*
Editorial Assistant: *JoAnne von Zastrow*
Marketing Manager: *Caroline Concilla*
Signing Representative: *Dan Silverburg*
Project Editor: *Cathy Linberg*
Print Buyer: *April Reynolds*

Permissions Editor: *Joohee Lee*
Production Service: *Donna King, Progressive*
Copy Editor: *Progressive Publishing Alternatives*
Compositor: *Progressive Information Technologies*
Cover Designer: *Bill Stanton*
Cover Images: © *PhotoDisc*
Printer/Binder: *Webcom, Ltd.*

**Library of Congress Cataloging-in-
Publication Data**
Constructing gender: multicultural perspectives
  in working with women / Maria Julia, editor.
    p.   cm.
  Includes bibliographical references and index.
  ISBN 0-534-36473-x
  1. Social work with minority women—United
States. 2. Minority women—Services for—
United States. 3. Minority women—United
States. I. Julia, Maria.

HV1445 .C65 1999
364.83'089'00973—dc21   99-045865

For more information, contact
Wadsworth/Thomson Learning
10 Davis Drive
Belmont, CA 94002-3098
USA
http://www.wadsworth.com

International Headquarters
Thomson Learning
International Division
290 Harbor Drive, 2nd Floor
Stamford, CT 06902-7477
USA

UK/Europe/Middle East/South Africa
Thomson Learning
Berkshire House
168–173 High Holborn
London WC1V 7AA
United Kingdom

Asia
Thomson Learning
60 Albert Street #15-01
Albert Complex
Singapore 189969

Canada
Nelson Thomson Learning
1120 Birchmount Road
Toronto, Ontario M1K 5G4
Canada

This book is printed on acid-free recycled paper.

Brief Contents

Detailed Contents

Preface

PURPOSE

The authors of this book argue that the socialization of women differs among ethnic groups, and that this socialization process has a different effect on women in each of these groups. The authors go on to maintain that the lives of women need to be examined from a perspective that recognizes that the interactive effects of ethnicity and gender continue to be oppressive in American society, along with the additional but related effects of racism and sexism.

The contributing authors of this book intend to empower the reader with a better understanding and a more complete appreciation of the varieties, differences, and similarities of ethnicity-gender issues that exist across cultures from within some of the most prevalent ethnic groups in the United States. This volume has two primary aims and potential benefits. The book will help those interested in acquiring or strengthening their understanding of female gender issues that are shaped by ethnic constructions, and it will provide social scientists and human service practitioners with an ethnically-sensitive, feminist-oriented conceptual framework from which to analyze women's circumstances and to help improve them.

Knowledge and understanding of gender conceptions and perceptions provide the basis for a culturally competent model for interacting and working effectively with women. This book provides necessary knowledge for those engaged in learning about developing the necessary skills for approaching and interacting with women in multicultural settings and, in turn, the dynamics and techniques for multicultural practice. The ultimate goal is to provide a multi-professional text and resource that integrates a human-service orientation and that enhances competence in professional work with women from diverse cultural backgrounds.

RATIONALE

In the modern history of the United States, the socio-political context of the Civil Rights movement provided impetus to a reawakened awareness (or, in some cases, a new awareness) of the needs of sub cultural groups identified by ethnicity, race, religion, gender and so on. The women's liberation movement, and the advent of feminism, were among the forces that played a major role in opening a "niche where issues of gender, race, and ethnicity could be examined" (Comas-Díaz & Greene, 1994, p. 185).

With respect to the influence of ethnicity, in the decades since the "revolutionary 1960s" there has been increased realization that ethnic minorities constitute the fastest growing population in the United States, a demographic trend that contributes to an "ascendancy of cultural pluralism" (Comas-Díaz & Greene, 1994, p. 3). Demographics of the country continue to change rapidly, and the prognosis is for a third of the population of the United States to be identified as a racial or ethnic minority by the year 2010 (Jones, 1990). This increase in cultural diversity has implications for how we increase not only the majority population's awareness and appreciation of cultural differences, but the awareness and appreciation of helping professionals as well.

In addition to the influence of culture on the lives of each of us, there is growing research and recognition that gender evaluation and role specificity are culturally patterned. An understanding of the interactions of culture, social role, and ethnicity in society has become central for understanding women. "Biological gender exerts a powerful cultural influence on behavior, with men and women displaying distinct socially learned beliefs, attitudes, and values. The double standard that describes different social rules and expectations for men and women is a clear illustration of the cultural influence of gender" (Kreps & Kunimoto, 1994, p. 2). Operating in the other direction as well, are expectations and behaviors based on cultural influences and conceptions of gender, and interpretations of reality based on cultural expectations, motivations, and interpretations.

Helping professionals are recognizing the need to acquire the knowledge and competencies to work with and meet the challenges of such a diverse population as we experience in the United States. The failure to recognize the combined influence and impact of ethnicity and gender can seriously compromise the effectiveness of gaining an understanding of women in American society and any attempt at providing gender-sensitive services to women in areas such as health care or social services.

Competent professional practice involves ethnocultural knowledge, understanding, and appreciation of cultural values and beliefs of the various groups. Providing professional services is frequently ineffective because of lack of awareness, sensitivity, knowledge or understanding of cultural variables and the implications that these variables have on shaping professional intervention. Understanding the cultural values, attitudes, norms, beliefs, dynamics and behavior of women increases the potential success in the process of interacting and working with women. By pursuing cultural understanding, human service professionals can begin to overcome the cultural barriers that interfere with and affect successful communication and relationships in the helping process and in the responsiveness of the service delivery system to culture and gender, as well as in their ability to build a true sense of community in American society. This book is aimed in its own modest way at helping facilitate these processes.

PLAN AND STRATEGY

There is both a gender strategy and an ethnic strategy in the plan and design of this book. As Locke indicates in *Increasing Multicultural Understanding* (1992), we must ask the culturally different to write their own stories (p. xii). Culturally diverse individuals "should be the primary source of information about their situation, condition, or direction (and) any efforts directed at identifying, developing, or evaluating information related to the culturally diverse should involve individuals from the specific population[s]" (p. 159). Unless a special effort is directed at including ethnically diverse female voices, American society will continue to perpetuate a male-dominated exclusionary framework.

In an attempt to overcome a monocultural, ethnocentric focus, each chapter is written by a different woman who is indigenous to the ethnic group about which she writes. The authors' insights, descriptions, and analysis of their culture offers academicians, students, and helping professionals the opportunity to hear the female perspectives—the voices of women—and to learn from firsthand knowledge grounded in experiences that reflect the reality of the writers and their ethnic groups. The contributors also bring to the book a variety of professional orientations—anthropology, home economics, human ecology, nursing, social work, and sociology—which adds a multidisciplinary perspective to this multicultural work.

The book is divided into ten chapters. The first chapter introduces the conceptual and theoretical framework, the eight chapters that follow address different cultural groups, and the last is a concluding chapter. The chapters are organized according to key cultural variables essential in understanding female members of these groups—major historical themes, overviews of the group patterns of acculturation and assimilation, as well as typical values, traditions, beliefs, and day-to-day life practices.

The authors' information and observations are addressed within the conceptual and experiential framework of each particular culture. Each author—who is a self-identified member of the group about which she writes[1]—addresses the characteristics within the ethnic group, as well as the major in-group differences. Each contributor also identifies her particular identity within the group as a potential bias in making any generalizations about the group as a whole.

ORGANIZATION

The introductory chapter addresses the basic concepts of culture, ethnicity, and gender, and their relevance to the book's thrust and goal. Chapter one describes and applies systems theory as the theoretical model—a holistic view—which provides the organizing framework of this work.

The concluding chapter summarizes the reality of women as a reflection of the confluence of gender, race, and ethnicity, as well as the contextual variables of historical influences and sociopolitical forces. These variables are presented as simultaneous and interacting systems of relationships and meanings that are part of the experience that affects each of the groups.

Each of the remaining chapters presents a picture of the traditional and evolving socialization of females and cultural perceptions of women's roles in a particular ethnic group in the American society. Moreover, each chapter provides concrete and practical information about ethnic group variables. This specificity is provided in order to heighten cultural awareness and sensitize readers so that they may build a knowledge base and develop a cultural understanding that will enable them to work competently and confidently with women in a multicultural society.

Each author follows an established organizational and conceptual framework in providing a model for examining ethnic diversity and gender. The outline guides the authors to consider the relevant cultural variables. However, the weighted emphasis that the individual authors place on selected elements of the culture and their differing approaches to the common framework reflect the cultural significance and relevance of the variables to each group as viewed by the author of the chapter. Consequently, any perceived unevenness in the chapters is considered an asset, not a weakness of the book, as it will highlight the uniqueness of the cultures and underscore our purpose in exploring the diversity. In addition, there are sensitive topics that are difficult, if not impossible, to address in some cultures. The contributors develop these topics within the constraints posed by the cultural norms and values and within the framework of respect called for by the ethnic group. The outline at the end of this preface describes the major headings, concepts, and themes addressed in the chapters.

IN SUMMARY

This book does not attempt to be exhaustively inclusive of all ethnic groups present in the United States, nor does it attempt to address every aspect of the selected groups. The book is to serve as a springboard to expand understanding of cultural differences and to build on the strength of developing this understanding from the experiences of women in different ethnic groups. The idea is to promote and facilitate competency in daily encounters with ethnic women and to create a level of sensitivity and understanding of differences that will preserve and transcend the differences in cultural groups by bridging gaps of communication and relationships.

The multicultural and gender-focused content of the book and its generic approach makes it relevant for several disciplines, including helping professions, academics, researchers, students, and those with interest in and concern for women and their ethnic diversity. The book may be utilized with students and professionals in settings such as social work, psychology, health care education, law, theology/pastoral care, and others. In addition, the book will be a valuable resource and professional reference for practicing members of the helping professions.

Gender and ethnicity are not easy terms to define or easy subjects to study. However, as the literature indicates, they are concepts which must be recognized by the helping professional who wants to understand the significant impact that occurs at the intersection of gender and ethnicity.

CONTENTS

The following outline describes the major headings, concepts, and themes addressed in the chapters.

Introduction

Group Profile (overview)
Who are we? (categorization)
Where do we come from? (group
composition)
Historical background/where do we
come from? (reasons to be here
are political, socio–economic,
etc.); i.e., what triggered
migration to U.S.
Numbers and other demographics
(how many are we)
General notions about how we are
different/similar from each other
Issues/patterns of acculturation and
assimilation
Usage of language (communication
barriers)

Women
Socio–demographic/economic
characteristics
Is there a gender difference in
migration patterns to or within
the U.S.?
General perception/conception of
women within the culture
Gender/self-identity
Expectations of and from women
Traditional coping strategies
Roles

Culture
Roots
Language
Values and beliefs
Attitudes about women
Religion
Traditions ("unspoken rules");
customs
Laws/policies (including
"unwritten")
Social control/cultural norms
Diversity within the cultural group
Myths
Variations as a function of
generation

Gender Issues
Position/status in hierarchy of
society (social mobility)
Position within family structure
(roles)
Communication lines
Religious influence/spirituality
Opportunities for women
Education/higher education
Work/working conditions
Employment/income/credit/
occupational disparities
Participation
Political life/right/interest to vote
Groups (women or other)
Organizations
Positions of power
Decision making
power/opportunities
Leadership roles
Family life
Division of labor, housework, care-
taking roles (children and elderly)
Sexual activity, pregnancy, childbirth,
birth control
Fertility
Marriage customs and patterns
Motherhood and single mothers
Adolescents
Elderly
Female-headed family
Child (daughters) rearing practices
Support systems (traditional,
nontraditional)
Social activities/recreation

Problems
Violence/domestic violence
Lack of access to
contraception/abortion
Abuse/incest
Divorce
Adultery
Clitorectomy
Dowries

Effects of war
Intergenerational conflict
Matriarchy
Menstruation
Mental and physical health (drug
   and alcohol abuse)
Physical appearance
Premarital sex
Sexual identity/preferences
Virginity/virtue
Cultural Barriers in Accessing Women
   Segregation
   Myths/stereotypes

Morality
Disability
Internalization of culturally dictated
   roles/socialization
Suggestions for Working with Women in
   this Group
Women's Movements (chiefly related to the
   group)
Glossary (when applicable)
Suggested Readings

REFERENCES

Comas-Diaz, L., & Greene, B. (1994). *Women of Color: Integrating Ethnic and Gender Identities in Psychotherapy.* New York: The Guilford Press.

Jones, W. (1990). Perspectives on Ethnicity. *New Directions for Student Services, 51,* 59–72.

Locke, D. (1992). *Increasing Multicultural Understanding: A Comprehensive Model.* Newbury Park, CA: Sage.

Kreps, G., & Kunimoto, E. (1994). *Effective Communication in Multicultural Settings.* Thousand Oaks, CA: Sage.

ENDNOTES

1. The exceptions to this requirement are the authors of the chapters on the Amish and Southeast Asians. See chapters 3 and 9 for explanations on why women not indigenous to these groups wrote the chapters, and the cultural competence of the women who wrote them.

Acknowledgments

This book is the product of the collaboration of many individuals. I would like to express my appreciation to a number of persons who reviewed the manuscript at various stages of its development, making a significant contribution with their critical review: Diane Haslett, University of Maine; Patricia Kerstner, University of Phoenix; Carol Massat, University of Illinois, Chicago; Katherine Shank (student reviewer); Althea Truiit, Benedict College; Maria Vidal de Haymes, Loyola University of Chicago, Water Tower Campus; Evelyn Smith Williams, University of North Carolina, Chapel Hill. In particular, my gratitude to Lisa Gebo, Susan Wilson, JoAnne von Zastrow, Cathy Linberg, April Reynolds, and Joohee Lee for their continuing support and practical assistance.

On a personal note, I wish to express my gratefulness to Jim for his continued love, support, and encouragement. My indebtedness to my mother for her challenging messages on how one views gender, full of love.

Biographical Sketches of Authors

MARIA C. JULIA

Maria Julia is an Associate Professor at the Ohio State University College of Social Work, where she also received her doctorate. Previous to joining the OSU faculty, she served as a social work consultant for both the Ohio and Puerto Rico health departments. Dr. Julia is actively involved in over a dozen professional and citizens' task forces, committees, and boards, where she volunteers her time. She provides volunteer professional services to various state, national, and international organizations as well. All of these professional activities have provided much of the data and experiences for her numerous presentations and publications. Her interest in women's roles and cultures has gradually expanded into issues of women in international social development.

HILDA BURGOS-OCASIO

Hilda Burgos-Ocasio is a Ph.D. graduate from the Ohio State University, College of Social Work. She was born and raised in Puerto Rico and received her masters degree in social work from St. Louis University. She has extensive professional experience in the area of child abuse and neglect, especially with Hispanic families. Dr. Burgos-Ocasio's current research is in the area of maternal substance abuse and child drug exposure.

KAREN V. HARPER

Karen V. Harper is professor of social work in the School of Social Work and Public Administration at West Virginia University. She is Special Assistant in WVU's Eberly College of Arts and Sciences for developing distance education. She has masters degrees in social work and in public administration, and a doctoral degree in social work from the Ohio State University where she also served as a member of the faculty. She has taught in social work practice, child welfare, human behavior and administration, and managed numerous funded projects focusing on the welfare of children and families. Dr. Harper is involved in numerous board and committees where she volunteers time to address issues in social service delivery and development for rural families and children. Her numerous presentations and publications reflect her work with children and families and women in administration and higher education. She continues to focus her efforts in child welfare, mentoring, and distance learning opportunities for families and communities at the edge of welfare reform.

ANAHID DER VARTANIAN KULWICKI

Dr. Kulwicki has a B.S. in Nursing from the American University of Beirut, an M.S.N. and Doctorate degree in nursing from Indiana University, Indianapolis, Indiana. Dr. Kulwicki is an Associate professor of Nursing at Oakland University School of Nursing. She has served on several state committees in Michigan and is a community advocate for Arab American health care needs in Michigan. She has testified on several U.S. congressional and senatorial hearings on issues of providing health care services to Arab Americans in the areas of AIDS, cardiovascular diseases, diabetes, smoking cessation programs, and teen health. She is the Co-chair of the International Academy of Nursing, is on the Governor's Advisory Council on Minority Health, and was the past president of the Coalition on Diabetes Education and Minority Health. Dr. Kulwicki has conducted research and published in the areas of AIDS, smoking behavior among Arab Americans, and cross cultural issues. Her most recent research activities include a study on domestic violence among Arab Americans funded by the W.K. Kellogg Foundation and the Michigan Department of Public Health, and an assessment of cardiovascular risk factors among Jordan's population.

BEVERLY E. NEAL

Tribal affiliation—Miami Tribe of Oklahoma. Ms. Neal has a B.A. in sociology from Missouri Southern State College, and a M.A. in cultural anthropology from the Ohio State University. She is a Ph.D. Candidate in cultural anthropology at the Ohio State University. Her general area of research is on Native Americans who live or once lived in the Great Lakes Region, on the Miami, Shawnee, and Ottawa regions in particular, as well as on non-reservation Native Americans. More specific areas of her research interest include mortuary customs of the Miami Tribe, Indian in Northeastern Oklahoma, contemporary Native American women, and Indian Child Welfare. Ms. Neal is currently involved in a research project on the Indian Identity in Northeastern Oklahoma.

SHARON K. RATLIFF

Sharon K. Ratliff received her B.A. degree in Political Science from the University of Kentucky, her M.A. in Philosophy from San Diego State University, and her Ph.D. in Interdisciplinary Studies (Anthropology, Religious Studies, and Philosophy) from the Ohio State University. She is the author of Caring for Cambodian Americans: A Multidisciplinary Resource for the Helping Professions (Garland Publishing, 1997), and of several articles and chapters on cultural issues. Dr. Ratliff is an educator at Children's Hospital in Columbus, Ohio, and professor of World Religions and Philosophy at Franklin University. She is president of her own consulting firm, Culture Communications, Inc., and is founder and president of the Cambodian Humanitarian Foundation, which created and supports a small hospital in southeastern Cambodia.

DARYLE SPERO

Daryle Spero is a registered nurse, certified by the International Childbirth Education Association as a childbirth educator. She works as a perinatal educator at the Mount Sinai Medical Center of Cleveland, Ohio and at its affiliate, the Maternity Matters Centers. Her responsibilities include all aspects of the perinatal period—early pregnancy, labor and delivery, the postpartum period, infant care, and parenting classes. She previously worked as a R.N. in renal and gastrointestinal diseases at Mount Sinai Medical Center and at the Cleveland Clinic Foundation. She received her R.N. and her associate of arts and science degrees at the Cuyahoga Community College in Ohio.

GRETCHEN H. WALTMAN

Gretchen H. Waltman is a self-employed social work consultant and trainer, and an approved continuing education provider for the Ohio Counselor and Social Worker Board. She has a masters degree in social work from Ohio State University and has been an adjunct instructor for the university. Her clinical experience includes medical, family and children's services, and psychiatric settings. She is the author of published articles on rural social work, and on the Amish culture. Having lived among the Amish in Holmes and Tuscarawas Counties (Ohio) most of her life, Ms. Waltman has a unique opportunity to observe the Amish culture and lifestyle, and has business and personal relationships with Amish people. She conducts workshops to assist health care and human service professionals to understand and appreciate the strengths and special needs of the Amish population.

GRETA BERRY WINBUSH

Greta Berry Winbush, Ph.D., is currently an Assistant Professor at the Ohio State University's College of Social Work. She received a Ph.D. in human development and family studies and gerontology from the Pennsylvania State University. Graduate training was followed by a position as Executive Assistant to the Director at the Ohio Department of Aging and as Research Analyst with a California statewide family caregiver support program. She has conducted research and written publications on African American families, minority mental health issues, and community-based long-term care service delivery to older adults. Current research and practice interests include family and community caregiving, particularly to minority elders and minority mental health clients, and development of community caregiving support models.

AMY ZAHARLICK

Amy Zaharlick has a B.A. in sociology and philosophy, an M.A. in social relations (an interdisciplinary degree in sociology, anthropology, and social psychology), and a Ph.D. in anthropology and linguistics. She is currently an Associate Professor of Anthropology, and is working on her M.S.W. at Ohio State University. She is a cultural, linguistic, and applied anthropologist who has worked with American Indians, particularly Pueblo Indians, in the U.S. Southwest and, since the early 1980s, Southeast Asian refugees in the Midwest. Dr. Zaharlick has conducted ethnographic and linguistic research at Picuris Pueblo in New Mexico and with numerous other Southwest Indian groups and served for four years as an Assistant Professor and Director of the Native American Bilingual/Multicultural Teacher Education Program at the University of Albuquerque. Her Southeast Asian research interests focus upon the changing health beliefs and practices of Vietnamese, Lao, and Cambodian refugees, the fertility transition of the ethnic Lao, family violence and intergenerational conflicts with these refugee populations, maternal and child health issues, and mental health beliefs and practices. She is a past vice-chair of the Committee on Refugees and Immigrants of the American Anthropological Association and co-edited Volume III of the CORI series, Selected Papers on Refugee Issues. Dr. Zaharlick has published numerous articles on her American Indian and Southeast Asian refugee research, has served on the boards of many organizations concerned with ethnic minorities and refugee issues, and has acted as an advocate for American Indians and Southeast Asian refugees.

1

Ethnicity and Gender

Introduction of Concepts
and Theoretical Framework

M. JULIA

Gender and ethnicity are concepts not easily understood and even less easily defined. The concept of *gender* is rooted in the belief that the sexes—diametrically defined as "female" and "male"—are naturally distinct. The focus on this dichotomy often turns into self-fulfilling prophecies when sex-role socialization forces distinct and often unequal positions onto people, creating socially distinct genders. Sex-role socialization differs in historical and cultural contexts, resulting in different conceptions of appropriate gender behavior (Amott & Matthaei, 1991, pp. 13–16). As recent literature further describes the process, gender is institutionalized in the fabric of society and shapes material well-being, social identities, and group relationships (Chow, Wilkinson, & Zinn, 1996, p. ix).

Significantly, gender cannot be assumed to be the variable of most importance in all women's lives (Brown, in Brown & Root, 1990, p. 15). The female subject is characterized not only by her sex, but also by ethnicity, class, age, and sexual preference (Buikeman & Smelik, 1995, p. 180). Lorde (in Brown & Root, 1990), Walker (1993), Moraga and Anzaludua (1981), and Andersen and Collin (1992) have all pointed out that for women of color, the requirement that sexism be chosen as the ultimate oppression negates the validity of their internal realities.

Like gender, ethnicity is based on perceived physical differences and rationalized as natural or God-given. Whereas gender creates differences and inequality according to biological sex, ethnicity differentiates individuals according to skin color or other physical features (Amott & Matthaei, 1991, p. 17). In everyday life, people categorize themselves and each other on the basis of sex and ethnic membership and behave accordingly. Once institutionalized, these processes become the mechanisms that create and re-create the differences themselves, establishing the social arrangements that become seen as normal and natural and legitimizing ways of organizing social life and maintaining gender and ethnic order (Chow, Wilkinson, & Zinn, 1996, p. 332).

Ethnicity includes race but goes beyond it. It also encompasses the characteristics of people who share a common historical past, lifestyle, and value system. As Katlin (1982) indicates, not all ethnic groups embody all of these characteristics, although some share more than one (p. 168). Ethnicity is presumed to be a "constitutive element of life," not just a trait characteristic of individuals. Ethnicity is constructed through social interaction and manifested in the institutions of society, interpersonal interactions, and the minds and identities of those living in ethnically based social orders. Concepts and practices of ethnicity, usually justified by religion, vary over time, reflecting the politics, economics, and ideology of a particular era (Amott & Matthaei, 1991, p. 12). The notion of common ancestry and emergent cultural characteristics that we identify as ethnicity is often transmitted through messages from parents to children and from group to family.

Ethnicity is more than a *distinction* defined by race, religion, national origin, or geography. As used in this book, the concept of ethnicity will include culture. It involves conscious and unconscious processes that fulfill a deep psychological need for security, identity, and a sense of historical continuity (Katlin, 1982, p. 168). Ethnicity has the quality of the self-chosen appellation, and this aspect remains a central way of distinguishing it from race. The term ethnicity was once a favored term in social and cultural studies because it connoted a temporary state that eventually resulted in integration or assimilation. Cultural scientists viewed ethnicity in terms of individualism rather than relationship to a group, because the individual was not perceived to be as threatening or as potentially disruptive to the status quo as was the group (Gunew, in Gunew & Yeatman, 1993, p. 9).

It is clear that gender and ethnicity are not static qualities unaffected by the vagaries of history. Nor do they rest independently as natural or biological categories. As recent literature argues, gender and ethnicity are socially constructed concepts that arise in and are transformed by societies. Conversely, gender and ethnicity themselves transform societies (Amott & Matthaei, 1991, p. 11). Because hierarchies of ethnicity and gender are interlocking systems (Eitzen & Zinn, in Andersen & Collin, 1992, p. 181), gender is manifested differently according to ethnicity (Andersen & Collin, 1992). Thus, any attempt to understand women's experiences using gender alone will interfere with the construction of the broad-based movements experienced by women (Amott & Matthaei, 1991, p. 12).

Because ethnicity and gender are simultaneous, interconnected, interdetermining processes rather than separate systems, discussing them separately requires an artificial construction. Therefore, to determine what it means to be socialized in a particular culture, one *must* inquire about the salience of gender as an organizing principle and how cultural factors outside of the control of members of a particular group shape internal experience (Brown, in Brown & Root, 1990, pp. 13 and 17).

The norms, values, customs, and roles that are referred to as *culture* are handed down from one generation to another (Chow, in Chow, Wilkinson, & Zinn, 1996, p. xxv and p. 181), and may be defined as the collective sense making of members of social groups—the shared ways they make sense of reality. Culture also is often defined as accepted and patterned ways of behaving—the basis for individuals to become humanized (Kreps & Kunimoto, 1994, p. 1).

The purpose of this book is to provide a broader, more inclusive paradigm to illuminate the multiple facets of gender understanding. Furthermore, basic to a feminist transformation of knowledge is not only the discovery of the significance of gender, but also the incorporation of ethnicity as central to analysis. Therefore, this discussion examines the simultaneity of the dimensions of gender and ethnicity in understanding diversity and multicultural issues among women. Drawing on feminist principles and personal experiences, the authors advocate multiple methods of discovering and knowing. Using systems theory as an alternative analytical framework, this book also examines professional cultural competency.

EQUALITY VERSUS DIFFERENCE

The integration of gender and ethnicity creates a system of meanings that influences social institutions and affects individual identity, consciousness, and behavior (Chow, in Chow, Wilkinson, & Zinn, 1996, p. xix). As Amott and Matthaei (1991) clearly indicate, although the processes of gender and ethnicity are intrinsically interconnected and have been central forces determining and differentiating women's lives, gender itself does not create a common "women's oppression" (pp. 16–17; 27). Rather, ethnicity differentiates the experiences of women. Yet the mythical "uniformity" of sisterhood has led to the homogenization of women's diverse ethnicities, a construction that fails to acknowledge significant variables that underscore heterogeneity—skin color, racial features, socioeconomic class, English language proficiency, a legacy of slavery (as in women of African descent such as African-Americans, West Indians, and African-Caribbeans) (Comas-Diaz & Green, 1994, p. 6), or a patrimony of American political colonization (as is the case of Filipinos and Puerto Rican women). Too often, as Lorde emphasizes, we pour the energy needed for recognizing and exploring differences into pretending that either those differences are insurmountable barriers or that they do not exist at all (as cited in Andersen & Collin, 1992, p. 496).

The degree of acculturation and transculturation to the mainstream society is another variable pointing to the heterogeneity among women. Certainly there is a language, or the heritage of a language, a general historical experience, and certain cultural traditions and practices that are shared. But the idiosyncracies of individuals must also be considered. Thus, even when we have identified a commonality spanning ethnic and other major lines of difference, the particular ways that commonality is acted out and its consequences in the larger society may be manifested, in any number of ways (Cole, in Andersen & Collin, 1992, pp. 130–131).

Hence, to pinpoint commonalities without dealing with our differences is to misunderstand and distort that which separates women as well as that which binds them. Women in the United States clearly share a number of experiences, particularly the assumptions about the way that women think and behave. However, what women have in common must always be viewed in relation to the particularities of a group. Even when we narrow our focus to one particular group of women it is possible for differences within that group to challenge the primacy of the norm (Cole, in Andersen & Collin, 1992, pp. 129–130). Lorde makes this point quite clear: it is not differences that separate women, but the reluctance to recognize those differences and to deal effectively with the distortions that have resulted from ignoring and misnaming those differences (as cited in Andersen & Collin, 1992, p. 502).

This equality-versus-difference debate has characterized conflicting feminist strategies. The equality-versus-difference dichotomy equates equality with sameness and thereby defines the demand for equality as incompatible with the recognition of difference (Deitch, in Chow, Wilkinson, & Zinn, 1996, p. 289). Central to this argument is that treating each ethnic group of women separately accentuates the differences and conflicts among women of various ethnic groups. The counterargument, however, emphasizes that social transformation can occur only by recognizing, accepting, and building on differences (Amott & Matthaei, 1991, p. 28). Rather than homogenous exclusivity, a more inclusive way to view the world is to make the experience of previously excluded groups more visible and central in the construction of knowledge.

Inclusive thinking should shift our perspective from the White, male-centered forms of thinking that have characterized much of Western thought (Andersen & Collin, 1992, p. 4) to a multicultural, multidimensional paradigm.

Understanding the forces shaping women's history and the complex intersections of ethnicity and gender as simultaneous social processes that shape all societal relations (Andersen & Collin, 1992) will help capture the underlying social structures that produce women's oppression (Chow, Wilkinson, & Zinn, 1996, p. xi). Oppression can be experienced in multiple ways. For instance, in U.S. society, women of color are doubly marginalized. As a member of two groups whose positions are determined by oppression, a woman of color's experiences differ from those of the man of color and the White woman because her reality involves the dynamics of living in a society that is both racist and sexist. Therefore, understanding and empowering women so they can cope effectively with the consequences of their societal entrapment becomes a fundamental goal for the helping professions (Pinderhughes, in Comas-Diaz & Greene, 1994, p. xi–xii; 1989).

A FRAMEWORK FOR STUDYING
GENDER AND ETHNICITY

Social entropy/systems theory provides an integrative framework capable of dealing with what many see as excess fragmentation. This framework enables comparative analysis, both of the same ethnic group at different points in time and of different ethnic groups at the same point in time. Such a broad formulation allows a focus on relationships as well as their components, and studies not only the relationships themselves but also their systemic context, including the social environment. In this line of reasoning the subject is not autonomous, but dependent on a social and cultural context for her or his ontology. Systems theory framework comprises the most comprehensive multilevel analysis of processes and structure constructed by any perspective to date (Bailey, 1994, pp. 40–43).

As Sutherland (1973) has argued, systems theory offers a distinct epistemological alternative to the various theoretical extremes of social and behavioral sciences—strict empiricism, positivism, and phenomenology at one end and intuitionalism, subjectivism, and rhetoric-ideographic preferences at the other (Ballou, in Brown & Root, 1990, p. 6). Arguing that reality will be misconstructed by adherence to any single epistemology or method of knowing, general systems theory proposes that the real truth is to be found in the connective nexus among the many methods of knowing and their shaping of reality (Ballou, in Brown & Root, 1990, pp. 34–35). Systems theory and social entropy theory present an effective framework for this discussion of gender and ethnicity because they allow analysis of ethnic minorities and women in a manner in which they are excluded by narrower approaches (Bailey, 1994, p. 42).

This theoretical framework conceptualizes a system, such as an ethnic group or gender, as a set of interactive components along with a boundary that filters both the kind and rate of flow of inputs and outputs to and from the system. All system conceptualizations allow for the existence of a boundary and such framework likewise presumes the existence of an environment outside the boundary (Bailey, 1994, p. 46). Social scientists who make no attempt to understand a concrete system by simultaneously studying all of its properties and their interrelationships often obfuscate the holistic and systemic nature of the phenomena under study (p. 63). Losing this focus restricts a comprehensive analysis of perspectives that deals with fundamental issues crucial to the understanding of society. Systems theory offers a framework for analysis, not a panacea. Nevertheless, systems theory enables the helping professionals to explore the significance of the relationship between gender and ethnicity and to develop a model for understanding the complex and complicated intersection of these systems.[1]

Central to the theoretical underpinnings established for the present work are two principles: women's experience and pluralism. This work values women's experiences and, as Ballou explains, women can see their experiences not as their faults, deviations, or difficulties, but as the result of external forces (in Brown & Root, 1990, p. 35). Pluralism underscores the validity of differences.

IMPLICATIONS FOR
INTERVENTION/PRACTICE

For the helping professional, it is critical to understand the challenges facing ethnic minority women. Ethnic minority women must deal with helping professionals who may or may not be familiar with the world views of their cultures (Comas-Diaz & Greene, 1994, p. xv). This book attempts to address the problem by promoting practitioners' respect for ethnically different world views and practices, with an emphasis on the heterogeneity among groups of women, and especially on the diversity among women within a given ethnic group (Pinderhughes, in Comas-Diaz & Greene, 1994, p. xii). Informed context also necessitates a revision of the assumptions made about normalcy and deviance, adaptive and maladaptive behavior. Cultural competence underscores how practitioners, researchers, and authors see and diagnose problems, identify helping interventions, and assess service effectiveness (Brown, in de Anda, 1997, p. 25).

As it can be argued in its broadest sense, social interaction is cross-cultural in that it embodies two persons who, by definition, have different backgrounds and unique cultural identities (Lago & Thompson, 1996, p. 14). Thus, every helping professional should be trained to recognize the ways in which her or his own cultural upbringing is likely to affect perceptions of clients' problems (Murphy, 1986, p. 179, in Lago & Thompson, 1996). We need to understand the often unconscious impact that our own cultural heritage has upon our attitudes and perceptions toward others, especially those who are ethnically different. Yet many helping professionals begin their training by learning intervention strategies before developing preliminary awareness of biases, prejudices, and stereotypes (Brown, in de Anda, 1997, p. 14).

To create more hopeful and useful images in working with women, we must name and alter value orientations, philosophies of intervention, and professional habits that may decrease the effectiveness of our work with women (Suarez, Lewis, & Clark, in Van den Bergh, 1995, p. 195). Feminist principles point to the need to change the societal institutions that contribute to the oppression of women (Suarez, Lewis, & Clark, in Van den Bergh, 1995, p. 207), and helping professionals require an understanding of the political processes in society that continue to perpetuate discriminatory practices (Lago & Thompson, 1996, p. 14). Helping professionals are not necessarily aware of the nature or extent of the structural inequalities that so pervasively affect people's lives, nor are they clearly aware of their own position on these issues. Even if not actively involved in the various modes of oppression, their role in the perpetuation of discrimination is characterized by lack of awareness, passivity, blind acceptance, and indifference (Lago & Thompson, 1996, p. 17).

REFERENCES

Amott, T., & Matthae, J. (1991). *Race, gender, and work: A multicultural economic history of women in the United States.* Boston: End Press.

Andersen, M., & Collins, P. (1992). *Race, class, and gender: An anthology.* California: Wadsworth Publishing Company.

Bailey, K. (1994). *Sociology and the new systems theory: Toward a theoretical synthesis.* New York: State University of New York Press.

Brown, L., & Root, M. (Eds.). (1990). *Diversity and complexity in feminist therapy.* New York: Haworth Press.

Buikeman, R., & Smelik, A. (1995). *Women's studies and culture: A feminist introduction.* London and New Jersey: Sed Books.

Chow, E., Wilkinson, D., & Zinn, M. (1996). *Race, class, and gender: Common bonds different voices*. London: Sage Publications.

Comas-Diaz, L., & Greene, B. (1994). *Women of color: Integrating ethnic and gender identities in psychotherapy*. New York: The Guilford Press.

de Anda, D. (1997). *Controversial issues in multiculturalism*. Boston: Allyn & Bacon.

Gunew, S., & Yeatman, A. (1993). *Feminism and the politics of difference*. San Francisco: Westview Press.

Lago, C., & Thompson, J. (1996). *Race, culture, and counseling*. Philadelphia: Open University Press.

Moraga, C., & Anzaldua, G. (Eds.). (1981). *This bridge called my back: Writings by radical women of color*. Watertown, MA: Persephone Press.

Pinderhughes, E. (1989). *Understanding race, ethnicity, and power: The key of efficacy in clinical practice*. New York: The Free Press.

Van den Bergh, N. (Ed.). (1995). *Feminist practice in the 21st century*. Washington D.C.: N.A.S.W. Press.

Walker, A. (1993). Teaching about race, gender, and class diversity in the United States families. *Family Relations, 42*(3), 342–350.

RECOMMENDED READINGS AND RESOURCES

Adams, M. (1996). *The multicultural imagination: Race, color, and the unconscious*. London: Routledge.

Albrecht, L., & Brewer, R. (1990). *Bridges of power: Women's multicultural alliances*. Philadelphia: New Society Publishers.

Bergh, N. (1995). *Feminist practice in the 21st century*. Washington D.C.: NASW Press.

Bottomley, G., de Lepervanche, M., & Martin, J. (1991). *Intersections: Gender, class, culture, ethnicity*. NSW, Australia: Allen and Unwin.

Clayton, O. (1996). *An american dilemma revisited: Race relations in a changing world*. New York: Russell Sage Foundation.

Cook, R. (1994). *Human rights of women: National and international perspectives*. Philadelphia: University of Philadelphia Press.

DuBois, C., & Ruiz, V. (Eds.). (1990). *Unequal sisters: A multicultural reader in U.S. women's history*. New York: Routledge.

Dujo, D., & Withorn, A. (1996). *For crying out loud: Women's poverty in the United States*. Boston: South End Press.

Ferguson, B., & Barnes, D. (Eds.). (1997). *Perspectives on transcultural mental health*. Parramatta, Australia: Transcultural Mental Health Center.

Gordon, A., & Newfield, C. (Eds.). (1996). *Mapping multi-culturalism*. Minneapolis: University of Minnesota Press.

Healey, J. (1998). *Race, ethnicity, gender, and class*. Thousand Oaks, CA: Pine Forge Press.

Henderson, G., & Spigner-Littles, D. (1996). *A practitioner's guide to understanding indigenous and foreign cultures* (2nd ed.). Springfield, Illinois: C.C. Thomas.

John, D., Shelton, B., & Luschen, K. (1995). Race, ethnicity, gender, and perceptions of fairness. *Journal of Family Issues*, 16(3), 357–379.

Katlin, F. (1982). The impact of ethnicity. *Social Casework: The Journal of Contemporary Social Work*, 4(2), 168–171.

Kesselman, A., McNair, L., & Schniedewind, N. (1995). *Women images and realities: A multicultural anthology*. Mountain View, CA: Mayfield Publishing Company.

Lambert, R., & Heston, A. (1981). *America as a multicultural society*. Philadelphia: The American Academy of Political and Social Science.

Lefley, H. (1991). *Women in cross cultural perspective*. New York: Praeger.

Leonardo, M. (1991). *Gender at the crossroads of knowledge: Feminist anthropology in the postmodern era*. Los Angeles: University of California.

Leontis, A., & Galin, M. (Eds.). (1992). *Understanding women: The challenge of cross-cultural perspectives*. Columbus, OH: OSU.

Ling, L. (1995). The promise and pitfalls of teaching feminist international relations. *Women's Studies Quarterly*, 3(4), 187–191.

Mac Cormack, C., & Strathern, M. (1980). *Nature, culture, and gender*. Cambridge: Cambridge University Press.

Maynard, M., & Purvis, J. (1994). *Researching women's lives from a feminist perspective*. Philadelphia: Taylor & Francis Inc.

Narayan, U. (1997). *Dislocating cultures*. New York: Routledge.

Neuman, S., & Stephenson, G. (Eds.). (1993). *Reimagining women: Representations of women in culture*. Toronto: University of Toronto Press.

Olds, L. (1992). *Metaphors of interrelatedness: Toward a systems theory of psychology*. Albany, NY: State University of New York Press.

Oskamp, S., & Costanzo, M. (1993). *Gender issues in contemporary society*. New Delhi: Sage Publications.

Peters, J., & Wolper, A. (1995). *Women's rights human rights: International feminist perspectives*. New York, London: Routledge.

Peterson, V. S., & Runyan, A. (1993). *Global gender issues*. Boulder, CO: Westview Press.

Rosaldo, M. (1980). The use and abuse of anthropology: reflections on feminism and cross cultural understanding. *Signs: Journal of Women in Culture and Society*, 5, 389–417.

Roschelle, A. R. (1997). *No more kin: exploring race, class, and gender in family networks*. Thousand Oaks; London; and New Delhi: Sage Publications.

Ruiz, V., & DuBois, E. (1994). *Unequal sisters: a multicultural reader in U.S. women's history*. New York: Routledge.

Sainsbury, D. (1996). *Gender, equality, and welfare states*. Cambridge; and New York: Cambridge University Press.

Saulnier, C. (1996). *Feminist theories and social work: approaches and applications*. New York: The Haworth Press.

Torres, A., & del Rosario, R. (1994). *Gender and development: making the bureaucracy gender-responsive*. London: United Nations University Press.

Van Horne, W., & Tonnesen, T. (1986). *Ethnicity and women*. Madison: University of Wisconsin.

Waldman, M., Leontis, A., & Galin, M. (1991–92). *Understanding women: The challenge of cross-cultural perspectives*. Papers in comparative studies 7. Columbus: The Ohio State University.

Womack, M., & Marti, J. (1993). (Eds.). *The other fifty percent: Multicultural perspectives on gender relations*. Prospect Heights, Illinois: Waveland Press, Inc.

Wyche, K., & Crosby, F. (1996). *Women's ethnicities: journeys through psychology*. Boulder, CO: Westview Press.

NOTES

1. This discussion inevitably leads us to the concept of deconstruction, the critical inquiry into the intersection of power and knowledge and the ways in which they support practices of exclusion and domination. The deconstruction approach consists of unveiling the complexity and ubiquity of masculinization, racialization, heterosexualization, and classification, understood as a constant process of formation of "pejorative others." The crucial point here is that politics for diversity involve a political position that stresses differences. Such an approach is opposed to "identity politics" because the counter-affirmation of oppositional identities ends up reasserting the very dualism it is trying to dismantle (Braidotti, in Buikema & Smelik, 1995, pp. 182–183).

2

African American Women

G. WINBUSH

INTRODUCTION

This chapter focuses on African American women. Focusing on a few key factors, the chapter provides a sociodemographic profile of those African American women who are United States women of African descent. That which is shared in this chapter is both prompted by and based on works that have recently emerged on African American women and on experiences witnessed by the author during her life. Therefore, the chapter not only considers some of the scholarly work pertaining to African American women, but provides some anecdotal information about some of the prevailing strengths and challenges which confront this group of African American women. Included in the discussion are the often omitted, yet noteworthy, personal experiences of the commonplace African American woman in our homes, in our schools, in the workplace, in our churches, and in our communities.

Personal experiences carry inherent biases, but many shared experiences can provide a collective "voice" for African American women. As Boyd-Franklin and Garcia-Preto (1994) mentioned in their text on psychotherapy, women of color may label similar experiences differently. We differ individually and in our perceptions. However, along with these differences, this chapter will provide insight into some of the similarities and trends that have shaped this group of women. It is hoped that such a discussion will be useful in understanding the dynamics of service delivery to African American women.

This chapter will present answers to the following questions:

1. Who are African American women?
2. What are some of the cultural variables that influence the construction and shape of their perceptions of their roles?
3. What strengths enable them to overcome challenges or sustain themselves despite adversities?
4. What difficulties confront African American women today?

Answers to these questions will draw from history, some perceptions, and some truths and misconceptions about this particular group of women.

WHO ARE AFRICAN AMERICAN WOMEN?

There is much debate about which variables are the most influential in defining "self." Questions about identity are complex because of the impact of pertinent variables (i.e., race, gender, heritage, and class) and also because an individual's interactions influence perceptions of identity. Higginbotham's (1994) notion of a meta-language is relevant as is the idea that we must view the lives of African American women through the lens of race and gender. While race and gender have been the prevailing variables in previous scholarship, this writer wants to add another variable—spirituality. Spirituality is one's relationship with something greater and more powerful than the self. Intertwined with perceptions of self is the degree of one's spirituality. I would like to emphasize the importance of including spirituality in uncovering realities about any population and contend that it can be more powerful than race or gender in influencing perceptions of both self and others. With its focus on ontology, spirituality supersedes mere cultural "values" and "traditions." Spirituality is crucial to uncovering realities about any population and may in some religious doctrines be more powerful than race or gender in influencing perceptions of both self and others. To many, it is their catalyst for "being or existing" and/or their blueprint for living.

For African Americans, spirituality is embedded in their traditions of unity (family, tribe, village, and community) and survival. Spirituality is significant to how African American women perceive themselves. Peterson (1992) has recently given credence to spirituality in her work on the will of African American women. The women interviewed in her study stated they "found it difficult to separate their religious views from the way they live their lives" (p. 80).

Perceptions of African American Women

The perceptions of others can color one's perception of self. African American women often identify themselves with how others view them, whether as matriarchs, Jezebels, and "controlling sapphires," or as powerless mammies. These perceptions have been particularly perpetuated in the media. Yet, despite the dominant notions that African American women are either strong and controlling or "victims—women suffering from multiple risk-factors such as racism, sexism, and poverty" (Sudarkasa, 1996)—according to Gordon (1987), the majority of African American women have managed to maintain a positive self-identity despite negative and often contradictory stereotyping. A number of factors have attributed to their positive self-identities. Among these, spirituality has been viewed as significant to African American women's perception of themselves. Positive self-perceptions might also have resulted from the roles African American women have had to assume. Additionally, various sociodemographic factors (e.g., income, education, employment, and power) might shape the self-perceptions of African American women (Falik, 1996). It should come as no surprise that the African American woman who has acquired a professional degree, who is following a professional career path, and who earns a high income might have a more positive self-image and be considered more powerful and resourceful than her African American sister with a less favorable sociodemographic profile (Comas-Diaz & Greene, 1994).

Roles of African American Women

Although the perceptions of outsiders do not necessarily influence African American women's views of "self," the roles of African American women in African American communities are derived from perceptions of what their own communities expect from them. While some see flexibility in gender roles among African Americans (Harley, 1995), African women traditionally are expected to be caretakers (Greene, 1994) and not the primary breadwinners. Motherhood is an important role for African American women and childrearing is frequently a joint effort among mothers, grandmothers, and girlfriends (Greene, 1994). In African American cultures, women have played a pivotal role in the family and have chief caretaking responsibility at home and in their communities (Boyd-Franklin & Garcia-Preto, 1994; Greene, 1994). African American girls are taught early in life to take responsibility for themselves and their families. They learn from first-hand experience that the African American mother is the conduit of traditional culture and values of African American family life (Greene, 1994; Peterson, 1992).

In addition to success as caretakers, African American women have experienced levels of success as leaders, activists, and in their work outside the home. Furthermore, they have also contributed immeasurably to the quality

of life within African American communities (Gordon, 1987). Although not at
the same rate as White women, African American women are now moving
into more professional and leadership roles, which have been traditionally
held by White males, including those of physicians, administrators, ministers,
and policy makers (Comas-Diaz & Greene, 1994). The level of success in
these nontraditional roles is based upon how well African American women
deal with *multiple roles*—simultaneously performing as wife, mother, and
teacher for instance—or whether how well they handle *conflicting demands,*
which can be characterized as a rivalry between family, work, and personal
demands. Successfully managing multiple roles puts African American women
in a favorable light with respect to their personal strengths (Robinson & Guy-
Sheftall, 1990); but prolonged multiple responsibilities, and sometimes sole
responsibility for a family, can often result in chronic illness, mental health
problems, and poverty. Conflicting demands, on the other hand, imply a
woman's competition with and/or deviation from her primary role as caregiver. We must weigh both benefits and losses to African American women, to
their families, to their communities, and to society at large when we scrutinize
the impact of their multiple roles or conflicting demands.

African American Women and Power

Power is defined here as decision-making capacities among African American
women through their leadership roles, political participation, and participation
in the feminist movement. Women in general have had and continue to have
far less power in decision-making than have men, and African American
women are no exception (Sudarkasa, 1996). According to Sudarkasa, "women
of color nor those of the majority group status will never have power comparable to their numerical representation unless and until commonality of focus
and voice prevail" (p. 301). Daniel (1996) states that we must be sensitive to
the conditions perpetuating powerlessness for African American women—
that is, psychological, cultural, and legal barriers to their decision making,
their lack of economic choices, and their primary roles as caretakers.

For most African American women, opportunities for social status or
power exist not in the labor market, but instead in their families, neighborhoods, organizations, and church lives (Harley, 1995). In spite of their
powerlessness in the economic and professional spheres, African American
women and other women of color generally have a dramatic impact within
and beyond their communities (Gilkes, 1994). The literature records the
strengths of African American women in the home, their input in household
decisions, and their tradition of outspokenness in domestic situations (Sudarkasa, 1996). Peterson (1992) also identifies some major themes that facilitate a
"strong self-determined Black female": family relationships, Black women as
sisters, and Black community connectedness. Gilkes found that African

American women's community work connects many "small pieces" of community life and contributes to the process of empowerment. It is this demonstrative commitment to family and community that projects power and a source to be reckoned with by the dominant society. Some even view African American women's role as primary caretakers potentially threatening to the dominant society (Gilkes, 1994) because of the subtle forms of resistance or blatant protest portrayed when there is harm or danger to their families and communities.

Smith (1995) speaks specifically about the social service work and political activity of African American women during the Black health reform of the 1890s–1950s. Although at that time men held most of the formal leadership positions, the women did most of the grassroots organizing. According to Smith, African American women's contributions were greatest at the local level and through their involvement in mobilizing community participation. The author proposes that the Black health reform movement would not have occurred had it not been for the laywomen's volunteer labor.

The degree to which African American women support and participate in the feminist movement is debated in the literature. Some speak of the lack of support for the movement by African American women and some see African American women's involvement in the feminist movement as only an imitation of White women's commitment to it. While African American women's general acceptance of feminist values seem clear (Saulnier, 1996), some scholars believe that issues specific to African American women and their plight in society take precedence over discussions about sexism (Robnett, 1997). Daniels (1996) contends that many African American women feel the feminist movement does not adequately represent their interests. She further notes that for African American women, the concept of feminism is replaced by "womanism," which reflects their roots and ideals, and womanhood as perceived by them. The womanist movement stresses the uniqueness of women of African descent, their needs, and their feelings stemming from generations of oppression. It has also been noted that those African American women who work toward feminist goals tend to focus their efforts at the intersection of sex, race, and class struggles (Wilcox, 1990), and that African American women, along with all others who are oppressed by multiple systems of domination, must deal with more than one issue at a time (Saulnier, 1996).

Sociodemographic Profile of African American Women

Education has been part of the formula for freedom and upward mobility for African Americans for many decades (Gilkes, 1982). Our mothers, our grandmothers, and our great-grandmothers often made sacrifices to provide their children with a solid education (Peterson, 1992). Although the sacrifices have paid off for their daughters, it becomes questionable given that their sons are unlikely to attend college. Twice as many African American women earn college degrees, compared to African American men. The numbers for African American women show a marked increase over the past two decades (Nettles & Perna, 1997). Education has afforded the African American woman the opportunity for choices in jobs, broadening her options beyond domestic work. However, as noted by Higginbotham (1994), having these choices has not been without challenges. Kusum (1995) suggests that African American women face both racism and sexism in institutions of higher education, and Carter-Obayuwana (1995) has provided a method that helps African American women cope with the pressures they face in the pursuit of education. Her "Model of Hope," a four-step survival guide, is based on measures of hope and successful coping which enable African American women "under siege" in higher education to deal with the stresses from both their professional and personal lives. The guidelines suggest that African American women identify, assess, and utilize their own coping and hope measures.

The economic profile of African American women will be discussed in the context of their labor force participation, which is a major indicator of economic status. African American women's work outside the home has historically been labor forced by slave holders or menial labor demanded by poverty (Harley, 1995; Mullings, 1994). In more recent times, African American women have taken part in the trend of women entering into traditionally male dominated fields. Women of color have been increasingly visible in professional job settings, a development which can be largely attributed to federal legislation and affirmative action policies (Higginbotham, 1994). However, these gains have not been without costs. Exposure to racism and sexism, coping in the absence of role models and mentors, isolation, juggling competing personal and career demands, and experiencing shifting social norms and expectations have taken their toll (Farrant & Williams, 1990). While the number of African American women in this country with successful careers and businesses has grown (Ballard, 1997), most of these women have never married or are divorced. This observation needs further exploration in terms of its prevalence and its predictive capacity with respect to career and/or business success among African American women. Also, while women of color are increasingly entering male-dominated occupations, there are noticeable differences between the degree of their presence in the public and that in the private sectors (Higginbotham, 1994). Few women of color enter the private sector; their visibility in public sector jobs is the result of less discrimination in hiring practices in that sphere. But Higginbotham also notes that working in the public sector is not without its hazards. Never-ending budget cuts, reduced commitment to service delivery, and overwork are but a few of the problems faced by public sector employees. She exposes "the myth of

double advantage"—that of being both black and female—in both traditional male (Landry, 1987; Fulbright, 1986) and traditional female occupations, and proposes that because of both their race and gender, African
American women have not seen the advancement, mobility, or economic
gains to which their white or male counterparts have been exposed (Higginbotham, 1987). Instead, they have seen additional constraints particularly in
the private sector and the access thereof. Both gender and racial discrimination
continually steer them toward traditional female occupations and employment
in the public sector (Higginbotham, 1994).

THE STRENGTH OF AFRICAN AMERICAN
WOMEN: SOCIAL NETWORKS

Both individual and collective strengths are pillars of survival for African
American women, their families, and their communities. This section begins
with a discussion of their collective strengths followed by illustrations of their
individual strengths. When discussing collective strengths among U.S. women
of African descent, the social networks among this group of women are the
most prevailing. Evident through a history of relationships and activities
involving family, friends, work, church, community, and social causes, the
social networks of African American women are powerful tools for nurturing
and maintaining their individual coping skills. Family, friends, and church
make up the fabric of African American women's lives and are considered by
some to be their strongest mechanisms for survival (Daniels, 1996). African
American women have been committed to such communal, familial, and
spiritual institutions throughout history and they have maintained them
through the 20th century. With the help of cultural supports, many African
American women, including primary providers, single parents, and women
without significant others, have prevailed against social and economic adversities and disparities and have made necessary transformations in their roles and
responsibilities. It is to be hoped that this precedent of survival will be
maintained during the change in public supports through welfare reform,
reductions in entitlements, and program cuts.

African American Women and Social Networks

Despite the stereotype of primarily single female heads of households, most
African American families are comprised of both mothers and fathers. Unfortunately, most of the attention paid to female-headed families in African
American communities has been negative. Yet Sudarksa and others (Dickerson, 1995; Randolph, 1995; Staples, 1994; Staples & Johnson, 1993) disparage

popular negative views of female-headed households and contend that these households are not inherently unstable nor are the children in them necessarily disadvantaged. As Sudarkasa (1996) states, "female-headed households are alternative forms of family organization that mature African American women have adopted in the face of the demographic, economic, political, and social negative realities of life in America for African Americans" (p. 6). They have survived with the support of their adaptive familial systems (George & Dickerson, 1995). Yet although Staples suggests that frequently the children of single-parent families are better off than those in two-parent families, this writer recommends caution when interpreting these findings. While we should make known successful adaptations among African American female-headed households, we should not do so at the expense of minimizing the negative impact on African American communities of father-absent or one-parent families. Most important, such findings should not encourage the fallacy that this family type is the most prevalent and most preferred among African American women and families.

Friendships

Social scientists are now acknowledging the implications of friendship among African American women. We now recognize the importance of "girl friends or sisters" to the emotional, social, and in many cases, the economic well-being of African American women and their families. African American women depend on other females within and outside the extended family system for support (Boyd-Franklin & Garcia-Preto, 1995) and they have created "formal" structures such as sororities, churchwomen's groups, and women's social clubs to facilitate this camaraderie (Smith, 1995). In fact, groups of African American women such as these are credited with initiating the first Black health reform movement (1890–1950s) (Smith, 1995). Next to family, female friendships are a powerful social support for African American women, and for some, friends become synonymous with family. Sadly, many African American women, particularly those in large urban areas, feel isolated in their struggles and sorely miss and express a need for sisterhood with other African American women (Boyd-Franklin, 1989).

Churches

Along with family and friends, African American women also derive strength from their church involvement. African American women comprise the majority of church membership and attendance and are crucial to the strength of this social network in providing support to its members and surrounding communities. Often both family and friends participate in church activities with these women, thus promoting a connection between the two types of social supports for African American women. They not only seek overall spiritual guidance from within their churches, but they often go there for support themselves and in many instances for the friendships discussed earlier. Like all women, African American women have experienced resistance to their participation in church leadership roles. Yet they continue to be the mainstay of church activities and church support (Peterson, 1992).

[Individual] Strengths of African American Women

African American women demonstrate individual strength in many different ways. Based on personal experiences and observations of African American women, I can attest to a diversity of strengths among African American women. Growing up in a two-parent household and yet observing a variety of family structures in my community, I saw many African American women demonstrate strength by their commitment to family and to causes pertinent to African American communities. For some of these women, strength was the knowledge used to acquire necessary external supports to sustain their families in times of need. These women simply knew how to locate and tap into the systems of help to secure basic life necessities—food, shelter, and medical care. Strength in other African American women came from the ability to support others in challenging times. I often saw women provide words of comfort, offer a place of refuge, give advice, offer food and shelter, and nurture children other than their own. Such help was provided to blood relatives, fictive kin and others, both women and men. Some of African American women managed to present their families in a positive light despite serious problems including poor marital relations, financial constraints, and the presence of dysfunctional family members. Some women were also concerned about the broader community. One woman, a social worker, was responsible for developing a safe place for recreation in my neighborhood and surrounding communities. Today, this same facility has expanded to one that offers multiple services to children, to young and older women, and to families.

As a child growing up in a working class community during the 1950s and 1960s, I observed African American women demonstrating strengths in a wide variety of ways. Women active in school and church life were numerous in my community. There was the elementary school teacher who took me under her wing, made clothes for my school performances, and taught me cultural/ethnic dance routines. Then there was that vocal and highly visible mother in the PTA, that Sunday school teacher who made us memorize Bible verses, and that guidance counselor who affectionately became known as "mom" or "best friend."

As discussed earlier, decision-making is yet another strength evident among African American women. A number of African American women in my community clearly made the major decisions in their households, even those with a male partner in the home. For some African American women, sole decision-making was thrust upon them and for others, the ability to make decisions was enhanced by choice. Growing up in a working class family, I did not see many African American women with careers or businesses outside the home. The few who engaged in paid employment were involved in real estate, cosmetology, nursing, teaching, or clerical professions. In fact, most of the professional women of my childhood are still going strong in their careers today.

In sum, the strengths of African American women are many and diverse; analysis of their strengths provide implications for how best to help and which kinds of help are needed by these women. Whereas many of the strengths identified among African American women are also exhibited by women in other cultural groups, their presence among other women has not been subjected to the combination of race and gender controversies that has always accompanied African American women. For example, discussions about troubled African American male-female relationships include perceptions of African American women's domineering, confrontational, highly vocal, and unyielding behaviors, which could be seen as strengths in one situation and problems in another.

CHALLENGES CONFRONTING AFRICAN AMERICAN WOMEN

With their strengths as our foundation, this section will examine some of the personal, familial, and societal challenges that are confronting African American women today. It is well documented that African American women often face precarious socioeconomic status, sometimes to the extent of impoverishment, little education, substandard housing, and frequently the burden of single parenthood (Boyd-Franklin & Garcia-Preto, 1994). Studies have shown that the cumulative effects of poverty, being African American and female, and single parenthood are chronic sources of stress (Boyd-Franklin & Garcia-Preto, 1994). More specifically, these authors note that chronic stress may be more detrimental to physical and mental health than distinctly stressful events that occur sporadically. Health problems increasingly affecting African American women include AIDS/HIV, substance abuse, and lupus.

Personal Health-Related Challenges

In spite of the implementation of an overdue initiative to examine major health concerns of women, problems specific to African American women have yet to receive comparable attention. Collins (1996), in her discussion of a number of health concerns among African American women, also states that

"African American women remain the sickest of all racial and gender groups in America" (p. 1). She concludes that they have the highest mortality rates for the leading causes of death, more undetected diseases, and higher mortality rates than any other group of women in this country.

Although the cancer rate for all women has improved, African American women have not experienced such a favorable trend. African American women have higher cancer mortality rates than other racial groups in the areas of breast, stomach, esophagus, cervix, and the corpus uteri (Collins, 1996) and lower overall survival rates (Roberson, 1996). Roberson proposes that African American women's placement in the social structure and societal stereotypes about their health-related behavior are factors contributing to such a gloomy report. She suggests that real efforts to address this problem must thoroughly investigate such factors among African American women. Routine cancer screening has been identified as an effective tool in early detection and one that could possibly change the rising trend in cancer mortality for African American women. However, African American women do not traditionally participate in mainstream screening mechanisms. Possibly, they neglect themselves in their tradition of applying "grandma's homemade remedies" to address or prevent illnesses among their family members. As well, the problem may lie in their use of folk remedies instead of mainstream health care services. In response to low participation among African American women in intervention programs, Forte (1997) describes a community-based breast cancer intervention program in beauty salons for older African American women, which proved to be a successful outreach effort.

Systemic lupus erythematosus (SLE) is of personal concern as a result of the loss of a close friend and the diagnosis of lupus among a number of female family members and friends. SLE is a multisystem disorder of the immune system, the prevalence rate for which is highest for women between the ages of 20 and 64, and occurs more frequently among African American women than among White women (Collins, 1996; Sullivan, 1996). The prognosis has improved: 90% of lupus patients in the U.S. now survive at least 15 years (Sullivan, 1996). A cure is yet to be found, but oftentimes pharmacological intervention can address symptoms and lead to remission. Little is known about the origin or cause of lupus; genetic factors are strongly suggested, and hormonal factors are suspected, as are environmental factors. The disease often goes undetected or misdiagnosed, resulting in devastating consequences given the lack of treatment. These risks are experienced more frequently by African American women than others, mostly because of insufficient insurance coverage (Collins, 1996; Sullivan, 1996). Awareness of available lupus resources, lupus research, and lupus outreach programs is critical to improvement in lupus outcomes for women in general, and for African American women in particular.

African American women comprise 72% of the women's population diagnosed with HIV/AIDS (Daniel, 1996). African American women and children are experiencing the greatest increase in the number of reported cases of HIV/AIDS (Hunter, 1996), and particularly affected are those women ages 15–44. Daniel identifies sociocultural factors that surround the pandemic of HIV/AIDS among African American women and speaks of the importance of empowerment among such women. Daniel stresses that African Amercian women have not personally benefited from their history of strength, problem-solving, and caretaking. Consequently, their prolonged self-neglect now confronts them with its consequence–illness, personal problems, and minimal use of help-seeking behaviors and resources (Daniel, 1996). Because of their connection to those who themselves have had risky lifestyle behavior(s) (i.e., drug abuse, needle sharing, bisexual relationship), the implication is that Afriian Amercian women are themselves highly susceptible to the consequences of such lifestyle choices.

Substance abuse exists regardless of gender, race, class or age. Women have become more frequently involved over the past several decades in the abuse of alcohol and drugs, and again, African American women are no exception (Jackson, 1996). African American women are experiencing the first- and second-hand consequences of substance abuse in ever-growing numbers (Collins, 1996; Jackson, 1996). African American women report more alcohol-related health problems, have the highest reports of fetal alcohol syndrome, and are more likely to have used crack cocaine than any other ethnic group (Bass, 1997; Collins, 1996; Jackson, 1996). Grandmothers raising grandchildren have exacerbated the cost of substance abuse, a dilemma frequently faced by minority group women. The number of African American women in our criminal systems for drug related offenses is also on the upswing (Burris-Kitchen, 1997; Collins, 1997). Often it is the children of incarcerated women who are under the care of grandparents.

What must be done to reduce or alleviate these above mentioned health-related concerns among African American women? Clearly, solutions might be rooted in policies and in programs; but regardless, they must be community-based, culturally, gender-, and age-sensitive. For instance, Daniel (1996) emphasizes that HIV/AIDS treatment of all women will be more effective if it is based on an understanding of the societal context in which women live as well as women's emotional needs. Gender-relevant and culturally sensitive programs that provide self-development have been identified as effective interventions among African American women (DiClemente, 1995). Concerned about HIV prevention among young urban women, Bond (1997) speaks to the importance of realistic messages in the printed media geared to young women 15 to 34 years of age. In her group work with African American women on drug and alcohol issues, Saulnier (1996) found that women felt strongly about interacting with staff of their own racial and cultural group. They also wanted such experts to discuss potential solutions to their health issues in a holistic manner, not viewing race, gender, class, and sexual orientation as isolated dimensions of the difficulties confronting them. Jackson (1996) contends that to understand the overrepresentation of African American women in the heavy drinking/alcoholic population, etiological factors must be explored. More specifically, consideration needs to be given to historical and generational stressors (e.g., slavery, primary role as caretakers, political and economic powerlessness), internal stressors (rejection/acceptance of fallacies and stereotypes about individual biophysical, political-economic, psychosocial, and spiritual functioning), and external stressors relating to family and community. Jackson further notes that strategies for addressing health-related concerns must be collaborative, involving African American women, their communities, and service agencies focusing on balancing the demands placed on African American women and the resources available to assist them. Many scholars fear that African American women will remain in a population unlikely to receive adequate treatment (Rhodes, 1997). However, Poitier, Niliwwaambieni, and Rowe (1997) insist that any attempts to ameliorate the problems of African American women must draw from the traditional African culture, and in particular, cultural values such as the importance of home and family.

Poverty Among African American Families

Although poverty among older women is a growing concern, so is poverty among working class families and female one-parent and teen families (Peake, 1997). The solutions to or remedies for improving the economic position for these family types among African Americans are varied and oftentimes controversial. Some scholars believe the solutions should be person-centered, focusing on self-improvement; some believe that community development centers should play a role; some believe solutions should emerge from policies or social movements; and some stress the value of a combination of these options. Regardless of the difference in strategies for solutions, all agree the problem needs immediate attention.

Homelessness

Along with the proliferation of health concerns, homelessness is increasing among African Americans, particularly among those in urban areas, among single women, and among women with children (Hunter, 1996). This is discouraging for African American women when we consider the risk factors that often accompany homelessness, such as domestic violence, life threatening diseases, rape, and illegal drug and sexual activities. Increasingly, more single African American women are among what I call the "hidden homeless," those persons without permanent addresses who routinely reside with relatives and/or friends, so-called "house skipping." In general, support-ive services for homeless persons are male-centered, family oriented, and not culturally sensitive. There are few supportive services targeted specifically for homeless single African American women, a phenomenon which in itself shows the overarching inadequacy of research on and services for homeless single African American women. Attempts to meet the needs of homeless women with children are fraught with family preservation or child endanger-ment issues. But, we have learned that even if an outsider views a mother as "bad," most children do not hold similar views. Oftentimes, for better or for worse, Mom is all that they have and the only one they trust. The homeless family might not have permanent housing, but at least they are all together. How do we help homeless, one-parent families without threatening their only sense of stability—their solidarity? As a worker at a family shelter for the homeless in Pennsylvania, we had to revamp our intervention strategy to include not only securing permanent housing and a job, but we also had to make parenting skills and household and financial management part of the available services. This change in programming is probably the experience of most family shelter providers today. Many of the families clearly lacked in these areas, which may explain the repeat visits by many.

Some of the challenges confronting African American women such as poverty, unemployment, substance abuse, and mental instability appear to be among the contributors to the growing homelessness rate of these women. Hunter (1996) also identifies racism, a decreasing number of male partners, changes in the family structure, and diminishing extended family support as extenuating factors leading to homelessness. She suggests that solutions lie with policy makers and community supports. Given the historical precedence of African American women's social clubs, church groups, and sororities in initiating grass roots efforts (Smith, 1995), we would do well to invest dollars, time, and service to troubled and high-risk families to promote their health, success, and well-being in the next millennium. We can offer financial assis-tance to these single homeless mothers, and we can also offer help with survival skills where the absence of such skills has placed some African Ameri-can women in high-risk status. Increasing their self-worth and family-worth, promoting their employable job skills, implementing service coordination, offering them financial and household management strategies, providing them with parenting skills, and improving their housing options will benefit all of us. We must not make these efforts just an annual event, but a lifelong com-mitment. I term this concept of community intervention as "community caregiving." Community caregiving might well be the next grass roots movement in African American and other minority communities.

Older African American Women

Older women living alone comprise over fifty percent of the adult population, and for African American women, the proportion is even larger. While some enjoy good health and secured finances, a growing number who live alone fall below the poverty line (Schulz, 1997; U.S. Bureau of Census, 1993), are facing debilitating health conditions with little or no health benefits, and are living in substandard housing (Coward, 1997; Mouton, 1997). Case managers have shared stories in which their African American clients cannot buy necessary medications and postpone or avoid doctor visits because of limited finances. Stories reveal how clients' once immaculate homes are now dilapidated, with poor roofing, plumbing, and other structural defects. Their once respectable neighborhoods have likewise deteriorated, adding safety concerns to their problems. These dilemmas will only become more pronounced in the wake of decreased entitlement and governmental support (Wells, 1997).

People on the whole are living longer, and children taking care of older parents is becoming more customary. Although the life expectancy rates for African American men and women continue to lag behind those of their white counterparts (National Center for Health Statistics, 1995), like them they have experienced increased rates over the past decade and with this brings new family demands. A commonplace assumption is that African Americans take care of their own through their extended familial systems. The challenges to their continued support of single older adult women are mounting. Some of the factors that diminish family support among the general population are increasingly threatening African Americans—i.e., mobility of adult children, fewer children, multiple/conflicting demands, financial hardships, and so forth (Atchley, 1997). Agencies are attempting to address these issues, but the problems of minority elders still warrant special attention when consideration is given to racial and economic disparities relative to availability and use. African American churches are a venue by which to fill some of the gaps, but little is known about the extent, the consistency, and the effectiveness of church support for African American elderly. Based on community service in this area and research (Winbush & Balaswamy, 1998), challenges that confront church-affiliated support include organizational issues such as structure, administration, financing, and accountability. Program models such as the Interfaith Volunteer Caregiving Project, in which churches of different denominations and community organizations collaborate to generate volunteers to provide supportive services for dependent populations, are quite promising, but they, too, have faced difficulties. More research is needed to examine the response of African American churches to the needs of African American elderly. Most mainstream churches have housing for the elderly and some have service components. However, we still need to know more about these church-based supports and their rates of utilization by African American elderly.

Another challenge facing single older African American women that has become of considerable concern is the parenting of grandchildren (Burnette, 1997; Fuller-Thomson, 1997; George & Dickerson, 1995; Minkler, 1997). Grandmothers raising grandchildren often need supportive services because of preexisting constraints including meager incomes, poor health, and poor housing (Burnette, 1997). Some older African American women are providing care not only to troubled grandchildren but to their troubled children as well. We need to document this trend in African American families and provide viable solutions that will assist these women, their children, and their grandchildren. A number of aging-specific organizations have taken some initiative in these areas through advocacy and program development.

African American Teenage Mothers

Even though rates of teenage pregnancy are declining (National Center for Health Statistics, 1996), teenage motherhood is still a challenge facing African American women. Some argue that publicizing the problem contributes to negative depictions relative to race, gender, class, and religion (Elise, 1995; Leslie, 1995). The proceeding discussion of teenage motherhood is not to indulge in the deficits of African Americans, but to direct focus to some of the negative consequences of early parenting for all women, and in particular, for African American women. Whereas debates have centered on the reasons for teenage pregnancy (Elise, 1995) and the immorality of teen pregnancy (Leslie, 1995), there is a consensus on the difficulties that attend early parenting, particularly for women of color. Some of the negative consequences of early parenting are far reaching and of an economical, educational, and social nature. Research shows that having a baby before age 20 reduces eventual academic achievement, reduces the likelihood of marriage, and increases the likelihood of being abused, abandoned, and divorced (Klepinger, Lundberg, & Plotnick, 1995; Lillard & Waite, 1993). Life-long negative consequences are not just limited to the young mother, but to her children, who over the life course are at risk for prenatal and birth complications, low birth weight, child abuse, low academic achievement or dropping out of school, drug abuse, delinquency, and early parenting themselves (Furstenberg, Brooks-Gunn, & Morgan, 1987; Hoffman, Foster, & Furstenberg, 1993). Although explanations for why there is teen pregnancy might be useful in prevention and support strategies, empowerment and sex education at an early age are seen as more valuable for encouraging awareness and behavioral change (Elise, 1995). Elise suggests educating young African American women on the kinds of ideological processes that affect them. Such ideologies encompass those of race, gender, and upward mobility. Therefore, we must continue to generate support for these young women, including child care, continued education, profitable jobs, affordable housing, sound financial support, health benefits, and emotional support to offset some of the negative consequences of this particular family situation.

Domestic Violence

Domestic violence is another problem facing African American women. There is the belief that violence against African American women is rooted in the patriarchal culture that prevails in African American communities (Smith, 1997). No matter what the reason, it is clear that African American women have not been exempt from domestic violence experienced by women in general. In fact, race has not been shown as consistently related to any type of violence among women, but there are some groups of women who are at high risk for certain types of violence (Plichta, 1996). Women found to be at highest risk are those with unfavorable economic status, college educated, residing in urban areas, and unmarried. Many of these high risk factors are prevalent among many African American women, and therefore we must assume that many are experiencing domestic violence and need help.

Kanuha (1994) described the inadequacy of services for battered women of color. She also notes that service providers need to be sensitive to the negative consequences of reporting domestic violence for women of color. Some women of color are reluctant to report domestic violence because it feeds into the stereotypes of people of color as being pathological; it advances family dissolution when family cohesiveness is culturally important; it defies societal attributions and subsequent self-perceptions of "strength and resiliency" (Kanuha, 1994); and it perpetuates the absence of men in these communities. More specifically, these factors should be considered in inquiries of help seeking and service delivery to African American women. Again, cultural competence is the solution presented most often for developing workable service models for women of color (Kanuha, 1994). Another suggestion is the combination of ethnic-sensitive models coupled with traditional methods which might positively influence African American men who batter (Williams, 1992).

CONCLUSION

The challenges facing African American women are many, but the most pressing are welfare reform and affirmative action. What have policy changes in each of these areas meant for minority groups in general, and for African American women in particular? The controversies surrounding each during discussions of possible change have now moved to implementation of these policies and subsequent outcomes. Welfare reform has been considered devastating for some and a welcome change for others. Most concerns have focused on the survival of welfare recipients without government assistance, who or what now appropriately fills the void, and whether the cost savings from implementation of welfare reform are greater than the costs to implement it. Productive job training and childcare are the prevailing issues. However, "gainful employment" is also needed once training has been completed. Some need transportation to their jobs, some need work socialization, and affordable and quality childcare is a must. With the proliferation of statistical data and studies demonstrating the pros and cons of welfare reform, they are sure to be as controversial as was the execution of initial welfare policies and procedures.

Clearly, diversity is present in any subgroup, and the strengths of African American women as well as their challenges are multivalent and complex. Thus, when formulating policies or interventions to assist them, the impulse to conceptualize African American women as somehow homogeneous is to be discouraged. In fact, acknowledging their multiplicity might be the best strategy for understanding and assisting African America women.

SUGGESTIONS FOR WORKING WITH WOMEN IN THIS GROUP

Approaches for assisting African American women, implicitly or explicitly stated throughout the chapter, stress the importance of sensitivity to their racial, gender, and spiritual experiences. Spirituality, which has been typically ignored, might be a critical component to successful outreach, programming, and assessment of services for this particular group of women. It is telling that the medical profession is now considering the impact of spirituality and is embracing concepts of "faith and prayer" in their health practices. Social service providers likewise need to consider the importance of this factor in all their venues of help.

Intervention strategies must also take advantage of the historical and evolving individual and collective strengths of African American women. For example, African American organized women's groups come to mind as one of the collective responses to homelessness among African American single mothers. A sorority, social, or professional African American women's group could "adopt a homeless family." Communities and orga-

SUGGESTIONS FOR WORKING WITH WOMEN IN THIS GROUP *(Cont.)*

nizations often adopt schools, pets, streets, and so forth, why not adopt troubled families? Because of the collective resources of organized women's groups, mechanisms for successful living can be shared with such troubled African American families to help minimize risk factors at the individual, family, and community levels. African American organized women's groups continue to be a powerful support network in African American communities, and collective activities similar to these reinforce or redirect us to African American cultural traditions of helping one another. In fact, some perceive a return to such traditions as critical in preparation for the millennium (Massey, Guy-Shetfall, Hefner, & Fennel, 1996). So why not support communities or subgroups in communities in caring for its troubled members? Why continue to invest dollars and energies on one-time projects with little and short-term impact when instead dollars and energies could be directed toward confirmed helping strategies?

In conclusion, barriers that stand in the way of assisting African American women can be best minimized or removed only when we take into consideration all facets of their lives. In spite of preconceived notions on what's best for them, emphasis must be placed on meeting African American women on their own ground and being committed to equity in interactions with them.

REFERENCES

Atchley, R. (1997). *Social forces and aging: An introduction to social gerontology*. Belmont, CA: Wadsworth Publishing.

Ballard, D. (1997). *Doing it for ourselves: Success stories of African American-women in business*. New York: Berkley Books.

Bass, L. (1997). A study of drug abusing African–American pregnant women. *Journal of Drug Issues, 27,* 659–671.

Burris-Kitchen, D. (1997). Female gang participation. *The role of African American women in the informal gang drug economy and gang activities*. Lewiston, NY: Edwin Mellen Press.

Boyd-Franklin, N., & Garcia-Preto, N. (1994). Family therapy: A closer look at African American women and Hispanic women. In L. Comas-Diaz & B. Greene. (Eds.), *Women of color: Integrating ethnic and gender identities in psychotherapy* (pp. 239–264). New York: Guilford Press.

Boyd-Franklin, N. (1989). *Black families in therapy: A multisystems approach*. New York: Guilford Press.

Burnette, D. (1997). Grandparents raising grandchildren in the inner city. *Families in Society, 78,* 489–499.

Bond, L (1997). Developing non-traditional print media for HIV prevention: Role model stories for young urban women. *American Journal of Public Health, 87,* 289–290.

Carter-Obayuwana, A. (1995). A model of hope and caring for African American women in higher education. *Black Scholar, 25,* 72–73.

Clark-Hine, D., King, W., & Reed, L. (Eds.) (1995). *We specialize in the wholly impossible: A reader in Black women's history.* Brooklyn, NY: Carlson Publishing Co.

Collins, C. F. (1997). *The imprisonment of African American women: Causes, conditions, and future implications.* Jefferson, NC: McFarland.

Collins, C. F. (Ed.) (1996). *African American women's health and social issues.* Westport, CT: Auburn House.

Comas-Diaz, L., & Greene, B. (Eds.) (1994). *Women of color: Integrating ethnic and gender identities in psychotherapy.* New York: The Guilford Press.

Comas-Diaz, L., & Greene, B. (1994). Women of color with professional status. In L. Comas-Diaz & B. Greene (Eds.), *Women of color: Integrating ethnic and gender identities in psychotherapy* (pp. 347–388). New York: Guilford Press.

Coward, R. (1997). Race differences in the health of elders who live alone. *Journal of Aging and Health, 9,* 147–170.

Daniel, R. B. (1996). Lupus: The silent killer. In C. F. Collins (Ed.), *African American women's health and social issues* (pp. 13–24). Westport, CT: Auburn House.

Daniels, S. (1996). Reproductive rights: Who speaks for African American women? In C. F. Collins (Ed.), *African American women's health and social issues* (pp. 187–197). Westport, CT: Auburn House.

DiClemente, R. (1995). A randomized controlled trial of an HIV sexual risk-reduction intervention for young African American women. *The Journal of the American Medical Association, 27,* 1271–1276.

Dickerson, B. J. (Ed.) (1995). *African American single mothers.* Thousand Oaks, CA: Sage Publications.

Elise, S. (1995). Teenaged mothers: A sense of self. In B. J. Dickerson (Ed.), *African American single mothers* (pp. 53–79). Thousand Oaks, CA: Sage Publications.

Falik, M. (1996). Introduction: Listening to women's voices, learning from women's experiences. In M. Falik & K. Collins (Eds.), *Women's health: The Commonwealth fund survey* (pp. 1–18). Baltimore & London: John Hopkins University Press.

Farrant, P., & Williams, J. (Eds.) (1990). Black women in higher education. *Journal of National Association of Women Deans, Administrators and Counselors, 53.*

Feagin, J., & Feagin, C. (1996). *Racial and ethnic relations.* Upper Saddle River, NJ: Prentice-Hall.

Forte, D. A. (1997). Community-based breast cancer intervention program for older African American women in beauty saloons. *Public Health Reports, 110,* 179–183.

Fulbright, K. (1986). The myth of the double-advantage: Black female managers. In M. Simon & J. Malveau (Eds.), *Slipping through the cracks*. New Jersey: Transaction Press.

Fuller-Thomson, E. (1997). A profile of grandparents raising grandchildren in the United States. *The Gerontologist, 37,* 406–411.

Furstenberg, F., Brooks-Gunn, J., & Morgan, P. (1987). *Adolescent mothers in later life*. New York: Cambridge University Press.

George, S., & Dickerson, B. J. (1995). The role of the grandmother in poor single-mother families and households. In B. J. Dickerson (Ed.), *African American single mothers* (pp. 146–163). Thousand Oaks, CA: Sage Publications.

Gilkes, C. T. (1982). Successful rebellious professionals: The Black woman's professional identity and community commitment. *Psychology of Women Quarterly, 6,* 289–311.

Gilkes, C. T. (1994). If it wasn't for women . . . : African American women, community work, and social change. In M. Zinn & B. Dill (Eds.), *Women of color in the U.S. society* (pp. 229–246). Philadelphia: Temple University Press.

Greene, B. (1994). African American women. In L. Comas-Diaz & B. Greene (Eds.), *Women of color: Integrating ethnic and gender identities in psychotherapy* (pp. 10–29). New York: Guilford Press.

Harley, S. (1995). When your work is not who you are: The development of a working-class consciousness among Afro-American women. In D. Clark-Hine, W. King, & L. Reed (Eds.), *We specialize in the wholly impossible: A reader in Black women's history* (pp. 25–38). Brooklyn, NY: Carlson Publishing Co.

Higginbotham, E. (1994). Black professional women: Job ceilings and employment sectors. In M. Zinn & B. Dill (Eds.), *Women of color in the U.S. society* (pp. 113–131). Philadelphia: Temple University Press.

Higginbotham, E. (1987). Employment for Black professional women in the twentieth century. In E. Bose & G. Spitze (Eds.), *Ingredients for women's employment policy* (pp. 73–91). Albany: State University of New York Press.

Hoffman, S., Foster, E., & Furstenberg, F. (1993). Reevaluating the costs of teenage childbearing. *Demography, 30,* 1–3.

Hunter, J. K. (1996). African American homeless women. In C. F. Collins (Ed.), *African American women's health and social issues* (pp. 135–148). Westport, CT: Auburn House.

Jackson, J. S. (1996). Alcohol abuse and stress among African American women. In C. F. Collins (Ed.), *African American women's health and social issues* (pp. 87–106). Westport, CT: Auburn House.

Kanuha, V. (1994). Women of color in battering relationships. In L. Comas-Diaz & B. Greene (Eds.), *Women of color: Integrating ethnic and gender identities in psychotherapy*

(pp. 428–454). New York: The
Guilford Press.

Klepinger, D., Lundberg, S., &
Plotnick, R. (1995). Adolescent
fertility and the educational
attainment of young women.
Family Practice Perspectives, 27,
23–28.

Kusum, S. (1995). Differences in
perceptions of African American
women and men faculty and
administrators. *Journal of Negro
Education, 64,* 401–408.

Landry, B. (1987). *The new black middle
class.* Berkeley: University of
California Press.

Leslie, A. R. (1995). Women's life-
affirming morals and the cultural
unity of African peoples. In B. J.
Dickerson (Ed.), *African American
single mothers* (pp. 37–52).
Thousand Oaks, CA: Sage
Publications.

Lillard, L., & Waite, L. (1993). A joint
model of marital Childbearing and
marital disruption. *Demography, 30,*
653–681.

Massey, W., Guy-Sheftall, B., Hefner, J.,
& Fennell, A. (1996). How to
prepare for the next 50 years.
Ebony, 117.

Minkler, M. (1997). Raising grandchildren from crack-cocaine
household: Effects on family and
friendship ties of African-Amercan
women. *American Journal of
Orthopsychiatry, 64,* 20–29.

Mouton, C. P. (1997). Special health
considerations in African
American elders. *American Family
Physician, 55,* 1243–1253.

Mullings, L. (1994). Images, ideology,
and women of color. In M. Zinn

& B. Dill (Eds.), *Women of color in
the U.S. society* (pp. 265–289).
Philadelphia: Temple University
Press.

National Center for Health Statistics
(1996). *Health, United States 1996.*
Hyattsville, MD: Public Health
Service.

National Center for Health Statistics
(1995). *Vital Statistics of the United
States, 1990.* Volume II-Mortality,
Part A. Washington, DC: U.S.
Government Printing Office.

Nettles, M., & Perna, L. (1997). *The
African American education data book.*
Fairfax, VA: Frederick D. Patterson
Research Institute of the College
Fund / UNCF.

Peake, L. J. (1997). Toward a social
geography of the city. Race and
dimensions of urban poverty in
women's lives. *Journal of Urban
Affairs, 19,* 335–361.

Peterson, E. A. (1992). *African American
women: A study of will and success.*
Jefferson, NC: McFarland & Co.

Plichta, S. (1996). Violence and abuse:
Implications for women's health.
In M. Falik & K. Collins (Eds.),
*Women's health: The Commonwealth
fund survey* (pp. 237–270).
Baltimore & London: John
Hopkins University Press.

Poitier, V. L., Niliwwaambieni, M., &
Rowe, C. L. (1997). A rite of
passage approach designed to preserve the families of substance-
abusing African American women.
Child Welfare, 76, 173–195.

Randolph, S. (1995). African American
children in single-mother families.
In B. J. Dickerson (Ed.), *African
American single mothers* (pp. 117–

145). Thousand Oaks, CA: Sage Publications.

Rhodes, R. (1997). A feminist approach to treating alcohol and drug-addicted African American women. *Women and Therapy, 20,* 23–37.

Roberson, N. L. (1996). Exploring health issues and health status of African American women with emphasis on cancer. In C. F. Collins (Ed.), *African American women's health and social issues* (pp. 37–57). Westport, CT: Auburn House.

Robinson, P., & Guy-Sheftall, B. (1990). Balkissa Adamou and Fatoumo Daouda Hamani, Medical students: Juggling family obligations and professional aspirations. *Sage, 7,* 57–58.

Robnett, B. (1997). *How long? How long?: African-American women in the struggle for civil rights.* New York: Oxford University Press.

Saulnier, C. F. (1996). *Feminist theories and social work.* New York: Hawthorne Press.

Schulz, J. (1997). Ask older women: Are the elderly better off? *Journal of Aging of Orthopsychiatry, 64,* 20–29.

Smith, M. (1997). When violence strikes home. *Nation, 264,* 23–24.

Smith, S. L. (1995). *Sick and tired of being sick and tired: Black women's health activism in America, 1890–1950s.* Philadelphia, PA: University of Pennsylvania.

Staples, R. (1994). *The Black family: Essays and studies.* Belmont, CA: Wadsworth Publishing.

Staples, R., & Johnson, L. (1993). *Black families at the crossroads: Challenges and prospects.* San Francisco: Jossey-Bass Publishers.

Sudarkasa, N. (1996). *The strengths of our mothers: African and African American women and families.* Trenton, NJ: Africa World Press, Inc.

Sullivan, G. (1996). Exploring issues and health status of African American women with emphasis on cancer. In Collins, C. F. (Ed.), *African American women's health and social issues* (pp. 25–35). Westport, CT: Auburn House.

Wells, R. M. (1997). Subsidies for Section 8 programs are on the chopping block. *Congressional Quarterly Weekly Report, 55,* 539–541.

Wilcox, C. (1990). Black women and feminism. *Women and Politics, 10,* 65–84.

Williams, O. J. (1992). Ethnically sensitive practice to enhance treatment participation of African American men who batter. *Families in Society, 73,* 588–595.

Winbush, G. B., & Balaswamy, S. (Spring 1998). Changing role of sectarian organizations as service providers: Challenges relative to administration and accountability. *Proceedings of the ASA the 44th Annual Meeting,* San Francisco, CA.

U.S. Bureau of Census (1993). Money income of households, families and persons in the United States: 1992. *Current population reports, Series P60-184.* Washington, DC: U.S. Government Printing Office.

RECOMMENDED READINGS
AND RESOURCES

Bayne-Smith, M. (Ed.) (1996). *Race, gender, and health.* Thousand Oaks, CA: Sage Publications.

Bolden, T. (1996). *The book of African American women.* Holbrook, MA: Adams Media Corporation.

Dance, D. C. (Ed.) (1998). *Honey hush!: An anthology of AfricanAmerican women's humor.* New York: W.W. Norton.

Gordon, V. (1987). *Black woman, feminism and Black liberation.* Chicago: Third World Press.

Guy-Sheftall, B. (1990). *Daughters of sorrow: Attitudes toward Black women, 1880–1920.* Brooklyn, NY: Carlson Publishing Co.

Guy-Sheftall, B. (Ed.) (1995). *Words of fire: An anthology of African American feminist thought.* New York: New Press.

Harrison, D., Wodarski, J., & Thyer, B. (Eds.) (1992). *Cultural diversity and social work practice.* Springfield, IL: Charles C. Thomas.

Hemmons, W. M. (1996). *Black women in the new world order: Social justice and the African American female.* Westport, CT: Praeger.

Singh, K. (1995). Differences in perceptions of African American women and men faculty and administrators. *Journal of Negro Education, 54,* 401–408.

Winters, W. G. (1993). *African American mothers and urban schools.* New York: Lexington Books.

Womack, M., & Marti, J. (Eds.) (1993). *The other fifty percent: Multicultural perspectives on gender relations.* Prospect, IL: Waveland Press, Inc.

Zinn, M., & Dill, B. (Eds.) (1994). *Women of color in the U.S. society.* Philadelphia: Temple University Press.

3

Amish Women: From Martyrs to Entrepreneurs

G. WALTMAN

This chapter provides an overview and insights into the Amish culture, with a focus on Amish women. Except where noted, the term—*Amish* refers to the Old Order Amish, the most prevalent Amish group in the United States.

John A. Hostetler (1993), a noted authority on the Amish, describes them as "a church, a community, a spiritual union, a conservative branch of Christianity, a religion, a community whose members practice simple and austere living, a familistic entrepreneuring system, and an adaptive human community" (p. 4). This chapter describes how this complex culture persists and adapts to change as it co-exists with modern society. Past and present lifestyle experiences and current trends in the lives of Amish women will be examined. Specific information is offered on how Amish culture affects women's roles, lifestyles, and behaviors, and how Amish women respond to cultural influences.

OVERVIEW

The Amish are a religious and social ethnic group who resist assimilation into modern society. Their lifestyle, based on European peasant culture, serves as a boundary from the outside world. They have their own language, called Pennsylvania Dutch; a distinctive, plain clothing style; work and family life which shuns the use of electricity, home telephones, modern farming equipment, and home appliances. They use horses for farming and horse-and-buggy for transportation, kerosene or gas powered lights and appliances, treadle sewing machines to make clothing, and they grow and preserve much of their food. Hostetler (1982) explains that "the Amish **believe** they must be separate from the world in order to attain eternal **life**" (p. 5). This belief is based on Romans 12:2, "Be not conformed to this world" (Holy Bible, King James Version).

The boundaries observed by the Amish are of several dimensions:

1. between their society and the outside world;
2. among different Amish groups, such as Swartzentruber, Old Order, and New Order; and
3. among different church districts within the group.

The Amish church rules set the boundaries that are then enforced by church officials. The more conservative Amish groups have more traditional and rigid boundaries.

Examples of boundaries that set the Amish apart from the outside world are:

- Language— the oral Pennsylvania Dutch or written and spoken High German;
- Distinctive dress and hairstyles— plain clothing styles for men, women, and children; beards for all married men and uncut hair for women;
- Transportation— use of the horse and buggy;
- Education— not beyond the eighth grade, and having their own parochial schools where Amish parents can control the education and socialization of their children;
- Modern Conveniences— no telephone, electricity, or gas from public utilities; horses and horse-drawn machinery are used for farming;
- Religious Practices— use of homes for worship, special holidays such as "Old Christmas" (January 6) and "Ascension Day" (forty days after Easter);
- Social Rituals— weddings, funerals, and mutual aid activities such as harvesting crops and barn raising;
- Silent Discourse— use of silence in worship services, expressing traditions in exemplary living rather than in written words, practicing pacifism and turning the other cheek.

The boundaries among different Amish groups such as Swartzentruber, Old Order, and New Order are expressed in several ways, such as different clothing and buggy styles. For example, the Swartzentruber Amish men wear a flat crown straw hat with a four-inch brim, but Holmes County (Ohio) Old

Order Amish men wear hats with depressed or creased crown and a narrower three-inch brim. Swartzentruber Amish women wear longer dresses, usually very dark-colored, than those of Old Order Amish women. Rubber tires are permitted on New Order Amish buggies, where Old Order buggy tires have metal rims. Kraybill (1994) describes detailed differences in buggies, household technology, tractor usage, farm equipment, shop technology, and general technology use by Amish group affiliation (pp. 61–71).

There are also regional variations in boundaries among the Old Order Amish. For example, women's black bonnets in Lancaster County, Pennsylvania, feature pleats while Holmes County, Ohio, gathers the back to the brim. The heart-shaped, white head covering in Lancaster County, Pennsylvania differs from the more rounded shape found in Holmes County, Ohio.

Among different church districts within an Amish group, there are differences in expected behavior and use of technology. Kraybill (1994) observes that, "Among the nine hundred plus Amish congregations in North America, there is enormous variation in everyday practice. One bishop may permit the use of bicycles but a neighboring bishop may not" (p. 4). Other variations are in the use of power mowers, weedeaters, artificial insemination of dairy cattle, and even eating in restaurants.

The Amish religion is intertwined with Amish life. An unwritten set of rules called the *Ordnung* dictates the lifestyle and religious practices of an Amish community. Each church district, comprised of twenty-five to thirty-five families, has its own *Ordnung*, prescribing hairstyles, dress, home furnishings, acceptable farming equipment, worship practices, and other rules and regulations to maintain separation from the outside world.

The concept of *Gelassenheit*, submission or yielding to a higher authority, embodies the Amish philosophy of life. It emphasizes humility, obedience, thrift, simplicity, and community well-being over individual rights (Kraybill, 1989).[1] This emphasis on community is also illustrated in the strong Amish mutual aid system, where community members work together to harvest crops, build a shed or a barn, and give emotional support and assistance to a family coping with sudden death, serious illness, or an accident.

Kraybill (1989) summarizes the basic values of Amish culture as follows:

- The individual is not the supreme reality.
- Communal goals transcend personal ones.
- The past is as important as the future.
- Tradition is valued equally with change.
- Personal sacrifice is esteemed over pleasure.

---

[1] This explains why Amish people who participate in research or talk to authors of Amish literature request anonymity so that their identity is protected.

- Local involvement outweighs national acclaim.
- Work is more satisfying than consumption.
- Obeying, waiting, and yielding are embraced.
- Newer, bigger, and faster are not better.
- Preservation eclipses progress.
- Staying together is the supreme value (p. 45).

HISTORICAL BACKGROUND
AND DEMOGRAPHICS

The Amish faith evolved from the Anabaptist movement during the sixteenth century European Reformation. The Anabaptists, meaning "rebaptizers," believed in adult baptism, separation of church and state, peace and nonresistance, literal interpretation of the Bible, and mutual aid (Kraybill, 1989, pp. 3–7). Catholics and Reformation Protestants persecuted them for their beliefs and customs. Martyrs Mirror (Van Braght, 1660/1972), a book found in most Amish homes, contains stories and illustrations of the torture and murder of early Christian and Anabaptist martyrs.

Among these Anabaptist martyrs were women who were persecuted for the expression of their beliefs or for refusing to renounce their Anabaptist husbands. Martyrs Mirror includes the story of Anneken Heyndricks, A.D. 1571, who was tortured to extort from her the names of her fellow believers. She refused and was sentenced to be burned alive. Her persecutors filled her mouth with gunpowder, tied her to a ladder, and thrust her into a fire (pp. 872–873).

A second example is that of Anneken Van Den Hove, 1597, who was imprisoned for two years and tortured to force her to return to the Roman Catholic faith. She refused and was eventually buried alive (1093–1094).

Still a third example is that of Lijskin, wife of an Anabaptist named Jerome, who was imprisoned for speaking in favor of adult baptism. As she was singing a hymn, she was taken from prison, thrust into a bag, and drowned in a river (pp. 521–522). The account contains a letter written by Jerome, also imprisoned, to his wife, encouraging her to be steadfast in her faith (pp. 520–521).

The traditional suffering of the Anabaptists continues, although in a different form, in today's Amish society. Amish women often express their martyred Anabaptist heritage by enduring pain and suffering quietly. For example, an Amish woman in labor will stifle her pain so as not to call attention to herself.

Even though women were actively involved in the Anabaptist movement four centuries ago, contemporary Amish women are not permitted to hold any leadership position in the Amish church. Hostetler (1982) explains the selection process: "Amish bishops, preachers, and deacons are chosen from their own lay [male] members by 'lot' for life" (p. 12).

The Amish began in 1693 as a separate Anabaptist group when the followers of Jakob Ammann, a Swiss Anabaptist elder, broke away from the Mennonite followers of Menno Simons to establish a more conservative sect. They arrived in America in the early 1700s, at the invitation of William Penn and settled in southeast Pennsylvania (Kraybill, 1989, pp. 6–8). Hostetler (1993) estimated there were approximately 145,000 Old Order Amish living in the United States and Canada in 1992 (p. 98), and their numbers continue to increase. The Amish no longer live in Europe. The largest Amish settlement in the United States is located in East Central Ohio and is known as the Holmes County area settlement. Two other large settlements are located in Lancaster County and vicinity in Pennsylvania, and Elkhart and Lagrange Counties, Indiana.

The Old Order Amish comprises the majority of Amish groups in the United States. Swartzentruber Amish broke off from the Old Order Amish to follow a more conservative lifestyle. Two groups of Amish that are more liberal than the Old Order are New Order and Beachy Amish. Other Amish groups range from conservative to liberal in their lifestyle and adaptation to modern technology.

Generally speaking, the more conservative Amish groups are less likely to accept modern technology and professional or public services. For example, New Order Amish use rubber tires on their buggies and generators to cool bulk milk. The Beachy Amish people dress similarly to the Old or the New Order Amish, but have automobiles, electricity, and tractors. Heikes (1985) surveyed Wayne County (Ohio) Amish and found that 58 percent of the Old Order Amish had their children immunized against childhood diseases, while none of the Swartzentruber Amish children were immunized. Heikes also found that the Old Order Amish women were more likely to give birth in hospitals than at home.

Some Amish, especially the more conservative Amish groups, are migrating away from the larger settlements to escape the intrusion of tourists and to find less expensive farmland. According to Luthy (1994), 162 settlements were founded in the United States and Canada between 1972 and 1992, including 18 that failed. Luthy observes, "Just as Amish forebears [sic] in the eighteenth and nineteenth centuries thought it was necessary to leave Europe for North America, so today descendants are meandering across the continent searching for locations where they can practice their faith and unique way of life" (pp. 250, 252).

AMISH FAMILY LIFE

The family is at the center of Amish life. The father is considered head of the family and is to be approached first by outsiders wishing to communicate with the family members. Amish women make important contributions to family life as they produce food, clothing, and services essential to the family. They will be consulted on various decisions such as where to live, but the father is the spokesperson to the outside world. Property and checking accounts are held jointly, but the husband probably will not consult his wife on certain expenditures, such as for a piece of farm machinery.

Men and women are assigned definite roles in Amish culture, and rituals steeped in tradition are followed for courtship, marriage, childbearing and rearing, family life, death, and burial. Umble (1996) suggests that "rituals can express identification with community and can confirm and strengthen social identity and a sense of belonging" (p. 10). Thus, family and community rituals such as barn raising and mutual aid preserve the Amish community's cohesiveness.

After a somewhat structured courtship, Amish women usually marry in their early twenties. Because the Amish faith does not have infant baptism, the young couples are baptized as adults and join the Amish church prior to their marriage. An Amish wedding is an all day event that includes a preaching service, exchanging of vows, elaborate meals, singing, and visiting. The bride's mother may not be able to attend all the events, as she is busy supervising the preparation of a meal for several hundred guests. It is an honor for a non-Amish person to be invited to an Amish wedding.

Because birth control is not used to limit family size, Amish families have many children, one to two years apart. The average number of live births per Amish couple reported in most studies ranges from six to eight, with seven being most common (Acheson, 1994; Campenella, Korbin & Acheson, 1993; Cross & McKusick, 1970; Ericksen & Klein, 1981; Hostetler, 1993). An interesting trend is noted by Meyers (1994) and Wasao and Donnermeyer (1996) that the birth rate is lower in Amish families where the fathers are engaged in nonfarm occupations. Meyers (1994) comments, "The shift to factory employment is apparently weakening the Amish prohibition against family planning" (p. 178).

All children are welcome and cherished in an Amish family, regardless of their health status at birth. Children are cared for and disciplined by both parents, and older children, especially girls, are expected to help care for their younger brothers and sisters.

Children are an economic asset to the Amish family and they are expected to help with household and farm chores at an early age; such activities also teach them appropriate sex roles. This child-rearing practice also results in untimely accidents and death of Amish children (Brewer & Bonalumi, 1995; Jones, 1990). These injuries to Amish children are unintentional rather than abuse, neglect, or child endangerment (Acheson, 1994).

All Amish children attend public or Amish parochial schools through the eighth grade. Huntington (1994) observes that "parochial schools are enabling the Amish to maintain a strong, local, church community . . . this highly functional community protects the Amish family and reinforces the family as a strong and self-reliant unit, enabling Amish parents to educate and thereby socialize their children in order to perpetuate their unique culture" (p. 95).

The parochial schools consist of one or two rooms, with outside toilets and a play area with a ball diamond. The teacher is usually a young unmarried Amish woman with an eighth grade education, selected by the school board consisting of Amish fathers. She is paid a small salary and gives the money to her parents. Becoming an Amish school-teacher is one opportunity for a young Amish girl to work away from home.

The school curriculum is a very basic one: children are taught reading, writing, and arithmetic, with some geography. A publication, Blackboard Bulletin, published by Pathway Publishers in Aylmer, Ontario, gives the teacher suggestions for teaching methods and content. Schooling is conducted in English because the Amish recognize that this is the language needed for conducting business in the outside world. Formal German may be taught by another Amish or non-Amish person, if available.

After many years of conflict with state laws concerning compulsory education, the Amish gained the right to limit their children's education to eighth grade in 1972 by the United States Supreme Court's decision on Wisconsin v. Yoder et al. (Hostetler, 1989, pp. 142–143).

COMMUNICATION

With the exception of preschool age children, Amish persons are bilingual (Pennsylvania Dutch and English) and some are trilingual (Pennsylvania Dutch, English, German). Pennsylvania Dutch is primarily an oral language used in the home and the Amish community. English is used when conducting business or other contacts with the outside community. German is used in worship services, weddings and funerals, when reading the Bible, or singing hymns from an Amish hymnal called the *Ausband*. The *Ausband* was first published in 1564 and is the oldest Protestant hymnal in continuous use. The lyrics were written by imprisoned Anabaptists and emphasize keeping the faith in God while enduring pain and torture. Sermons are preached in a mixture of Pennsylvania Dutch, German, and English. In 1993, with assistance from Wycliff Bible Translators, a Pennsylvania Dutch-English edition of the

New Testament, *Es Nei Teshtament*, was published by The Bible League. A companion manual, *Ich Kann Pennsylvania Deitsh Laysa* (Committee for Translation, 1994), teaches how to read Pennsylvania Dutch. (Amish people refer to non-Amish persons as "English," because they do not speak Pennsylvania Dutch as a primary language.)

Face-to-face communication is valued in the Amish community as it preserves intimacy and cohesiveness. Umble (1994, 1996) traces debates about telephone use in Old Order Amish communities since the early part of the twentieth century and contends that the telephone threatened traditional patterns of communication. While home telephones are prohibited, telephone use is not. Therefore, an Amish person will use an English neighbor's telephone to call a local business or professional person.

The Amish use postcards and letters, written in English, to communicate among themselves and with others. Postcards are sent to neighbors and friends to announce a frolic for the men to build a shed, or a home products party for women to attend.

Nationally, the Amish communicate with each other through *The Budget* newspaper, published in Sugarcreek, Ohio, since 1890. Over 300 Amish writers, called scribes, send weekly letters to *The Budget* describing activities and conditions in their church communities. The letters report marriages, births, deaths, illnesses, weather conditions, progress of crops, church services, social gatherings, and unusual happenings. One Amish woman scribe reported:

> Sons [names omitted by author] had a hair-raising experience this winter when their stud horse broke into a pasture lot where another young stud was. He chased him into the barn and his life-saving escape was up a narrow flight of stairs which were only 4" wider than the horse's breast measured. Finding this young horse upstairs on the barn floor they did some thinking. Then called the vet from Baltic. He gave him a tranquilizer shot, then they worked him back down the narrow stairway and got him on all fours again, safe and sound (January 31, 1996, p. 24).

The newspaper also contains ads for patent medicines, Amish clothes, horse-drawn farm implements, windmills, battery-operated appliances, yard goods, and treadle sewing machines. *The Budget* is widely read by the Amish and this national communication helps to promote and preserve their cultural unity.

In the larger settlements, the Amish use a unique system of naming to help identify individual persons. This process is necessary because only a few surnames are used. Hostetler (1993) reports the most common Ohio names are Miller, Yoder, Troyer, Raber, and Hershberger, while Stoltzfus, King, Fisher, Beiler, and Lapp are found among the Pennsylvania Amish (p. 245). Biblical names are used for first names, such as Mary, Sarah, Lydia, Noah, Moses, and Eli. The commonality of names presents a problem in identifying individual Amish persons, because it is possible for several persons to have the same name (for example, "Eli Troyer"). To offset the problem, many Amish men and women in Ohio use the first letter of their father's first name as a middle initial. Thus, Eli M. Troyer might be the son of Moses Troyer. Francomano (1996) explains that "among the Old Order Amish of Lancaster County Pennsylvania, a child's middle initial is that of the mother's unmarried name" (p. 180).

The patriarchal nature of Amish society is reflected in informal references to "Moses' Eli" (Moses' son Eli) and "Eli's Katie" (Eli's wife, Katie). Francomano (1996) further advises health care professionals who work with Amish patients to refer to themselves informally as "Nurse Bill" or "Dr. Nancy" (p. 180).

Women's Roles

The primary roles of Amish women are wife, mother, and homemaker. Amish girls learn as they grow up that their role in Amish society is to please others: namely their husbands, children, parents, relatives, and other Amish brethren. A job description for an Amish wife is found in the Bible, Proverbs 31 (Today's English Version):

> How hard it is to find a capable wife! She is worth far more than jewels!
> Her husband puts his confidence in her, and he will never be poor.
> As long as she lives, she does him good and never harm.
> She keeps herself busy making wool and linen cloth.
> She gets up before daylight to prepare food for her family . . .
> She is a hard worker, strong and industrious.
> She knows the value of everything she makes, and works late into the night.
> She is generous to the poor and needy.
> She doesn't worry when it snows, because her family has warm clothing.
> She speaks with a gentle wisdom.
> She is always busy and looks after her family's needs.

An Amish wife is her husband's helper, but not his equal, and is expected to willingly submit to him. However, Huntington (1988) explains that "Important family decisions are made jointly. Unlike the corporation wife, the Amish wife participates actively in any decision to move to a different locality" (p. 378).

Erickson and Klein (1981) describe the economic importance of Amish women to the family: they grow and preserve food, make the family's clothing, and have many children to help with labor-intensive farming practices. Generally, Amish women take care of the house, garden, and yard, while men do the farm work. Children help their parents according to their assigned roles. For example, letters to *The Budget* newspaper will announce the birth of a "woodchopper" (a boy) or a "dishwasher" (a girl). Because the family is the center of Amish life, all members contribute toward strengthening and perpetuating the Amish family, but Amish wives are managers of the home, overseeing the completion of all the work.

A mature Amish woman's social life usually revolves around church, weddings, funerals, quilting or sewing gatherings, home products parties, and mutual assistance activities such as barn raising. These events are often reported by *The Budget* scribes (Yoder, 1990, pp. 305–317).

In contrast, a young unmarried Amish girl's social life is more intertwined with the outside world. Her Amish boyfriend may have a car and they can travel longer distances to go to movies, attend country music concerts, or go on overnight trips together. If her suitor does not have a car, they will use the traditional Amish buggy but may enjoy loud music from a portable radio/tape player, thus turning the buggy into a horse-drawn boom box. There may be some experimentation with alcohol and tobacco use and dressing in nontraditional clothing. This worldly courtship activity is called "running around." It is accepted by the Amish elders, as it is considered a rite of passage to becoming an Amish adult. When the couple makes a conscious decision to give up the exposure to the modern world and embrace the Amish lifestyle, they then are baptized, join the Amish church, and assume their prescribed male and female roles in Amish society.

Changes in Women's Roles Two developments that are influencing and reshaping women's roles in Amish society are the increasing number of Amish husbands working in off farm jobs, and the influx of tourism, especially in the larger Amish communities in Ohio, Pennsylvania, and Indiana. Both of these developments are economically driven and generally not under control of the Amish community, examples of economic acculturation.

The declining availability of farmland in Amish communities has resulted in an increase in nonfarm occupations among Amish men. Using the 1988 Ohio Amish Directory: Holmes County and Vicinity, Kreps, Donnermeyer, and Kreps (1994) found 57.5% of Amish males in nonfarm occupations; Kreps, Donnermeyer, Hurst, Blair, and Kreps (1997) report an increase to 68% employed in nonfarm occupations in 1995. The conservative Swartzentruber Amish are not listed in the Amish Directory, and Kraybill (1994) estimates that more than three-fourths of them are farming (p. 11).

Many Amish men seek off-farm employment as carpenters, masons, or laborers in factories and businesses. This removes them from the home during the day and lessens their influence on family life. Kraybill (1989) refers to this development as the "lunch pail threat" (p. 192), explaining that Amish church leaders fear that the exposure to the modern world will undermine the Amish way of life. The consequence is that the Amish mother has to manage the home and family alone during the day, without the support of her husband; in addition, many young Amish boys are not learning farming skills alongside their fathers.

Some Amish entrepreneurs have home-based businesses such as furniture making or harness repair, and family members can assist with these enterprises, thus maintaining the family work unit. Kraybill and Nolt (1994) studied these microenterprises in the Lancaster, Pennsylvania, Amish settlement and found they were very successful, with "no bankruptcy and virtually no evidence of business failures" (p. 152). The business owners learn their trade by apprenticeship or mentoring, rather than business or technical training. Their success is rooted in a strong work ethic, low overhead costs, and emphasis on quality products that are appreciated and sought out by Amish and non-Amish customers.

Tourism is big business in "Amish Country," as it is called in Ohio. Tourists come into Amish communities year-round to observe the Amish lifestyle, eat at Amish-style restaurants, buy furniture and crafts, and stay at local motels and bed and breakfast facilities. Although not all the Amish appreciate these uninvited guests, many enterprising Amish men and women work in tourist-related businesses or develop their own business catering to the tourists. An Amish man may sell handmade baskets or an Amish woman home-baked bread and pastries, from the back of a buggy parked along a busy highway. Tourists also enjoy shopping at bulk food stores operated by some Amish families, usually in a small separate building at their homes.

Young unmarried Amish women now have a variety of vocational opportunities, many of which are related to the tourist industry. They can work as waitresses in restaurants, clerks in stores, *and* housekeepers in motels and bed and breakfast establishments. Others work in nursing homes and retirement centers as cooks, housekeepers, and nursing assistants.

A local public school district in the Holmes County, Ohio, Amish settlement offers training in office skills for young Amish students who complete their education in the eighth grade. In the past, these vocational opportunities were limited to housecleaning and baby-sitting for non-Amish families, being a "Maud" (temporary maid) for Amish families with a new baby, or sewing for others.

Kreps et al. (1997) studied the impact of tourism on the Amish in the Holmes County, Ohio, settlement area and concluded that tourism has not yet threatened core elements of Amish culture. However, the increased traffic and numbers of tourists cause some inconvenience for Amish people trying to conduct their daily business in the local towns, so some will avoid going to town when they know it will be crowded with tourists. Also, land prices have increased in tourist areas, making it more difficult for young Amish couples to purchase farmland.

Because of the decline in family income from farming and the opportunities presented to them by tourism, Amish women are starting their own businesses. Farm wives are motivated by a need to supplement the farm income, and wives of husbands who work away from the farm want to be productive in something other than their domestic duties. An Amish woman would need her husband's approval and support to start a business, but as Hostetler (1993) explains, "Important family decisions typically are joint decisions" (p. 150).

Kraybill and Nolt (1994) report that twenty percent of the Amish business owners they surveyed are women whose business activities "conform to traditional gender expectations—bakeries, greenhouses, quilts, handicrafts, and vegetable markets. The women, however, are managers, which introduces a new twist into this patriarchal society" (p. 156).

Two recent studies are helpful in understanding this entrepreneurial activity among Amish women. Taylor (1995) studied a group of married Amish women entrepreneurs in Pennsylvania, and Hawley (1995) conducted an in-depth study of one Amish woman entrepreneur in Indiana.

Taylor (1995) created a demographic and developmental profile of married and recently widowed Old Order Amish women entrepreneurs and studied the factors leading to entrepreneurial activities, how they run their businesses, and the effects of the entrepreneurial activities on their personal, family, and social lives and on their Amish community. Taylor found that the women ventured into entrepreneurial activities to supplement farm income, to support nonfarm households or to raise their standard of living. This information supports earlier findings by Kraybill and Nolt (1994). Other reasons for their business activities were to keep busy with something other than domestic and childcare duties, or to help people by providing a needed product. These women are capable managers who operate their businesses on flexible work schedules to maintain their family and community social obligations. Another strategy is to keep the business small enough so that it can be operated by the Amish women and a few family members or relatives.

Similar to their non-Amish counterparts, these Amish working women juggle the demands of their business with the demands of husband, family, and social life. Taylor (1995) reports one Amish man saying, "The business is okay as long as I get supper" (p. 90). Some of the Amish women expressed frustration at not being able to run a household as their mothers did because they enjoy the traditional work (p. 93). They reported having smaller gardens, preserving less food, and sewing less of the family's clothing. In addition, some reported having less time to visit family and friends, a community value among the Amish.

According to Taylor's study, Amish women reported positive changes in their lives, such as having more money to spend on vacations, prepared food, and ready-made clothing. Others mentioned the opportunity to meet outsiders and giving support to their Amish community by giving money and jobs to people. Taylor concludes that these Amish women entrepreneurs "continue to honor the mores of their family and group-oriented society which dictates that they keep their businesses small so they do not take priority over family responsibilities or the social rituals and functions that are an integral part of their culture" (p. 98).

Hawley's (1995) research, on the other hand, is based on a year of fieldwork and participant observation with an individual Amish woman entrepreneur, "Anna," who operates a country store for Amish customers and non-Amish tourists. Anna's motivation to go into business was to supplement the family income, and she also provides income for other Amish people who work for her or consign food products to be sold in the store. The area she lives in is a growing tourist attraction and her business is successful. However, she operates the business within the boundaries of the Amish culture; for example, she converted electronic cash registers to dry cell battery power registers, and she does not have a computer to place orders with suppliers. Hawley concludes:

> The primary purpose of business enterprise for Anna is to provide goods and services to an insular community that formulates the rules that allow them to remain distinct and separate from the larger American system, thereby ensuring the survival of the Amish community. Success for the Amish is measured, not by accumulation of money, and thus material possessions, but rather by contributions to the Amish community that are seen as perpetual safeguards of the Amish cultural system (p. 327).

BOUNDARIES

Burns (1996) studied ethnic boundary maintenance in an Old Order Amish settlement in Ohio, and defines boundaries as "those markers that distinguish the people of one culture from another. Religion, language, dress, and transportation are just some culture markers that create the boundaries that separate these individuals" (p. 7).

As Amish women have historically moved from early Anabaptist martyrs to successful entrepreneurial businesswomen, the issues of maintaining cultural boundaries persist. These boundaries are important to preserve the cohesiveness and strength of the Amish community.

"Anna," the Amish woman entrepreneur in Hawley's (1995) study, made several adjustments in operating her business when she overstepped the boundaries and was confronted by Amish church officials:

> She acquired a meat case, converted it to diesel power in order to meet the church rules concerning the use of electrical power and purchased meats and cheeses to be sold. The new meat case was rebuilt, stocked, and ready to be used on a Saturday, but by Monday, the meat case was gone because church elders had decided that selling meat was not a necessary product for the Amish, since most Amish butcher their own meat. Instead, they saw it as product offerings primarily for the tourist market merchandised in a way that was too worldly by Old Order Amish standards (p. 321).

In two other instances, Anna was forced to terminate an employee who was old enough to join the Amish church but had not done so, and to dissolve a partnership with a non-Amish woman in operating a fabric store. Hawley and Hamilton (1996) conclude that "Amish entrepreneurs often find themselves in a state of negotiation between contradictory values of their own cultural system and those of the dominant world" (p. 639).

Boundary Maintenance

Because the Amish work, socialize, and worship together and value face-to-face communication, there is a constant monitoring of adherence to the boundaries. Amish neighbors and relatives visit frequently in each others' homes and are aware of their lifestyle practices. Burns (1996) suggests that "visiting is a very strong thread of boundary maintenance" (p. 37), and also observes that an Amish parochial school ties Amish families together and reinforces the boundaries as the Amish parents work together to maintain the school (p. 73).

When an Amish person or family breaches the boundaries by not following the *Ordnung* rules and becoming too worldly, church leaders point out their transgression and encourage a change in behavior to conform with the rules. If a baptized member of the Amish church violates the *Ordnung* and will not repent, then they may be excommunicated and shunned (also known as the ban or Meindung). Deviant members are socially avoided by other church members until they confess their sins and are reinstated. For a married Amish woman whose husband is the transgressor, shunning presents a dilemma. Does she uphold the church's teachings and shun her husband, or does she voluntarily join him in excommunication and preserve family unity?

Blurring of Boundaries

Some of the Amish cultural boundaries are becoming blurred. For example, English words such as "shopping center" or "computer" are creeping into the Pennsylvania Dutch language because there is no comparable Pennsylvania Dutch term. Some Amish women continue to work after marriage, in a nursing home or restaurant. Amish men may work at a factory or business, using modern equipment, computers, Fax machines, and microwave ovens to heat their lunch. Other Amish families may cooperate with the tourism business by consigning baked goods and crafts to a local shop, selling "Amish made" products such as quilts or furniture directly to tourists or serving meals to tourists at an Amish home.

Boundary Compromises

Some boundary compromises are necessary as the Amish strive to remain separate from, but interacting with the outside world. These compromises are often economically driven. An Amish home-based business selling a product to a national manufacturer needs telephone communication with the manufacturer. The solution is to install a telephone in a location separate from the house, inside the business building, or in a small adjoining shed. Umble (1996) believes "this compromise maintains a degree of separation from worldly habits while acknowledging economic pressures" (p. 153). An Amish woman may use a wringer washing machine powered by a gasoline engine or a sewing machine with compressed air power, still maintaining the boundary of not having public utility electricity in the home. The cultural boundaries continually evolve as the Amish negotiate with the outside world, balancing the rights of individuals with community needs.

Leaving the Boundaries

Some Amish young adults choose not to be baptized nor join the Amish church. Other Amish church members choose to leave Amish society and become "English." Leaving after baptism and becoming church members represents the ultimate crossing of the boundaries and is a very difficult decision for the individuals who leave and painful for the Amish parents left behind.

The reasons for leaving are varied: they include emotional, social, intellectual, and economic factors as well as rebellion against authority. The social and economic consequences for the person leaving are also varied. Persons not baptized into the Amish church are not ostracized or shunned, although their parents will be disappointed about their leaving. Baptized persons are seen as breaking a sacred covenant to uphold the teachings of the *Ordnung* and may be shunned. However, Hostetler (1993) explains that different Amish communities have differing views on shunning. Some of the more liberal Amish groups feel that "moral transgressors should be excommunicated and shunned, but if the offender is restored to some other congregation of the pacifist Anabaptist faith, then shunning should be discontinued" (p. 86). Because many people who leave the Amish faith become Mennonites, also an Anabaptist faith, they may still retain close ties to their Amish family of origin.

Those crossing the boundaries and leaving the Amish church are not eroding Amish society, because most Amish children do grow up to join the church of their birth. Kraybill (1994) observes that "the vigorous population growth [of Amish society] in the twentieth century has been bolstered by large families, the growing use of modern medicines, the rise of Amish parochial schools, and the ability of the church to retain over 80 percent of its progeny" (p. 10).

If a young Amish woman decides to leave, she enters the outside world with an eighth grade education, no driver's license or car, and few modern clothes. Hostetler (1993) describes the following case history of Rebecca, who left her Amish background at eighteen without being baptized:

> "I read a great many books and anything I could get my hands on. I tried to persuade my father to let me go to high school. But he would not. After grade school I was Amish another six years and this was a very difficult time in my life. My dissatisfaction began to show in physical ways. I had no energy, I was anemic. Nothing interested me. I didn't fit in with the Amish young people and I sort of despised them for their lack of learning. I made attempts to be popular among the Amish and dated a few times, but I didn't like it very much. I was the oldest of eight, and mother kept on having children, and this tied me down and I was constantly resenting this. I was always running away to read, and I hid books. When mother was not watching I would read everything I could."

> "When I was eighteen, I thought mother had reached the age when she could have no more children. Finally, I thought, I could begin to see daylight, have a little more time to myself, and to keep the house neat without working so hard. Then I learned that mother was pregnant again, and this was the last straw. I simply could not face this. I went to the basement and just cried. I told father I had had enough, I was leaving. While I packed my suitcase, mother became very upset. Father knew that mother needed my help. So we worked out a compromise. Father said if I would stay until the baby was born, the next year I could go to Bible school. Two of my father's brothers had gone away for a six-week term of school. This was enough for me; then I could get away and go where there was a library and read."

Rebecca went to college and left the Amish way of life. Later her brothers and sisters followed her example, and after several more years the whole family left the Old Order Amish faith and joined a Mennonite group. It is not uncommon for one or two children in a family to break with the tradition with the result that the parents do so later (pp. 313–314).[2]

It is the author's observation that formerly Amish persons react to their Amish upbringing in several ways: some distance themselves but still respect and cherish their Amish background, others may romanticize their experiences in the Amish culture and ignore serious problems such as child abuse, while still others are bitter, critical, and demeaning toward their Amish heritage. Thus it is important to evaluate the formerly Amish person's views on an individual basis.

WOMEN'S ISSUES AND CONCERNS

Amish women have the same social problems and health concerns as women in the larger society. The following issues are examined within the context of Amish society.

Pregnancy and Childbirth

A young Amish woman marries in her early twenties, and has a long reproductive span that extends to menopause. The first baby may arrive before the couple's first wedding anniversary. She typically will have a new baby every other year; or some have a baby every year. Although the average is about seven live births during the reproductive years, some Amish women have ten or twelve or even eighteen children.

Birth control is prohibited in traditional Amish groups, as it is seen as interfering with God's will for the family. Some Amish couples from the more progressive New Order Amish inquire about natural family planning, not to limit the size of their family but to space the births farther apart. It is possible that some Amish couples use artificial means of birth control. An Amish woman, in consultation with her physician and husband, may have a tubal ligation for medical reasons if having more children is a serious threat to her health or life.

Prenatal care will be obtained early in a first pregnancy, but delayed until the second or third trimester in subsequent pregnancies if the mother feels well. Transportation and economic factors affect decisions concerning when to initiate prenatal care. It is costly to pay a hired automobile driver to take

---

[2] The stories of Rebecca and J. Hostetler are used with permission from publisher: John A. Hostetter. Amish Society. pp. 312–14. © 1993. The Johns Hopkins University Press. Used by permission.

the pregnant mother to a doctor's office or clinic every month. Some physicians accommodate this concern by encouraging prenatal visits every six weeks if there are no complications.

The first baby may be born in a hospital and if all goes well the next births may be at home with a midwife or physician in attendance. Heikes (1985) found that Amish women from the more conservative Swartzentruber group preferred home deliveries, either in their own home or at an Amish lay midwife's home, while Old Order Amish women were more likely to deliver in a hospital (pp. 54–56).

Another alternative for childbirth available in some areas is a freestanding birthing center that caters to the Amish with its plain decor, no telephones or television in the rooms, and overnight accommodations for the father or other relatives. Two of these birthing centers are available in Ohio Amish communities. Used for low-risk normal deliveries, these centers are staffed by physicians, nurses, and midwives who are sensitive to the Amish culture; for example, Huntington (1993) explains the need for the Amish mother to wear her head covering during labor and delivery (pp. 288–289). The birthing center offers professional care to the Amish mother at a reasonable cost, which is important because the Amish community's self-insurance generally does not cover maternity costs.

If an Amish woman gives birth to a baby with a congenital defect or abnormality, it is not considered a terrible tragedy. All children are welcomed and cherished in Amish society, and a child with a disability or serious medical problem is called a "special child." The child will be cared for at home if possible, by the parents, siblings, and extended family members. Because of high medical costs and the limited availability of Amish self-insurance, some families are accepting governmental assistance for medical care. The Amish, however, are very sensitive about accepting free care and one Amish community in Ohio held a benefit auction to raise money for a state program to benefit children with medical handicaps. Because they are supported by the Amish community such efforts help the families receiving benefits to be more comfortable as recipients.

If a baby is critically ill or has serious congenital malfunctions and there is not a reasonable chance of survival, the parents may request to take the baby home and trust in "God's will" regarding outcome. Waltman (1996) advises, "Health care professionals need to respect the parents' wishes in these cases" (p. 31).

When a young Amish woman becomes pregnant before marriage, she is encouraged to marry the father, if he is Amish; he may be her intended spouse. When the parents do not marry, the mother may keep the baby or place it for adoption with another Amish couple. Sympathetic physicians and attorneys will assist the Amish family with the adoption process.

Childlessness occurs in Amish couples but the rate is less than the U.S. population as a whole (Hostetler, 1993, p. 100). Because of the strong emphasis on having children in Amish culture, childless couples are viewed sympathetically. These couples may adopt a child born to an unmarried Amish mother, or they may enjoy close ties with extended family members with children.

Midwives

The use of midwives for delivery at home, at a birthing center, or in a hospital is increasing in popularity, for comfort and economic reasons, with Amish and non-Amish mothers. The midwife is a registered nurse with a degree in nursing and certification in midwifery, or a lay Amish or non-Amish midwife trained by apprenticeship. Nurse midwives meet national standards and are licensed by individual states. The licensing and recognition of lay midwives varies from state to state.

Midwives are more likely to accommodate an Amish expectant mother's desire to use herbs as part of prenatal, perinatal, and postnatal care, and may provide herbs in capsules or teas to the mother. Ginger tea is given for morning sickness and catnip tea is used during labor. Campenella, Korbin, and Acheson (1993) report the use of brown sugar applied topically to heal vaginal tears, blue cohosh to speed labor, and red raspberry capsules throughout the pregnancy (p. 335).

Midwives are an important resource to promote Amish women's access to health care. An Amish woman may feel more comfortable talking with a nurse midwife about gynecological concerns, as she probably did not have a premarital exam by a physician to discuss birth control options. Finn (1995) observes that "Amish women separate public and private sexual expression. There are no public displays of affection, and they do not discuss sexuality with their children" (p. 33). The nurse midwife has an opportunity to educate Amish women about sensitive subjects through informal conversation or providing educational literature.

Health Care The Amish, like many other people, use several health care systems, often simultaneously. Wenger (1995) classifies these health care systems as professional care, alternative care, and folk care (p. 6). Regardless of the health care system or systems used, Amish persons value a practitioner with a holistic approach who will take time to listen to the patient, consider transportation and cost issues, and tolerate the patient's use of other health care systems. Thus a nurse–midwife will engage in some small talk during examinations, schedule appointments in a cluster of time for several Amish women who can share a ride with a paid driver, and provide herbal teas and remedies preferred by their Amish patients.

Amish people get medical care from professionals such as family physicians, medical specialists, dentists, and nurses. Because their training requires higher education, these medical professionals are all non-Amish. However, some practitioners may have grown up in Amish culture and speak Pennsylvania Dutch with their patients to make them more comfortable with medical care. If a preschool Amish child is the patient, the mother or father may have to interpret from English to Pennsylvania Dutch to aid in examination and treatment.

Chiropractors, herbalists, and reflexologists are examples of alternative medical care providers used by the Amish. Wenger (1995) describes alternative care as "an intermediate system of care and cure services which are used by both Amish and non-Amish, but are generally not identified with the professional health care system" (p. 6).

Folk care is defined by Wenger (1995) as "the indigenous system that provides traditional care and cure practices, usually in the home or community context, using home remedies and the services of Amish healers" (p. 6). These home remedies may include teas, tonics, ointments, liniments, or poultices. Many Amish folk care traditions and recipes are passed by mothers from one generation to another. The ingredients for home remedies may be grown in home gardens or purchased commercially from health food stores or mail order companies.

Patent (prepackaged nonprescription) medicines are popular with the Amish and are purchased at local pharmacies. Examples are Lydia Pinkham Herbal Compound and Hyland's homeopathic combinations. The Lydia Pinkham label proclaims its existence since 1875, compounded from natural medicinal herbs and used to relieve menstrual and menopausal distress. This tonic also contains $13\frac{1}{2}$ percent ethyl alcohol. Hyland's pills are offered for a variety of non-lifethreatening medical problems such as headache, flu, arthritis, and women's problems such as bladder irritation, menopause, menstrual cramps, and premenstrual syndrome. *The Budget* newspaper contains testimonials and advertisements for mail order remedies to treat a variety of ailments. Although these items may be very expensive, this advertising approach appeals to the Amish customer because it is based on self-diagnosis and convenient to obtain.

An Amish folk practitioner called a "pow-wow" uses words, charms, and physical manipulation to relieve symptoms such as backaches, headaches, arthritis, and fever. The pow-wow techniques are learned from other practitioners; most of these practitioners are men, but some are women. The pow-wow does not charge a fee for services but accepts donations and does not prescribe but suggests helpful herbs and vitamins, thus avoiding a charge of practicing medicine without a license. Amish and some non-Amish people patronize pow-wow practitioners because they are easily accessible as they live in the Amish community, are low cost, and their success is based on trust and inspired hope.

According to Wenger (1995), the Amish use folk care "because they want to be involved in their own health care and believe that they have a responsibility to do all they can to help themselves first" before using professional care (p. 6). Huntington (1993) further explains that "they are reluctant to depend exclusively on medical professionals to make decisions involving the health of their families" (p. 163). Health care professionals treating Amish patients need to inquire about the use of alternative and folk medical care and not criticize or interfere with this practice, so long as it is not detrimental to the patient's health.

Family Breakdown

Although Amish culture emphasizes strong families and family life, Amish families do experience family breakdown in instances of desertion, divorce, child abuse, and domestic violence. Huntington (1993) suggests that "in spite of strong moral teachings and close community surveillance, a population of well over 130,000 living in diverse communities in twenty-two states can be expected to have problems" (p. 184).

Desertion is documented only anecdotally, but does occur in Amish communities. An Amish man may leave his Amish wife, children, and church to enter the outside world. The wife and children left behind will be supported and cared for by relatives and others in their Amish community, but there can be complex issues of child custody and visitation rights. Because divorce is not permitted in Amish society, the deserting spouse would have to obtain a divorce through the usual legal procedures. If there is no divorce, the couple lives separately for an indefinite time.

Child abuse, including sexual abuse, also occurs in Amish families but it is not condoned. If Amish church officials become aware of abuse, they may try to correct the behavior within the congregation but will cooperate with outside agencies if it becomes necessary. Social service agencies serving Amish communities need to use culturally-sensitive approaches such as recognizing the patriarchal nature of Amish families and including their bishop in discussions of alleged abuse. As an outreach effort, the Holmes County (Ohio) Department of Human Services printed and distributed to area Amish families a resource booklet on child abuse. The booklet focuses on understanding, identifying, and reporting child abuse.

There are no studies available on domestic violence in Amish families, so it is not known whether Amish women are victims of physical abuse. Olshan and Schmidt (1994) suggest that because of the Amish religious values of pacifism and nonviolence, aggression is constrained in Amish society (p. 225).

If it happens at all, abuse toward Amish women is more likely to be verbal than physical.

Occasionally a very dysfunctional Amish family receives disproportionate attention in the national news media, with the risk of readers and viewers generalizing the dysfunctional behavior to all Amish families. This causes distress in Amish communities and concern from their non-Amish friends and neighbors who are knowledgeable about Amish society.

Coping Strategies

Most Amish women do not experience family breakdown but they, as all of us, experience serious illness, death, accidents, and the ravages of natural disasters such as fire, flood, and tornadoes. They cope with a strong faith in God and acceptance of whatever happens as "God's will." This individual faith is buoyed by a community of faith, exemplified in the strong Amish mutual aid system, which provides concern and care for Amish persons from cradle to grave. This mutual support exists nationally and is reported in *The Budget*. For example, one scribe describes a circle letter for girls who have no sisters, and another reports a reunion for Amish parents who experienced sudden death of a child (*The Budget*, August 25, 1993, pp. 10, 12).

Other coping strategies observed by the author and documented by others are the use of humor, silence, and passivity. Yoder (1990) describes social banter among *The Budget* scribes and quotes a response from a woman scribe: "To [name omitted] your question about grammar is a bit tricky, but I would say, 'The yolk of an egg is yellow' instead of 'is white' or 'are white.' Hah! I'm smarter than you thought" (p. 321).

The use of silence is pervasive in Amish society and is a very effective coping strategy. Relatives, neighbors, and friends sit silently with family members experiencing serious illness, death, or accidents. Surrounded by silence, the family members are comforted by this expression of concern. During disagreements or potential conflicts, it is better to remain silent because spoken words can never be taken back. Rather than get into an argument, an Amish person may literally walk away from an awkward situation.

Feminist Movements and Amish Women

From a feminist perspective, Olshan and Schmidt (1994) ask, "Do Amish women constitute an exploited resource or are they empowered by their work?" (p. 221). They answer that "Amish society in spite of its anachronistic ways and domineering patriarchy, accords respect and dignity to women" (p. 221). Amish women are excellent managers in overseeing their households, and their contributions to strengthening and maintaining Amish families are valued. They also teach homemaking and parenting skills to the next generation of Amish wives and mothers. Amish women are empowered in ways other than earning high salaries and promotions.

Feminists emphasize self-determination for women in making lifestyle choices (Van Den Bergh & Cooper, 1987, p. 613). Amish women deliberately choose their lifestyle when they join and are married in the Amish church. Their roles in Amish society are clear and they know what is expected of them in their adult life. In contrast, Alma Kaufman, a retired journalist who grew up in an Amish family and chose to leave before joining the Amish church, explains why she did not want to be an Amish wife: "I was a feminist before feminism . . . I didn't like the idea of leaving my own name and it seemed really stupid to promise to obey somebody who wasn't as smart as I was!" (The Holmes County Hub, June, 1992, p. 8).

Yet Kraybill (1989) warns that "it would be wrong to conclude that Amish women are discontent" (p. 73). He explains:

> As self-employed people, Amish wives, ironically, have greater control over their work and daily affairs than do many modern women who hold full-time clerical and nonprofessional jobs. Unfettered by the pressure to succeed in a career, Amish women devote their energies to family living. And while their work is hard, it is *their* work and it brings as much, if not more, satisfaction than a professional career (p. 73).

Sue Bender (1989), an author, artist, and feminist, lived for several months with Amish families in Ohio and Iowa and describes her experiences in *Plain and Simple: A Woman's Journey to the Amish*. Bender was astonished at the Amish women's contentment in performing their daily tasks and their sense of accomplishment at the end of each day. She concluded that "their view of the world is different than mine, so they reached different conclusions about how to live. Their conclusions are not THE WAY, but one way—a way that works for them. Their life is a celebration of the ordinary" (p. 145).

An alternative assessment of Amish women's contentment is presented in a study of health risk factors among a sample of Amish and non-Amish adults in Holmes County, Ohio. Fuchs, Levinson, Stoddard, Mullet, and Jones (1990) found that more Amish women (46.7%) than non-Amish women (37.5%) reported feeling depressed or low, and a higher proportion of Amish than non-Amish women (30.6% vs. 14.9%) indicated that anxiety or nerves interfere with regular activities (p. 205). The limitations of this study are that all of the findings are based on self-reports rather than direct observations or clinical measures, and some of the response variations may be a result of cultural differences and expectations.

Because Amish women grow up in a culture that teaches suppression of feelings and emotional expressions, particularly negative feelings and emotions, they may not reveal their negative feelings to others. Also it would be considered impolite for an outsider to inquire about these private matters. Therefore, a scholarly assessment of Amish women's emotional state or degree of contentment is not available.

Fallacies and Stereotypes

A number of fallacies and stereotypes, some perpetuated by portrayal of Amish people in commercial movies and television programs, exist about the Amish and their lifestyle. Some fallacies have been addressed elsewhere in this chapter and are summarized as follows:

Fallacy: The Amish lifestyle is simple, idyllic, and problem-free.

Fact: Amish people experience many of the same health, mental health, and social problems and issues as non-Amish persons.

Fallacy: All Amish people are alike in appearance, lifestyle, and religious practices.

Fact: There are a number of different Amish groups, with their own clothing styles, lifestyle, and religious practices.

Fallacy: Amish people are uneducated and backward.

Fact: Although formal education for Amish children ends in the eighth grade, many Amish people are knowledgeable and competent in agricultural, business, and entrepreneurial pursuits. Lack of fluency in English should not be interpreted as illiteracy.

Fallacy: The Amish lifestyle is very primitive, like early settlers or pioneers.

Fact: Most Amish families, especially Old Order and New Order, live in homes that are plain in decor but have basic amenities such as indoor plumbing and modern-looking appliances. A non-Amish visitor may not realize there is no electricity in the home until darkness appears and the camping-type gaslights are lit.

Fallacy: All Amish men are farmers and are forbidden to work in factories or other non-Amish owned businesses.

Fact: Because of the declining availability of farmland, many Amish men are working in their own cottage industries or in area factories and businesses.

Fallacy: The Amish reject all modern technology, including modern medical care.

Fact: Amish people are adept at selective use of technology, adapting it to conform to their lifestyle. They also use modern medical care along with their own traditional and folk medicine.

Fallacy: Anyone who leaves the Amish culture is automatically shunned, for life.

SUGGESTIONS FOR WORKING WITH WOMEN IN THIS GROUP

We can learn about other cultures through direct observation, asking others who are knowledgeable about the culture, attending workshops, and reading culture-specific literature. Health, mental health, legal, and other professionals need to develop an appreciation for and sensitivity to Amish persons in order to work effectively with them. Suggested guidelines are:

1. Individualize the Amish client/patient:
    *   Ask which Amish group the family belongs to, on a continuum of conservative to liberal, as this will influence decisions about accepting professional care and services.
    *   Remember that Amish persons value face-to-face relationships.
    *   Amish clients or patients may ask personal questions of the professional, such as about marital status, children, place of residence, and blood relations. Such inquiries help them to individualize the professional and determine his/her place in the overall community. Respond to these questions briefly, but be open and honest.
    *   Don't be concerned if formal titles are not used to address you. Such a practice is not meant to be disrespectful, but only to establish a genuine relationship.
2. Start where the Amish client/patient is, physically, intellectually, and emotionally:
    *   Accept Amish values, beliefs, customs, and attitudes.
    *   Modify service delivery to accommodate Amish preferences and to overcome the barriers of distance, transportation, and cost. Taking services to the Amish community, for example offering childhood immunizations at a local livestock auction barn, is appreciated.
    *   Provide a hitching rail for the Amish horse and buggy at public buildings, professional offices, and business places.
    *   Observe Amish holidays and Sunday as a day of rest.
3. Move at the Amish client/patient's pace:
    *   Remember the pace of Amish life is slow—an Amish buggy travels at about ten to twenty miles per hour.
    *   Talk slowly and allow enough time for discussion of an issue.
    *   Learn the art of "chit-chat" and spend a few minutes initially talking about the weather, crops, local news.
    *   Remember that language is not a barrier between Amish and non-Amish, except for preschool children who may not speak English. Don't "talk down" to an Amish client/patient.
4. Remember the Amish client/patient's right to self-determination:
    *   Accept parallel health care practices using home remedies and folk practitioners in addition to professional care.

SUGGESTIONS FOR WORKING WITH WOMEN
IN THIS GROUP (Cont.)

- Avoid aggressive legal action to force an Amish family to accept heroic medical care for a family member. They prefer to die at home and accept death as part of God's plan for their lives.
- Involve Amish bishops or other representatives in planning programs and services targeted for the Amish community.

5. Above all, treat Amish client/patients with dignity and respect:
  - Recognize the patriarchal nature of Amish society, but also be aware that Amish women will participate in decision making.
  - Dress appropriately, especially when visiting an Amish home.
  - Speak with a soft voice and do not use jargon or slang unless it is commonly used in the local community.
  - Allow a comfortable physical space between you and the Amish client/patient.
  - Avoid physical touch, especially between genders, unless appropriate and necessary for professional care.

These guidelines will assist professionals in establishing working relationships with Amish people, with mutual benefits as each group learns from the other.

Fact: Some divisions among the Amish groups have occurred over the issue of shunning, as different Amish groups have varied views on shunning. It is not necessarily automatic or indefinite.

Fallacy: Amish society is dying out and will be extinct in the future.

Fact: Amish society is continually growing, owing to a high birth rate, low infant mortality, and longer-lived elderly members. In recent years their population has doubled about every twenty years (Kraybill, 1989, p. 9).

Other fallacies and stereotypes include:

Fallacy: Amish people do not pay taxes or vote.

Fact: They pay real estate and local, state, and federal income taxes. Some pay Social Security taxes, depending on their employment situation. Many Amish will vote if there is a ballot issue that directly affects them; for example, a recent Ohio referendum exempted Amish employers from paying Workers' Compensation premiums.

Fallacy: Amish fathers paint a door or a gate blue to announce a daughter of marriageable age.

Fact: Although blue is a popular color among the Amish and is often used in clothing and window curtains, there is no connection between blue paint and an eligible daughter.

Fallacy: Amish dating couples practice bundling (courting in bed, fully clothed).

Fact: This courtship practice carried over from medieval Europe and colonial America into Amish culture. It is not believed to be widely practiced now. Whether or not they practice bundling, Amish groups maintain that sexual relations should occur only within marriage.

Fallacy: Amish people are indifferent to current events.

Fact: Although they do not watch television news, many Amish families read local newspapers and farm or religious magazines. They also like to travel, via bus, train, or hired van, and enjoy visiting and learning about historical places and events.

Conclusion Amish society has been in existence for over three hundred years and Amish women make valuable contributions to sustaining the unique Amish way of life. Women are important to the life of an Amish community, as they contribute to the economic base of their community as farm wives or business managers. They also produce, nurture, and train the next generation of Amish men and women who will continue Amish society in the future.

Amish women choose to embrace the Amish lifestyle and assume their roles in a patriarchal society, living within cultural boundaries. They adapt to these boundaries and cope with life's problems through their religious faith, acceptance of life's events, sense of humor, and reassurance of support from a strong community mutual aid system.

Some interesting trends are occurring in Amish women's lives that affect their traditional roles. Young unmarried Amish women have a variety of vocational opportunities, such as teaching in the growing number of Amish parochial schools and working in the burgeoning hospitality industry in Amish tourist areas. Some married Amish women continue to work outside the home or start their own entrepreneurial businesses serving the Amish community or tourists. Because increasing numbers of Amish husbands and fathers are working in nonfarm occupations and away from the family farm, Amish women homemakers are assuming greater responsibility for managing the household and rearing the children.

The Amish way of life reflects respect for the past, acceptance of the present, and hope for the future. Their religion guides and dominates their life, exemplified in a passage from the Bible, Ecclesiastes 3 (Revised Standard Version):

For everything there is a season, and a time for every matter under heaven:

a time to be born, and a time to die;

a time to sow, and a time to reap . . .

a time to weep, and a time to laugh . . .

a time to seek, and a time to lose . . .

a time to keep silence, and a time to speak . . .

Professionals working with Amish people need to be mindful of the Amish values and beliefs, in order to work effectively with them.

REFERENCES

Acheson, L. S. (1994). Perinatal, infant, and child death rates among the Old Order Amish. *American Journal of Epidemiology, 139*(2), 173–183.

Ausband (Selection) (1989). Lancaster, PA: Lancaster Press.

Bender, S. (1989). *Plain and simple: A woman's journey to the Amish.* San Francisco: Harper & Row.

Brewer, J. A., & Bonalumi, N. M. (1995). Cultural diversity in the emergency department: Health care beliefs and practices among the Pennsylvania Amish. *Journal of Emergency Nursing, 21*(6), 494–497.

Burns, E. (1996). *Cultural identity and ethnic boundary maintenance: The Old Order Amish.* Unpublished master's thesis, Kent State University, Kent, OH.

Campenella, K., Korbin, J., & Acheson, L. (1993). Pregnancy and childbirth among the Amish. *Social Science and Medicine, 36*(3), 333–342.

Cross, H. E., & McKusick, V. A. (1970). Amish demography. *Social Biology 17*(2), 83–101.

Eis Nei Teshtament. (1993). South Holland, IL: The Bible League.

Erickson, J., & Klein, G. (1981). Women's roles and family production among the Old Order Amish. *Rural Sociology, 46*(2), 282–296.

Finn, J. (1995). Leininger's model for discoveries at The Farm and midwifery services to the Amish. *Journal of Transcultural Nursing, 7*(1), 28–35.

Francomano, C. (1996). Amish culture. In N. L. Fisher (Ed.), *Cultural and ethnic diversity: A guide for genetics professionals* (pp. 177–197). Baltimore: The Johns Hopkins University Press.

Fuchs, J. A., Levinson, R. M., Stoddard, R. R., Mullet, M. E., & Jones, D. H. (1990). Health risk factors among the Amish: Results of a survey. *Health Education Quarterly, 17*(2), 197–211.

Hawley, J. M. (1995). Maintaining business while maintaining boundaries: An Amish women's entrepreneurial experience. *Entrepreneurship, Innovation, and Change, 4*(4), 315–328.

Hawley, J. M., & Hamilton, J. A. (1996). Retail Entrepreneurial values in a bicultural community: Cultural and economic contentions and negotiation. *Journal of Socio-Economics, 25*(6), 639–661.

Heikes, J. K. (1985). *Differences among the Old Order Amish of Wayne County, Ohio, and their use of health care services.* Unpublished master's thesis, The Ohio State University, Columbus.

Hostetler, J. A. (1982). *The Amish.* Scottdale, PA: Herald Press.

_____. (1989). *Amish roots.* Baltimore: The Johns Hopkins University Press.

_____. (1993). *Amish society* (4th ed.). Baltimore: The Johns Hopkins University Press.

Huntington, G. E. (1988). The Amish family. In C. H. Mindel, R. W. Habenstein, & R. Wright, Jr. (Eds.), *Ethnic families in America: Patterns and variations* (3rd. ed.) (pp. 367–399). New York: Elsevier.

_____. (1993). Health care. In D. B. Kraybill (Ed.), *The Amish and the state* (pp. 163–189). Baltimore: The Johns Hopkins University Press.

Huntington, G. E. (1994). Persistence and change in Amish education. In D. B. Kraybill & M. A. Olshan (Eds.), *The Amish struggle with modernity* (pp. 77–95). Hanover, NH: University Press of New England.

Ich Kann Pennsylvania Deitsh Laysa. (1993). Sugarcreek, OH: Committee for Translation, 3864 Township Road 162, 44681.

Jones, M. W. (1990). A study of trauma in an Amish community. *The Journal of Trauma, 30*(7), 899–902.

Kraybill, D. B. (1989). *The riddle of Amish culture.* Baltimore: The Johns Hopkins University Press.

Kraybill, D. B. (1994). Introduction: The struggle to be separate. In D. B. Kraybill & M. A. Olshan (Eds.), *The Amish struggle with modernity* (pp. 1–17). Hanover, NH: University Press of New England.

Kraybill, D. B., & Nolt, S. M. (1994). The rise of microenterprises. In D. B. Kraybill & M. A. Olshan (Eds.), *The Amish struggle with modernity* (pp. 149–163). Hanover, NH: University Press of New England.

Kreps, G. M., Donnermeyer, J. F., Hurst, C., Blair, R., & Kreps, M. (1997). The impact of tourism on the Amish subculture: A case study. *Community Development Journal, 32*(4), 354–367.

Kreps, G. M., Donnermeyer, J. F., & Kreps, M. W. (1994). The changing occupational structure of Amish males. *Rural Sociology, 59*(4), 708–719.

Luthy, D. (1994). Amish migration patterns: 1972–1992. In D. B. Kraybill & M. A. Olshan, *The Amish struggle with modernity* (pp. 243–259). Hanover, NH: University Press of New England.

Meyers, T. J. (1994). Lunch pails and factories. In D. B. Kraybill & M. A. Olshan, *The Amish struggle with modernity* (pp. 165–181). Hanover, NH: University Press of New England.

Olshan, M. A., & Schmidt, K. D. (1994). Amish women and the feminist conundrum. In D. B. Kraybill & M. A. Olshan, *The Amish struggle with modernity* (pp. 215–229). Hanover,

NH: University Press of New England.

Taylor, A. S. (1995). *A demographic and developmental profile of newly-emerging entrepreneurs among married women in the Old-Order Amish society of Lancaster County, Pennsylvania* (Doctoral dissertation, Temple University, 1995). UMI Dissertation Services, Ann Arbor, MI. UMI Number: 9600082.

The Holmes County Hub, Millersburg, Ohio (1992). Special edition, The Amish: A culture, a religion, a way of life.

Umble, D. Z. (1994). Amish on the line: The telephone debates. In D. B. Kraybill & M. A. Olshan (Eds.), *The Amish struggle with modernity* (pp. 97–111). Hanover, NH: University Press of New England.

_____. (1996). *Holding the line: The telephone in Old Order Mennonite and Amish life*. Baltimore, MD: The Johns Hopkins University Press.

Van Braght, T. J. (1972). *The bloody theater of martyrs mirror of the defenseless Christians*. (J. F. Sohm, Trans.). Scottdale, PA: Herald Press. (Original work published 1660).

Van Den Bergh, N., & Cooper, L. B. (1987). Feminist Social Work. In *Encyclopedia of Social Work* (18th. ed., pp. 611–618). Silver Spring, MD: National Association of Social Workers.

Waltman, G. H. (1996). Amish health care beliefs and practices. In M. C. Juliá (Ed.), *Multicultural awareness in the health care professions* (pp. 23–41). Boston: Allyn & Bacon.

Wasao, S. W., & Donnermeyer, J. F. (1996). An analysis of factors related to parity among the Amish in northeast Ohio. *Population Studies, 50,* 235–246.

Wenger, A. F. Z. (1995). Cultural context, health and health care decision making. *Journal of Transcultural Nursing, 7*(1), 3–13.

Yoder, E. S. (1990). *I saw it in The Budget*. Hartville, OH: Diakonia Ministries.

RECOMMENDED READINGS AND RESOURCES

Armstrong, P., & Feldman, S. (1986). *A midwife's story*. New York: Arbor House.

Beachy, A., Hershberger, E., Davidhizar, R., & Giger, J. N. (1997). Cultural implications for nursing care of the Amish. *Journal of Cultural Diversity, 4*(4), (118–126).

Dauwalder-Troyer, L. (Producer), & Bowers, R. F. (Director) (1993). *The Amish: Between two worlds*. Millersburg, OH: Amish Heartland Production, 6005 County Road 77, Millersburg, OH 44654.

Emery, E. (1996). Amish families. In M. McGoldrick, J. Giordano, & J. K. Pearce (Eds.), *Ethnicity and family therapy* (2nd ed.) (pp. 442–450). New York: The Guilford Press.

Good, M., & Good, P. (1979). *Twenty most asked questions about the Amish* and *Mennonites*. Lancaster, PA: Good Books.

Hall, B.Y. (1980). *Born Amish*. Randolph, OH: Jacbar Publications.

Hershberger, A. (undated). *Amish life through a child's eyes*. Danville, OH: Amish Taste Cooking Company, Post Office Box 375, 43014.

_____. (1992). *Amish women*. Danville, OH: Art of Amish Taste, Post Office Box 375, 43014.

Journal of Multicultural Nursing and Health, 3(2), 1997. Special issue on the Amish culture. Chautauqua, NY: Riley Publications, Post Office Box 889, 14722.

Kaiser, G. H. (1986). *Dr. Frau: A woman doctor among the Amish*. Intercourse, PA: Good Books.

Kreps, G. M., Donnermeyer, J. F., & Kreps, M. W. (1997). *A quiet moment in time*. Sugarcreek, OH: Carlisle Press.

Kult, P. K. (1986). *Through my eyes: The Amish way*. Dover, OH: Newhouse Printing.

Miller, L. (1989). *Ben's Wayne*. Intercourse, PA: Good Books.

Nolt, S. M. (1992). *A history of the Amish*. Intercourse, PA: Good Books.

Ruth, J. L. (Producer & Director). (1991). *The Amish: A people of preservation*. Harleysville, PA: Heritage Productions, 1191 Sumneytown Pike, Harleysville, PA 19438.

Scott, S. (1986). *Why do they dress that way?* Intercourse, PA: Good Books.

_____. (1988). *The Amish wedding*. Intercourse, PA: Good Books.

Stoltzfus, L. (1994). *Amish women: Lives and stories*. Intercourse, PA: Good Books.

Stoltzfus, L. (1998). *Traces of wisdom: Amish women and the pursuit of life's simple pleasures*. New York: Hyperion.

Weaver, W. (1997). *Dust between my toes: An Amish boy's journey*. Wooster, OH: The Wooster Book Company.

GLOSSARY

Amish: a socioreligious ethnic group who aspire to live separately from the modern world through manner of dress, language, family life, and avoiding the use of modern conveniences or higher education

Anabaptist: a name, meaning "re-baptizer," given to a religious group during the Protestant Reformation who advocated adult baptism, separation of church and state, peace and non-resistance, literal interpretation of the Bible, and mutual aid

Ausband: Amish hymnal, first published in 1564, containing lyrics composed by imprisoned martyrs; the Ausband has only German lyrics, no musical tunes or notes; the hymns are sung a cappella. English translations of some songs are available in a recently (1999) published version, available from the Ohio Amish

Library, 4292 SR 39, Millersburg, OH 44654.

English "Outsider": the name given by Amish to non-Amish people

Gelassenheit: the Amish philosophy of life, meaning submission or yielding to a higher authority and emphasizing community well-being over individual rights

head covering: also called a prayer cap; a white organdy cap worn by Amish girls and women, symbolizing subjection to God and man; styles vary in different Amish groups and in different settlements; some younger Amish girls wear a black cap

Martyrs' Mirror: a large book found in most Amish homes that contains stories and vivid illustrations of early Christian and Anabaptist martyrs being tortured and murdered

maud: a temporary maid or "mother's helper"; an Amish girl who lives with an Amish family for about a month after the birth of a baby, to help with child care and housework

Ordnung: unwritten set of rules that sets the lifestyle and religious practices of an Amish congregation; each church district has its own Ordnung which, if violated by a member, can result in excommunication

Pennsylvania Dutch: primarily an oral language used by Amish people at home and in the Amish community; it is derived from German dialects, Swiss, and English

Pow-Wow: Amish folk medicine practitioner who uses words, charms, or physical manipulation to treat symptoms of illness; evidence of healing by a pow-wow practitioner is supported mainly by oral testimonies

reflexologist: practitioner who manipulates the feet to treat symptoms of illness

running around: Amish courtship which involves worldly activity prior to joining the Amish church and marriage; considered a rite of passage to becoming an Amish adult

scribe: a person who writes weekly letters to *The Budget* describing events in a local Amish or Mennonite community

shunning: social avoidance of an excommunicated Amish church member; the purpose of shunning is to show the deviant member his or her errors and to encourage repentance and reinstatement in the church

The Budget: an English-language newspaper that serves Amish and Mennonite communities throughout the Americas; published weekly by Sugarcreek Budget Publishers, Inc., 134 North Factory Street, P.O. Box 249, Sugarcreek, Ohio 44681. Telephone: (330) 852-4634

Wisconsin v. Yoder et al.: case brought before the United States Supreme Court resulting in the 1972 decision granting the

Amish release from compulsory education beyond the eighth grade

work away: working off the farm, in local factories or businesses

ACKNOWLEDGMENTS

The author gratefully acknowledges the following key informants, who contributed their knowledge about and experiences with the Amish for this chapter:

Sarah Early, M.S.N., C.N.M.
Certified Nurse Midwife
Millersburg, Ohio

Alma J. Kaufman
Retired Journalist
Millersburg, Ohio

George M. Kreps, Ph.D.
Associate Professor
The Ohio State University
Agricultural Technical Institute
Wooster, Ohio

Marty W. Kreps
Honey Run Traditions
Wooster, Ohio

Rebecca L. Mutschelknaus, ACSW, LISW
Director of Social Services
Joel Pomerene Memorial Hospital
Millersburg, Ohio

Donald A. Waltman, D.V.M.
Veterinarian
Baltic, Ohio

Numerous Amish informants who wish to remain anonymous.

4

Appalachian Women's Ways of Living: Within and Beyond Their Cultural Heritage

K. HARPER

As a young woman growing up in Appalachia in the 1950s and 1960s, I bridled at the stereotype of "barefoot and pregnant," the ethnic jokes, the Snuffy Smith cartoons in Sunday morning papers, and the generally poor regard toward my region from the dominant culture. Labels misinform and distort the perceptions of lifestyles, values, achievements, and strengths of individuals in ethnic minorities and regional subcultures. Voyaging into cities and states outside the region of my childhood has widened the lens through which I view my world and has provided a few answers to the existential question of how meaning is defined in the cultural context of life. Having returned to my native state after more than a quarter of a century of urban life and work, I fit the stereotype of Appalachians who return to the hills and valleys of their youth. My experiences and research bring me to this chapter.

My work and research include studies of women in administration (Harper, Ramey & Zook, 1991; Harper, 1991); impacts of caregiving on careers of men and women in higher education (Riemenschneider & Harper, 1990); and existential family practice with families of various races, social classes, and ethnicities (Lantz & Harper, 1989; Lantz & Harper, 1990; Harper & Lantz, 1992; Harper, 1994). I have practiced as a social worker and therapist; administered academic programs in higher education; and managed various training, demonstration, and research grants in areas such as child welfare, adoption, community practice for minority mental health, and family mentoring in current welfare reform initiatives. Such a background equips me to write about the experiences of life and gender and all contribute to my understanding of people in environments in which they live (Galbreath & Harper, 1992; Harper & Loadman, 1992; Harper, 1996).

APPALACHIA: A DESIGNATED REGION

The geographic region of the United States identified as Appalachia was politically constructed in the 1960s "war on poverty." National attention centered on negative economic and social indicators of small towns and rural areas along the Appalachian mountain range identified as a region of extreme poverty, extensive unemployment, inadequate health care, widespread illiteracy, and "backward" people (Appalachian Regional Commission, 1985). The purpose of the Appalachian Commission was ". . . to reduce or eliminate the social and economic problems that were perceived to be endemic in the area as a consequence of isolation and neglect" (Watts, 1983, p. 226).

Established in 1965, the Appalachian Regional Commission identified the boundaries of the region and created a series of grant and funding opportunities to address poverty, including programs in health, housing, food, training, education, employment, and development opportunities for people and communities throughout the Appalachian region. Gaps created by long-term low investment in social and economic development left the region without adequate housing, health care, environmental protection, sanitation, education and other basic resources to support its population.

Geographically, Appalachia stretches along the Appalachian mountains and is less than a day's drive to the eastern seaboard. Appalachia includes parts of thirteen states from northern Alabama to southern New York. West Virginia is the only state included in the region in its entirety and holds significant poverty in its isolated hollows and valleys. Obvious poverty marks a contiguous section of Virginia, West Virginia, Kentucky, and Tennessee in central Appalachia. Northern West Virginia to southern New York, once a center for rail and steel industries alongside the production of coal, now suffers major losses in employment as the workforce shifts in favor of automated mining and importation of much of the nation's steel. The high mountain ranges from southern Pennsylvania south into West Virginia, Kentucky, and Tennessee are home to those most closely associated with the stereotypes of "hillbilly" and "country bumpkin." Dominated by colorful folklore and Ozark traditions, southern Appalachia reaches into the Carolinas and Alabama (Campbell, 1983; Lantz & Harper, 1989).

Writers like Caudill (1962) and Ergood and Kuhre (1983) chronicled life and times in the region, particularly in the lives of people in remote areas and of their work in extracting coal from rich seams of minerals beneath land owned by generations of local families but devoid of mineral rights. Extractive industries ripped away the wealth of the land and stripped local economies of natural capital for renewing production and regional wealth. Unable to solve structural deficits in the economy, often men and women assumed personal failure as the cause of their poverty (Harper & Greenlee, 1991). Viewed as a culture of poverty, the perception of Appalachians is that of socially dysfunctional and economically dependent people with values that are counterproductive to social mobility. This perspective blames the victim and ignores the regional context and subcultural values.

Fiene (1993) contends that situational explanations, based on internal colonialist theory, more accurately recognize appropriate economic, political, and social contexts of life in Appalachia. She views strong familial boundaries and kinship systems as insular networks, protection against external hardship imposed by poverty, coal companies, and impersonal industries. Out-of-state corporate ownership and control of mineral resources negatively affect the lives of men and women in Appalachia and constrain the growth.

The past four decades have brought social and economic progress to the Appalachian region. Once encased by geographic barriers, the region has developed accessible highway and transportation systems, health care networks, quality higher education systems, and media links, and participates in the nation's communication highway. Nevertheless, the region lags behind the nation in overall economic growth with the greatest disparities evident in small towns and rural areas. Subcultural or regional values and traditional gender roles remain strong, especially for those whose livelihoods have been touched by coal mining, lumbering, and mica and textile industries. Life in Appalachia is multifaceted. Personal hardship, folklore, stereotypes, and traditional values have influenced men and women throughout the region's history and color the lives of many today.

BLENDED LIFESTYLES IN APPALACHIAN COMMUNITIES

Outward migration of its population has gone on for decades in Appalachia as mobile and educated young people left the region in search of employment in urban areas. A shift in this trend increased the region's population by 1.6% in the decade of the 1980s, 8.2% less than the increase in the national population (Couto, 1994). Many who migrated return to visit relatives and often to retire in familiar areas. Others, particularly professionals in manufacturing, education, and health care, are recruited to the region. Approximately 8% of the nation's population lives in Appalachia (Couto, 1994). The broad mix of people living in the region produces a blend of cultural experiences and mediates the intensity of traditional values. Subcultural values such as independence, self-reliance, stoicism, respect for elders, modesty, respect for traditions associated with living close to nature, and production of food and simple clothing and tools are revered by many, yet lessened and even absent in the lives of others.

Appalachia has become a region of diverse lifestyles where a wide spectrum of social classes lives in close proximity in small towns. Face-to-face contact among people of all classes is a reality of daily life in rural areas and small communities. Business and manufacturing executives, professionals, skilled workers, unskilled workers, underemployed, and unemployed travel the same roads, shop in local stores, use the local post office, courthouse, hospital, schools, and churches and are prepared for burial by the same mortician.

In Appalachia, as in most rural areas, the lack of resources demands that people work together. Poverty, unemployment, lack of education for job preparedness and unmet demand for economic growth are persistent problems throughout the region. Social stigma is directed against the lower class—the unemployed, poor, and welfare clients. Despite the seemingly bucolic world of rural Appalachia, distinction among upper, middle, and lower classes carries discrimination that is severe for the poor in the Appalachian subculture. Socio-economic hardships exist for many and are reflected by lagging employment trends, particularly in the region's rural areas. For example, in West Virginia an increasing number of non-goods producing jobs pay less and unemployment remains above the national average (Bureau of Employment Programs, September, 1996).

West Virginia, the only state with all of its counties in the Appalachian region, is the case example used in this chapter to report continuing poverty and discrepancies between employment of men and women. West Virginia's unemployment rate dropped to 6.5 percent in July 1996, and to 6.2 percent in November 1997, the lowest in the state since 1978. (Bureau of Employment Programs, September 1996; Bureau of Employment Programs, January 1998).

In 1990, 36% of West Virginia's population lived in urban areas as compared to 75% of urban dwellers nationally. An African American population of 4% in 1990 has grown only minimally and leaves the state racially homogeneous for the most part. West Virginia women represented 52% of the state's population of 1,793,477. About 43% of women were employed representing 37% of the state's labor force. Of women employees, 50% worked in service industries. Only one of 10 women over age 60 in West Virginia was employed. In 1990, 16% of women over age 65 lived below the poverty level of $5,947.00. In 1992, women in the United States earned $0.71 for every $1.00 earned by men. The same earnings statistic for West Virginia women dropped to $0.45 as compared to men's earnings in the state for the same year (West Virginia Women's Commission, 1995, pp. 1–16).

Nonfarm jobs held by women in West Virginia increased at the rate of 2.9% annually from 1990–1995 with increases in the service-producing sector, including services in health care, social services, and business services. In goods-producing sectors, women held only 15.8% of jobs (Women in the West Virginia Economy, 1996).

In 1990, 82% of West Virginia's families were in married households, 11.6% of which were at or below the level of poverty. Of the 14.1% of households headed by single women, 39.8% lived in poverty. In 1990, 26% of West Virginia children lived at or below the poverty level as compared to 18% nationally (West Virginia Women's Commission, 1995, pp. 1–16). By 1994, nearly 30% of West Virginia's children lived at or below the poverty level (West Virginia Kids Count, 1997).

Low educational attainment is a major labor force problem where national labor markets impinge on regional markets and automation reduces labor in industries such as coal mining and lumbering. In West Virginia and surrounding Appalachian regions, educational aspirations and achievements are linked to a labor intensive economy employing many able-bodied but poorly educated men in well-paying jobs, particularly in extractive industries such as coal mining. Literate, able-bodied men are often trained on the job to perform specialized and often dangerous jobs that pay well.

As recently as 1994, 16.2% of West Virginia youth dropped out of high school (West Virginia Kids Count, 1997). As late as 1993, West Virginia ranked 48th nationally in the percentage of adults completing high school (Zeller & Smith, 1993). Only 66% of West Virginia women over age 25 in 1990 held a high-school diploma with 11% holding bachelors degrees as compared to national figures of 75% and 18%, respectively. About 14% of males over age 25 held bachelor's degrees in 1990 as compared to 23% nationally. This gap is closing as the college-going rate for young people in West Virginia reached 32% in 1990, only slightly below the national figure of 34% (West Virginia Women's Commission, 1995, pp. 17–24). It is noted that close to one-third of professional school graduates in 1990 in medicine, law, pharmacy, and dentistry in West Virginia were women, not all of whom were residents of the state. Raising the level of education has been a long-term problem as available capital for investment in education has been less than needed, particularly in rural and isolated counties where economic growth has been slow. Access to education and life-long learning programs is particularly important to rural adults, especially for women who, more than ever, head households and search for meaningful jobs.

Women's Work in the Informal Economy

In Appalachia, work is defined by interpretations of environmental constraints and maintained by traditional family and community systems. The region's inhabitants place high value on production by a male, labor-oriented workforce. Women's production is generally viewed as less important and is concentrated in service industries, tourism, and home-based work. Needing additional income and having few job opportunities, many low-income women turn to informal economic activities to earn money essential for survival. Informal economies include numerous work activities which generate unreported income in typically female dominated and often irregular work performed outside usual workplaces. One study of twenty-three Appalachian women identified the informal economy as a source for providing necessary additional income for subsistence and for emergencies. This study identified four patterns of women's participation including anticipating regular monthly income, producing income for immediate economic crises, meeting family survival needs from transfers of money from extended family members, and collecting regular and large amounts of money from illegal activities including sales of drugs and sex (McInnis-Dittrich, 1995).

Olson (1988) singled out rural women as being a particularly vulnerable population in need of resources and opportunities. Many seek income outside the formal economy. Common and observable income producing activities in the informal economy include cleaning, baby-sitting, caring for elderly in their homes, word processing, hair styling, furniture refinishing, selling produce and eggs, and designing and selling knitwear and quilts. Often performed in the home, these activities blend public and private spheres of income generation and nurturing and are not linked to larger social or economic structures. Particularly relevant to rural areas, women contribute unpaid labor in the private sphere of their homes and personal lives. Potentially benefiting capitalism as compensable labor, these productive activities are frequently defined as "women's work," often by familiar and minimally employed males in depressed rural areas and serve to relegate women to continued dependence and powerlessness. For many women, blending public and private spheres in their lives to maintain subsistence blurs boundaries of production and reproduction (Glenn, 1985). Rural women who are caught in this confusion and subordination rarely view personal or political potential for themselves or others.

Oberhauser (1995) notes the importance of household economies where gender relations, parenting, and income production merge. These economies have the potential to produce stress within families. Rural women take on numerous responsibilities that often create stress and place women at further risk of social and economic hardship. Many assume a "superwoman" persona by trying to concurrently hold jobs and fulfill traditional family and community roles. The socially constructed "protection" afforded middle-class women who may be able to live in subordinate positions but with adequate economic support is unavailable to low class, rural women, particularly to those living in Appalachian poverty. Feminization of rural poverty places rural women who are employed heads of families at a 50% greater risk for living in poverty than their urban counterpart (Morris, 1986).

According to Ford, Arcury, and Porter (1985), joining the workforce probably provides some level of personal independence for Appalachian women. Nevertheless, informal and unreported production devalues women's work and obfuscates the accuracy of household income data. Production from Appalachian women's participation in the informal economy is not extensively studied and its impact on future economic restructuring in the Appalachian region is not understood.

Not all Appalachian women are poor or unskilled. Some have outstanding academic achievements and hold national leadership positions in higher education, banking, law, government, health care and other areas. Women from affluent, rural families reared in upper-income lifestyles began their successful career trajectory at early ages. Many differences exist among women in the region creating broad social diversity that further divides the sisterhood of women in Appalachia. Separating roles associated with class, gender, and subcultural membership is difficult in the diverse mix of lifestyles. The segment of impoverished women who are caught in intergenerational and unrelenting poverty is the population most in need of having their stories recorded. Generations of low-income women who hold deep subcultural values have taken serious and strong action so that they and their families could survive. Without marketable skills, transportation, childcare, or economically productive spouses, these women's efforts in formal and informal economies have ensured their survival.

Yet, historically, women have taken a backseat and have passively carried out roles congruent with expectations of traditionally defined gender in the Appalachian region. For much of rural America, particularly conservative Appalachian America, the empowerment of women calls for changes in traditional discriminatory practices toward women in the workplace and in attitudes toward women's economic value in general. Appalachia is experiencing changing lifestyles and increasing diversity in its population, particularly among rural women. The social construction of gender in the region, a phenomenon that historically has placed Appalachian males in dangerous extractive industries and relegated women to dependence, household maintenance, and child rearing, is more and more a phenomenon to be negotiated.

Gender and Negotiation of Identity

Social behaviors associated with gender roles reflect images and convey meanings of how a person should behave in locales or subcultures. Social construction of gender defines expectations, and negotiation of those expectations pushes and constricts acceptable boundaries. These definitions shape images of being male or female, not concrete images, but markers that are socially constructed and can be deconstructed by those who are both actors and interpreters of gender behaviors. Social construction of gender thwarts equality and awareness of personal potential. Markers of ethnicity, class, and gender are being challenged as working class people negotiate their identity and survival in the face of changing economic and social realities (Williams, 1989; Howell, 1989). Negotiating gender identity is a venture in locating, exchanging, and owning power.

Historically, power has been associated with the strength and productivity of males but not with females. The typical association in Appalachia of women is that of a less physical, less productive, even docile individual. "She's a good ol' girl. She pretty much just sets there . . ." (Parker, 1992, p. 149).

Gender role definitions in Appalachia partially emerged from the tremendous labor movements that unionized the production of the nation's coal, recognized as the most dangerous productive activity in the country. Masculinity was equated with the strength and courage of men who worked underground and risked their lives to bring this natural fuel from the vast reserves of the Appalachian mountains to the surface for industrial burning and home heating. Masculinity in the region became linked to the daily risk and images of bravery in face of threatened rock falls and cave-ins or underground explosions. These miners were powerless to change their lives and worked endlessly in situations where failures to prevent mining disasters and improve safety continued for decades. Victimized by coal companies and excluded from vast wealth associated with energy produced by coal, socially and politically unempowered miners participated in segregating women's work to home, family, daylight and activities external to the production of coal (Maggard, 1994).

Negotiation of gender is no different than negotiation of markers such as class, race, or ethnicity. In gender negotiation, femaleness and maleness are questioned and bartered. Appalachian girls learn to be dependent, caring, mothering and socially responsive to relatives and acquaintances. On the other hand, boys learn to be independent, stoic, hardworking, and reflective rather than verbal. The phenomenon of male dominance is evident in rural situations where males are victims of poverty, poor education, unemployment, and hazardous extractive industries. The view that differences in gender equate with different roles in society typically allows for male dominance and superiority (Freeman, 1984). One example from rural Arkansas identifies gender differences in a description of "back-talking boys, dirty politics, and supportive, but not subservient, women. Gender is symbolically represented in the silences of subjective girls and women, devaluing women in positions of authority, 'overstepping women' and 'watered-down men'" (Parker, 1992, p. 148).

In many cases, the demands of hard physical labor and formidable environmental challenges have contributed to images of strong, independent, rural women and men who live outside mainstream America. In this social construction of gender, men are sanctioned to maintain power. Women, on the other hand, experience subordination and have little recourse from oppression. Rural women are dual victims as they are socio-economically oppressed by rural social systems and victimized by politically powerless males who sometimes vent their frustration and despair on women in bursts of domestic violence and abuse.

Oppression of rural women includes diverse means of subjugation. Class, race, education, employment, marital status, age, and world experience (e.g., rural versus urban) are a few of the variables that set women apart from society and from each other. Isolation in small towns, farms, and remote hollows in Appalachia remove women not only from their urban sisters but also from their rural counterparts. Separatism by class, race, and ethnicity has divided the sisterhood of women throughout history. Women's occupations and economic contributions have been devalued, particularly in sparsely populated areas where the women's movement is less evident. Personal and social discrimination exclude many Appalachian women from contemporary marketplace competition, particularly those who hold low political power and few technical skills. Generally, the masses of working class and low-income women have suffered oppression and disregard in historical records of social and economic movements. Women in the Appalachian mountains provide few recorded accounts of their own contributions and importance to the southeastern United States. For the most part, women in the southeastern Appalachians have received about as much attention in research and economic development efforts as "walk-ons in the last act" (Smith, 1998).

There are exceptions. Mother Jones, a miners' union organizer, was an activist who fought for the rights of miners in her public orations in the Appalachian coalfields in the early 1900s (Lee, 1969). Maggard (1998) writes of those whose work and lives are not disregarded. For instance, women in eastern Kentucky led union activities and fueled labor strikes that brought about social and political changes that expanded health care in nonprofit institutions and changed labor relations laws at the national level. These women mounted labor strikes in the coalfields, even at risk to their lives. They put down their "women's work" to become activists in labor movements in the 1970s. Unfamiliar with picketing, these Kentucky women were successful in political action and in redefining their roles for themselves. Stepping out of their private roles into public roles of leadership and union activism proved to be an uncommon but successful demonstration of power for women who overcame oppression and disregard despite traditional social practices devaluing them and their participation in labor disputes.

Subordination of women in Appalachia is a practice to be overcome as both genders continue to negotiate their identity through familiar networks and subcultural ethos that are pervasive in the region. "Gendered identities are produced over time in people's lives through interactions that associate engendered narratives with empowerment and disempowerment, personally and institutionally" (Kingsolver, 1992). Negotiation of markers in daily life, including gender, is an intergenerational process with deconstruction and construction for those involved in the drama.

APPALACHIAN WOMEN: EMPOWERED
SELF-IMAGES IN PROCESS
OF EMERGENCE

Self-images of Appalachian women are as numerous as the women themselves. Yet, there is limited understanding of the influences and experiences in the lives of Appalachian women that open pathways for new understanding of "self" to emerge. Much of the literature about Appalachia reports the harshness of the region and its unrelenting poverty and lack of regard for gender. The literature repeats familiar images and carries the stereotype of Appalachian women linked to extended families, incest, pregnancy, religious fundamentalism, poor education, and dependence on home remedies and folk medicine rather than mainstream, allopathic medicine. In one Kentucky town, Puckett (1992) determined literacy to be linked to gender as a skill for women and not men. Illiteracy is high in Ash Creek, Kentucky, where reading is viewed as more "natural" for women. Women are sanctioned to read in church and teach Sunday school classes while physical labor is paid employment for men. Feminine imagery is associated with mothering, wiping hands on aprons, housekeeping, gardening, quilting, helping neighbors and awaiting the return of a husband at the end of his shift. The voices of Appalachian women are rarely chronicled, and they seldom write their own stories or sing their own songs of love, mothering, caring, toiling, succeeding, failing, studying, working, longing to join, and feeling different from women outside the region.

Appalachian women, like all people in every culture, amass a composite of personal values as confirmed by significant others and a warehouse of successes and failures gained from personal experiences. They hold values and images of individual worth versus ideal worth from ethnic and subcultural interpretations of appropriate gender, class and community roles. Experiences in the subcultural context of their daily lives hold significant impact, both in the experience and from the feedback each episode brings. Clearly, socially constructed public and private spheres define work for men and women in Appalachia.

Women bound to the Appalachian subculture often form self-images congruent with their immediate world and define themselves in terms of accomplishments in the traditional family context of their prescribed personal spheres. Others gain strength from their experiences to move beyond traditional regional lifestyles to realize personal ambitions. It is this difference in separating self from subcultural values and expectations that calls for investigation of the influences that foster self elaboration and empowerment exhibited by some women reared within Appalachian families.

One qualitative study of Appalachian women who entered higher education identifies three major streams of influence as those of role models and mentors, family support and expectations, and incremental processes in pursuing higher education (Egan, 1993). Role models and mentors are those who set examples and guide others to achievement and success and include ". . . grandmothers and grandfathers, parents, teachers and school counselors, coaches, siblings, other relatives, friends, and peers" (Egan, 1993, p. 270). Realization of ambitions to be like a successful teacher and to realize personal potentials identified by significant others enhance self-image and self-confidence.

Family support and expectations are powerful motivators and serve to break down stereotypes of traditional gender roles. Egan (1997) provides examples of families who encourage education and take pride in having a daughter in college. Fiene (1993) identifies traditional family values as being extremely important in the worldview of Appalachian women. A range of family values and respect for individual achievements are part of the diverse mix of lifestyles in the region, a region that can no longer be labeled socially or culturally homogeneous.

In a second study of rural women who established their own business, Egan (1997) found that the women viewed previous welfare assistance as a time of failure in their lives but that this failure did not stymie their work ethic or determination. She reports that women in her study stressed that a major influence in their lives was a strong father who encouraged his daughter to be self-reliant. "My dad always told me you can do anything you want" (Egan, 1997, p. 222). Family is centrally important to success for women from a subcultural context where early marriages, child bearing, and being good wives and mothers perpetuate socially constructed images of self. Along with this traditional worldview is the image of long-lasting mother-daughter bonds supporting intergenerational caring and loyalty. Fiene (1991) suggests that Appalachian women who combine traditional roles, occupational roles, and maternal-conjugal roles find congruency and empowerment in multiple roles and accomplishments.

Egan's (1993) finding that Appalachian women often approach higher education incrementally by finding success at local colleges or in other small academic settings before moving into larger settings suggests a need to gain familiarity and success in systems beyond the familiar context of rural life experiences. An incremental approach is found in the case example of Susan who was reared in Appalachia, abused physically and sexually, and eventually attended a small college near her hometown as a part-time student. She was encouraged by teachers and assisted by student loans. "Today, she teaches in a public high school not more than two hours driving distance from where she grew up. Viewed by the small community as 'uppity,' Susan rarely visits her hometown, seldom speaks of her family, and volunteers at a shelter for battered women" (Harper & Lantz, 1996, p. 137).

Another example of incrementalism is that of Mary, an African American woman from a rural Appalachian county who entered a small community college through the help of a social worker. Seven years later and with three small children in day care, she enrolled in graduate school.

> Having great pride, Mary came to my office to let me know she was dropping out of school but that she wanted to let me know how well she had been treated and that she hoped to return one day. Upon questioning why, Mary said, "I can't feed my children and buy gasoline to get to class. You see I have been divorced just four months, the kids' father is not working, and I won't get AFDC for another month. I am the first in my family to ever go to college and one day I'll finish, I know." A small student grant was made possible and Mary graduated with her class. (Author)

Mother-daughter relationships are perhaps the most stable of all family relationships in the lives of Appalachian women (Fiene, 1993). Loyal, life-long relationships are common as daughters often maintain close ties and seek guidance in their own roles as wives and mothers. Socialized in the importance of good daughter, wife, and mother roles, these internalized values define primary roles. Satisfactions gained from adequately carrying out such roles enable many to move to levels of personal ambitions and achievements. Women with strong fathers, mothers, and role models from an early age are better able to meet prescribed roles and to respond to their inner voice for need fulfillment at other levels. Belenky et al. (1986) report that women who respond to their inner voices "know" their personal and public realities. This response is believed to produce empowered realization of self-potential. This process of empowerment is not well understood nor clearly evidenced. The bridge from gaining satisfaction beyond accomplishing traditional roles to "a valuing of self-actualization outside that role" (Egan, 1993, p. 274) remains a question for further investigation.

SUGGESTIONS FOR WORKING WITH WOMEN IN THIS GROUP

According to Tice and Pabon (1988), people in rural areas are resistant to change and often wary of unfamiliar faces and names. Intervention within rural systems can produce change over time but requires relationship building and public education. From a feminist perspective, practice with rural women is action for social change. The social order that sets Appalachian women apart by class and gender in rural areas needs to be identified. Through consciousness raising efforts and coalition building, women can gain power over their lives. The imbalance of public and private membership and rewards can be addressed from joint efforts toward equality in both private and public spheres for women and men.

Helping rural women accomplish their goals of satisfaction in life and equal opportunity calls for intervention at personal and social levels. First, rural women need to identify gender roles that are characteristic of the area in which they live, the Appalachian region in this example. Second, self-help or support groups for women to share experiences can help to extend personal and social boundaries and reshape some of the restrictive roles they occupy. For example, learning to develop and utilize childcare centers can be truly empowering for a woman who has little respite from caring for children. Third, participation in the public or production arena demands job training and education. These are rights to be expected.

Feminist principles set forth by Van Den Bergh and Cooper (1986) guide feminist practice with rural women and can be applied in Appalachia as follows:

1. *Eliminate false dichotomies.* Enabling Appalachian women to distinguish their oppression as an interaction among class, race, gender and culture is a means to empowerment. Poor rural women often participate minimally as consumers and producers and experience greater oppression from social isolation. This separateness is forced by social and cultural beliefs and practices reflected in regional lifestyles and is particularly evident among rural poor and oppressed working poor.

2. *Reconceptualize power.* Empowerment of Appalachian women will be gradual but occurs every time an oppressed woman is helped to make a decision or to take action to direct her life. Empowerment becomes a metaphor for being in touch with self, finding meaning in life, and di-

SUGGESTIONS FOR WORKING WITH
WOMEN IN THIS GROUP (Cont.)

recting energy and emotions toward self-realization. Power is making
choices to act rather than being acted upon and redefines roles for
gaining self-actualization.

3. *Value process equally with product.* As Appalachian women make choices
   and take action needed to reach their goals, a new sense of belonging
   and involvement with others in their network is likely to emerge. This
   sense of belonging and of value to others is a process of membership
   that strengthens commitment for goal setting and attainment, provides
   feedback, and validates the experiences of success.

4. *Validity of renaming.* Having the right to name one's experience is an
   expression of self to be celebrated. Many Appalachian women find
   meaning in their rural heritage, take pride in their crafts and artifacts,
   and seek ways to share their music, poetry and folklore. Working together to bring recognition for cultural competence places greater
   value in sharing personal accomplishments. This act of renaming can
   establish pride and limit victimization in private and public spheres for
   impoverished Appalachian women.

5. *Personal is political.* Appalachian women often feel alone and isolated
   from not only mass society but from their closest neighbor living a
   farm away. Reconstructing regionally held beliefs and restructuring socially constructed lifestyles can decrease isolation and bring women together. By gaining personal power to break the socially constructed
   barriers, Appalachian women can move to greater participation in the
   public sphere of their community and work environment.

It is important to recognize that many Appalachian women may be
unfamiliar and unaccepting of feminist understandings of women's lives.
Experiences of those living traditionally and informed by subcultural values and practices are to be valued. Much is to be learned from empirical
investigation of the extent of women's informed choices as they live
within subcultural mores of Appalachian communities and rural areas.
"Women are influenced by their ethnicity and cultural heritage, and they
bring this perspective to their understanding of women's rights within
their own cultural boundaries" (Cervantes & Cervantes, 1993, p. 168). Appreciation for individual differences among women in oppressed ethnic
and regional subcultures is essential to providing culturally competent intervention.

The sisterhood of women must support diversity of women to include
ruralness. Oppressed Appalachian women suffer isolation, poverty and barriers to participation alongside those who reside in more mainstream mi-
lieu. Historically separated by isolation, the changing face of Appalachia is

> ## SUGGESTIONS FOR WORKING WITH
> ## WOMEN IN THIS GROUP (Cont.)
>
> in touch through communication, media, and transportation systems, which bring the region into participation with national and global economies. "Feminist researchers and advocates for women assert that the preservation of agriculture, family farming, and the diverse rural culture depend on the empower-ment and participation of women" (Hoff, 1992). Within the region's boundaries social and economic participation must be equitable across all markers of diversity.
>
> Finally, a feminist message that is important for all women is that oppression within the ranks of women themselves needs to be overcome. Only by overcoming separation created by markers of class, gender, race, ethnicity, and environment can women become participants in the struggle for equality of all women in both public and private spheres. By approaching the oppression of rural women from a feminist perspective, women can be empowered to take charge of their lives.

REFERENCES

Appalachian Regional Commission. (1985). A region of contradictions. *Appalachia, 18,* 7–11.

Belenky, M. F., Clinchy, B. M., Goldberger, N. R., & Tarule, J. M. (1986). *Women's ways of knowing.* New York: Basic Books, Inc.

Bureau of Employment Programs. (September, 1996). *West Virginia economic summary.* Charleston, WV: Office of Labor and Economic Research.

Bureau of Employment Programs. (January, 1998). *West Virginia economic summary.* Charleston, WV: Office of Labor and Economic Research.

Caudill, H. (1962). *Night comes to the Cumberlands: A biography of a depressed area.* Boston: Little, Brown and Company.

Campbell, J. (1983). The southern highlands and the southern highlander defined. In B. Ergood & B. Kuhre (Eds.), *Appalachia: Social context past and present.* Dubuque, IA: Kendall/Hunt Publishing Company.

Cervantes, N., & Cervantes, J. (1993). A multicultural perspective in the treatment of domestic violence. In M. Hansen & M. Harway (Eds.), *Battering and family therapy* (pp. 156–174). Newbury Park, CA: Sage Publications.

Couto, R. A. (1994), Political economy of Appalachia. In Couto, R. A., Simpson, N. K., & Harris, G. (Eds.), *Sowing seeds in the mountains* (pp. 29–42). Washington, D.C.: National Cancer Institute, NIH Publication No. 94-3779.

Egan, M. (1993). Appalachian Women: The path from the "hollows" to higher education. *Affilia: Journal of Women and Social Work, 3,* 265–276.

Egan, M. (1997). Getting down to business and off welfare: Rural women entrepreneurs. *Affilia: Journal of Women and Social Work, 12,* 215–228.

Ergood, B., & Kuhre, B. (Eds.) (1983). *Appalachia: Social context past and present.* Dubuque, IA: Kendall/Hunt Publishing Company.

Fiene, J. I. (1991). The construction of self by rural low-status Appalachian women. *Affilia: Journal of Women and Social Work, 6,* 45–60.

Fiene, J. I. (1993). *The social reality of a group of rural, low-status, Appalachian women.* New York: Garland Publishing, Inc.

Ford, T. R., Arcury, T. A., & Porter, J. D. (1985). The impact of economic change on central Appalachian households and families. *Sociological Focus, 18,* 289–299.

Freeman, J. (1984). Introduction. In J. Freeman (Ed.), *Women, a feminist perspective.* Palo Alto, CA: Mayfield, XIII–XVI.

Galbreath, W. B., & Harper, K. V. (1992). Rural child abuse: Incidence, substantiation, and barriers to service. In Borner, J., Doucck, H., & Jacobsen, M. (Eds.), *Emerging from the shadows* (pp. 127–138). Fredonia, NY: SUNY Fredonia.

Glen, E. N. (1985). Racial ethnic women's labor: The intersection of race, gender and class oppression. *Review of Radical Political Economics, 17,* 86–108.

Harper, K. V. (1991). Gender issues in academic administration: A second look at positions of BSW directors. *Affilia: Journal of Women and Social Work, 6,* 58–71.

Harper, K. V. (1994). Intervention in cultural confusion of relocated children. In B. L. Locke & M. Egan (Eds.), *Fulfilling our mission: Rural social work in the 1990's.* Morgantown, WV: West Virginia University School of Social Work.

Harper, K. V. (1996). Culturally relevant health care service delivery for Appalachia. In M. C. Julia (Ed.), *Multicultural awareness in the health care professions.* Boston, MA: Allyn and Bacon, 42–59.

Harper, K. V., & Greenlee, R. W. (1991). Workfare programs in rural America: Joblessness in Ohio's Appalachian counties. *Journal of Sociology and Social Welfare, 18,* 71–85.

Harper, K. V., & Lantz, J. (1992). Treating cultural confusion in the relocated rural child. *Social Work in Education, 14,* 177–183.

Harper, K. V., & Lantz, J. (1996). *Cross-cultural social work: An existentialist approach.* Chicago, IL: Lyceum Books, Inc.

Harper, K. V., & Loadman, W. E. (1992). Adoption disruption/dissolution: A predictive model. In *Discovering the new world of research and statistics: A federal/state partnership.* Proceedings of the 32nd National Workshop of the National Association for Welfare Research and Statistics. Columbus, OH, II, 107–131.

Harper, K. V., Ramey, J. H., & Zook, L. (1991). BSW program administration: BSW directors' perception of their power to manage. *Journal of Education for Social Work, Vol. 27,* 176–186.

Howell, B. J. (1989). Mountain foragers in Southeast Asia and Appalachia: Cross-Cultural perspectives on the "mountain man" stereotype. *Journal of the Appalachian Studies Association, 1,* 114–124.

Hoff, M. D. (1992). Women's perspectives on the rural crisis and priorities for rural development. *Affilia: Journal of Women and Social Work, 7,* 65–81.

Kingsolver, A. E. (1992). Five women negotiating the meaning of negotiation. *Anthropological Quarterly, 65,* 101–104.

Lantz, J., & Harper, K.V. (1989). Network intervention: Existential depression and the relocated Appalachian family. *Journal of Contemporary Family Therapy, 11,* 213–223.

Lantz, J., & Harper, K.V. (1990). Anomic depression and the migrating family. *Journal of Contemporary Family Therapy, 12,* 153–163.

Lee, H. B. (1969). *Bloodletting in Appalachia.* Morgantown, WV: West Virginia University.

Maggard, S. W. (1994). From farm to coal camp to back office and McDonald's: Living in the midst of Appalachia's latest transformation. *Journal of the Appalachian Studies Association, 6,* 14–38.

Maggard, S. W. (1998). Coalfield women making history. In G. Norman & D. Billings, (Eds.), *Re-*

cycling Appalachia: Back-talk from an American region. Lexington, KY: University of Kentucky Press.

McInnis-Dittrich, K. (1995). Women of the shadows: Appalachian women's participation in the informal economy. *Affilia: Journal of Women and Social Work, 10,* 398–412.

Morris, L. C. (1986). The changing and unchanging status of rural women in the workplace. *Affilia: Journal of Women and Social Work, 1,* 20–29.

Oberhauser, A. M. (1995). Gender and household economic strategies in rural Appalachia. *Gender, Place and Culture, 2,* 51–70.

Olson, C. S. (1988). Blue Ridge blues: The problems and strengths of rural women. *Affilia: Journal of Women and Social Work, 3,* 5–18.

Parker, J. H. (1992). Engendering identity(s) in a rural Arkansas Ozark community. *Anthropological Quarterly, 65,* 148–155.

Puckett, A. (1992). "Let the girls do the spelling and Dan will do the shooting": Literacy, the division of labor, and identity in a rural Appalachian community. *Anthropological Quarterly, 65,* 137–147.

Riemenschneider, A., & Harper, K.V. (1990). Women in academia: Guilty or not guilty? Conflict between care giving and employment. *Initiatives, 53,* 27–35.

Smith, B. E. (1998). Walk-ons in the fourth act: The role of women in Appalachian historiography. *Journal of Appalachian Studies,* Forthcoming.

Tice, K.W., & Pabon, A. (1988). From "fotched-on women" to the new feminist practice: Women and social work in Appalachia. In H. Roseberry (Ed.), *Remembrance, reunion and revival: Celebrating a decade of Appalachian studies*: Proceedings of the 10th annual Appalachian studies conference, 1987. Boone, NC: Appalachian Consortium Press.

Van Den Bergh, N., & Cooper, L. B. (Eds.) (1986). *Feminist visions for social work*. Silver Spring, MD: National Association of Social Workers.

Watts, A. (1983). Does the Appalachian Regional Commission really represent a region? In B. Ergood & B. E. Kuhre (Eds.), *Appalachia: Social context past and present*. Athens, OH: Kendall/Hunt 225–233.

West Virginia Kids Count (1997). *West Virginia kids count data book*.

Charleston, WV: West Virginia Kids Count Fund.

West Virginia Women's Commission (1995). *West Virginia women: In perspective 1980–1995*. Charleston, WV: West Virginia Women's Commission.

Williams, B. F. (1989). A class act: Anthropology and the race to nation across ethnic terrain. *Annual Review of Anthropology, 18,* 401–444.

Women in the West Virginia Economy (1996). *West Virginia Business and Economic Review, 2,* 1–4.

Zeller, F. A., & Smith, W. J. (1993). The West Virginia economy tomorrow. *Community and Economic Development Newsletter*. Morgantown, WV: West Virginia University Extension Service 2, 2–3.

RECOMMENDED READINGS
AND RESOURCES

Adams, P. (1992). *Appalshop: Film and video on culture and social issues* (Film and video). Whitesburg, KY: Appalshop.

Appalachian Regional Commission (1993). *Appalachia's hidden resource: A report on the status of women business owners in Appalachia*. Washington, DC: Appalachian Regional Commission.

Best, B. F. (1997). *One hundred years of Appalachian visions: 1897-1996*. Berea, KY: Appalachian Imprints.

Carden, G. (1993). Blow the tannery whistle (Video recording). Delaplane, VA: Davenport Films.

Collins, J. M. (1992). *Functional health, social support, and morale of older women living alone in Appalachia*. Unpublished doctoral thesis, University of Alabama, Birmingham, AL.

Crissman, J. K. (1994). *Death and dying in central Appalachia: Changing attitudes and practices*. Urbana, IL: University of Illinois Press.

Dabbs, J. M. (1994). *Women and men in Central Appalachia: A qualitative study of martial power*. Ann Arbor, MI: University of Michigan.

Dyer, J. (Ed.) (1998). *Bloodroot: Reflections on place by Appalachian women writers*. Lexington, KY: University Press of Kentucky.

Dotterer, R. L., & Bowers, S. (Eds.) (1992). *Politics, gender and the arts: Women, the arts, and society*.

Jones, L. (1994). *Appalachian values*. Ashland, KY: Jesse Stuart Foundation.

Lunsford, B. L. (1989). *Ballad of a mountain man: The story of Bascom Lamar Lunsford* (Video recording). Alexandria, VA: PBS Video.

Mujahid, R. (1996). *Diet and obesity among rural women in Appalachia: Rural and urban counties of West Virginia*. Unpublished master's thesis, University of West Virginia, Morgantown, West Virginia.

Seitz, V. R. (1995). *Women, development, and communities for empowerment in Appalachia*. Albany, NY: State University of New York Press.

Smith, H. E. (1995). *Beyond measure: Appalachian culture and economy* (Videorecording). Whitesburg, KY: Appalshop.

Stitzel, J. (1979). *Voices of Appalachian women* (Video recording). Morgantown, WV: WWVU-TV.

5

Arab Women

A. KULWICKI

INTRODUCTION

The term *Arab* refers to someone who considers himself or herself to be a member of the Arab Nation, sharing a common heritage, language and culture. Arabs originated from the Arabian peninsula and the Fertile Crescent, now the countries of Syria, Iraq, Jordan, and Lebanon.

The modern Arab world encompasses diverse and heterogeneous groups of people from various religions, racial groups, nationalities and political affiliations. The vast majority of Arab persons are Muslims, although Christianity is practiced by Maronites of Lebanon and Copts of Egypt; Judaism by a small group of Yemenites, Moroccans, Syrians, and Iraqis. Despite the many differences, the Arab people are linked by a common language (Arabic), a common history, and above all, a common cultural identity. Today, the Arab world includes inhabitants of 22 countries in North Africa and Southwest Asia, including Algeria, Bahrain, Djibouti, Egypt, Iraq, Jordan, Kuwait, Lebanon, Libya, Mauritania, Morocco, Oman, Palestine, Qatar, Saudi Arabia, Somalia, Sudan, Syria, Tunisia, United Arab Emirates, and Yemen. Currently, more than 150 million Arabs live in 22 Arab countries, constituting one of the fastest growing populations in the world (Zogby, 1990). Approximately three million Arabs reside in the United States. By 2000, it is expected that the number of Arab Americans will approach 12 million. Arab Americans in the United States represent all the 22 countries of Middle East, with the majority from Lebanon, Palestine, Syria, Egypt, and Yemen (Rice & Kulwicki, 1992).

The objective of this chapter is to discuss Arab American immigrants, highlighting history, religion, family structure, and other related topics. It discusses some of the most common values and behaviors of Arab women in general and, more specifically, of the Muslim Arab population. The information presented in this chapter is derived from the author's experience as a researcher in Michigan and Jordan, from her personal experience as a Middle Eastern woman, and from her knowledge of the Arabic language.

ARAB AMERICANS IN THE UNITED STATES

The history of Arab Americans encompasses two distinct waves of immigration. The first wave of immigrants came to the United States for economic reasons. The majority were Christians from Greater Syria (now known as Syria and Lebanon). Most of them were male, illiterate (44%), and unskilled mountain-village immigrants who became successful peddlers (90%). From 1887 to 1913, immigration increased sharply from 4,000 to 9,000 per year. During this period, women composed 47% of the Arab immigrants. They come to the United States for economic reasons, to join their spouses, or to increase their chances of marriage as their villages were emptied of single men. Seventy-five percent of the female immigrants during this period were between the ages of 15 and 45 and about 60% were single (Naff, 1980).

The second wave of immigrants came to the United States after World War II and included more educated and professional people than those in the first wave. These immigrants, primarily from Lebanon, Palestine, Egypt, Iraq, Syria and Yemen, came to the United States for better economic opportunity, to escape political instability in the Middle East, to pursue higher education, to find freedom from political conflicts, and to join family members. Most of them immigrated after the creation of the State of Israel in 1948, the expulsion of Palestinians from Palestine, the Arab Israeli war, the Lebanese civil war, the Yemeni, and the Iraqi Gulf war in the early 1980s. The majority (68%) came to the United States unmarried (Naff, 1980).

Most Arab Americans in the United States live in major urban areas such as New York, Washington, Boston, Pittsburgh, Philadelphia, Los Angeles, Chicago, Houston, Texas, Cleveland, and Detroit. More than two thirds of all Arab Americans live in 10 states, with one third concentrated in California, New York, and Michigan (Zogby, 1990). With approximately 250,000 residents, the metropolitan area of Detroit has one of the largest Arab American populations outside of the Middle East. According to the 1990 census, Arab Americans tend to be younger, better educated, more likely to own businesses, and overall, and more affluent than the general U.S. population. Eighty-two percent of the Arabs in the United States are U.S. citizens, 63%

are American born, and 54% are male (El–Badry, 1994). Although Christian Arabs currently outnumber Muslims at a ratio of nine to one (Thernstorm, 1980), most of the new immigrants to the United States are Muslims.

About half of Arab Americans are immigrants who arrived in the United States between 1890 and 1940. The other half of Arab American immigrants came after World War II. The new Arab American immigrants are generally younger; 47% are under the age of 25, while only 5.9% are 65 years and older. The median age is currently 29.2. About 28.8% live in households headed by two Arabs and 16.8% of Arab American households have five or more people. A sizeable percentage—42.2%—of Arab American immigrant males are single. By contrast, only 17.8% of the Arab American women are unmarried. Nearly half (46.5%) of Arab Americans 18 years and older speak a language other than English (Zogby, 1990).

Because of the large number of Arab immigrants in the United States and Americans' general curiosity about other cultures, the American public has developed an increasing interest in the Arab culture, particularly in their religious institutions, political ideologies and inclinations, and social organizations.

Religion

The majority of Arabs in the United States are Christians, in contrast to the Middle East, where the vast majority of Arabs are Muslims. A small number of Jews also live in the Arab world. Although Christians, Muslims and Jews have different religious orientations, they share common roots attributed to the prophet Abraham. The prophets of Judaism, Christianity, and Islam are all believed to be descended from Abraham's sons. Mohammed, considered the messenger of Islam, is believed to have been a descendant of Abraham's eldest son Ismael. Moses, the messenger of Judaism, and Jesus, the messenger of Christianity, are believed to be descendants of Isaac. Muslims respect Jesus and Moses and consider them God's messengers (Qur'an).

Arab Christians in the United States belong to several denominations, the majority of whom are Maronites, Copts, Greek Orthodox, and Greek Catholics. The majority acculturated to the Western lifestyle because of their historic, religious links with the Western world. Catholics tend to be more assimilated than the Orthodox Arab American immigrants because of their strong links with the Western Catholic denominations.

Arab Muslims belong to the religion of Islam, which is divided into Sunni and Shiite sects. Both sects believe in the fundamental issues of the Qur'an, the Holy book of Islam, and the Shari'ah, the Islamic law. Islam, unlike Christianity, is not only a religion but also a prescriptive way of life. Islam is concerned with many aspects of Muslim life, such as family roles, marriage, divorce, inheritance, child custody, dietary restrictions, and husband–wife relations.

Due to such diversity among Arab American immigrants in the United States, readers are cautioned that many of the values discussed in this paper will be based on common trends and on some generalizations. Arab Americans cannot be described as a single group of people with similar values and behaviors. Factors such as religion, socioeconomic status, country of origin, years of residency, age, rural or urban residence, tribal or urban/rural origins, political orientations, and local customs should be considered as key elements to individual differences among Arab Americans.

The Arab American Family

The traditional Arab Muslim family is the foundation of Islamic society. The family provides security to each individual member and, in return, expects each family member to respect and conform to family norms. The Arab family is organized around the norms and values of the Arab extended family, which include commitment, cooperation, interdependence, sacrifice of individual needs for the common good, respect for elders, and great love of children. Individuals in the family are expected to respect the rules of the family and contribute both emotionally and financially to the overall good of the family unit. The family provides a strong and dependable social, economic and emotional support to each family member. Consequently, the Arab culture places the needs of the family ahead of the needs of the individual family members (Kulwicki, 1996). The traditional Arab Muslim family is patrilineal in descent with individual inheriting certain rights through the father (Aswad, 1974). It is also patrilocal, in that the family resides with the father and paternal grandmother. The children are raised in the paternal extended family.

Within the Arab family, individual roles differ depending on the age and gender of the family member. The eldest son or daughter is given more responsibility than the younger ones, and they are expected to care for their younger siblings. Males are expected to protect their sisters and females are expected to nurture and support their male and female siblings (Aswad & Gray, 1996).

Women are included in their father's family unit and although they do not pass on the membership by lineage, they have definite rights and duties in the patrilineage. They usually do not adopt their husband's name but carry their father's family name. Men provide protection for women in their patrilineage, and in return, expect modesty and chastity from their female kinswomen.

Although Islam establishes property for women, and Christianity also prescribes it, the majority of the property remains in the patriline. Marriages within the family are preferred, among cousins. Although polygamy is accepted by Islamic law, it is rare in the majority of Arab countries and ranges from 2% in less traditional Arab countries to 10% in most traditional Arab countries (Hijab, 1989). Polygamy is limited to four wives and is allowed only if equality among the wives is ensured. There are rules for men who practice polygamy, such as separate residences for each wife and equal treatment of women. Polygamy occurs most often in villages, tribal areas, and in areas where state government is not in power. In the United States, Muslim Arabs rarely practice polygamy. The few cases of polygamy that are practiced in the United States usually occur when a man who has immigrated to the United States without his wife subsequently marries again while residing in this country.

Two distinct values control Arab behavior—the concepts of honor ("sharaf") and shame ("ayb") (Aswad, 1988). These concepts control individual behavior and reflect on the reputation of the family in Arab society. Mothers are held responsible for the proper upbringing of the children, especially their daughters. Girls are expected to remain virgins before marriage. Premarital sex is considered a sin and an affront to family honor. Girls' behavior usually is much more controlled than boys' behavior, a measure to ensure that the family honor is respected and intact. If shame is brought upon a family as a consequence of a girl's sexual behavior outside marriage, it may result in severe punishment and in some cases in death by the members of the patriline, that is, the brother or father. If the children bring honor to the family because of their exemplary behavior and they conform to cultural rules and norms, the family shares the pride.

The values of American Muslim may vary as a result of the social changes that immigrant families undergo after arriving in the United States. For instance, in the United States, the nuclear family is gradually replacing the extended family among Arab Americans. Despite the fact that the concepts of honor and shame persist, the strong, traditional Arab family value system appears to be losing its importance. Premarital sex, although still not condoned by Arab families, is not as severely punished by either the patriline among the first- or second-generation immigrants or by the more acculturated Arab Americans. The strict gender differences are also changing. Women are more active in the workforce, are taking leadership roles in the political system, and are gaining legal rights they were previously denied.

The Role of Women

Perhaps the most controversial issue drawing the attention of many Westerners is the status of women in the Arab culture. Westerners perceive Arab women as submissive and inferior, with few or no rights. In general, Arab Americans view the American perception of Arab women as stereotypical. Thus, by extension, conservative Arab Americans perceive the Western misunderstanding of Muslim Arab women as a criticism to the Arab family value system itself.

Traditional Arabs and Muslims view women as individuals who have rights and responsibilities toward themselves and their patriline. Most Arab females are socialized to be caring and sacrificing. They are primarily responsible for childrearing and domestic chores. They are usually nurturing and dependent on their parents or their spouses for most aspects of their life. Because of the differences in behavioral expectations between women and men, a traditional Arab woman sees herself as self-sacrificing, accepting the husband's misbehavior, meeting his physical and emotional needs, complying with her husband's decisions, and providing her unconditional support and commitment to her husband and her family. Often, Arab women are aware and accepting of gender differences prescribed to them by their religion or customs and may not view these differences as inequalities of power between the male and female. However, Arab women usually assume power behind the scenes and within the family circle and often gain status through motherhood and maturity. Adult married women with children are often approached with respect because of their experiences in motherhood.

Arab women are encouraged to attend school, but in some traditional families higher education for girls is not encouraged. Gender role differences, and, in most cases, gender role inequalities may represent a serious limitation to career-oriented Arab women. An Arab woman learns gender differences between herself and her male kin during the early ages of her life. In the more traditional Arab families, the female child may not be encouraged to pursue higher education or a career so that she can prepare to be a wife and a homemaker. Selecting a husband is considered more important for a young woman than pursuing a career. Arranged marriages may be accepted among traditional Arab families but it is not a common practice among Arab Americans. From an early age, women are socialized to be modest and isolated from their male counterparts for fear of sexual relations. Mothers are in charge of their daughters' upbringing and if a daughter dishonors the family, the mother is usually held responsible. For this reason, mothers tend to be more strict with their daughters than with their sons (Kulwicki, 1996).

The concept of honor and the fear of loss of virginity may further set limitations to women in pursuit of individual aspirations. In some traditional families, the sooner the girl marries, the sooner of the family's honor is no longer in jeopardy of being damaged. Consequently, many young women marry quite early. The results of a community assessment of low-income population of Arab Americans in the U.S. indicated that 45% of the Arab women married at a young age and as a result did not go beyond the eighth grade (Gold, 1987).

Traditional Arab women view the women's place as in the home. Work outside the home is frowned on, and in some cases is viewed as a source for the deterioration of Arab families in the West. It is true that in some Middle

Eastern countries such as Lebanon, Egypt, and Jordan, women are engaged in the workforce. However, the percentage of Middle Eastern women in the Arab world working outside the home is low and perhaps one of the lowest in the world (Hijab, 1989). The majority of women who are in the workforce in the Middle East and in the United States are often professionals, and belong to a higher socioeconomic class. Professions such as medicine and law are viewed as more prestigious than any other type of work.

Despite the many restrictions Arab women face, they do have advantages. For instance, a woman has the right to own property. In the United States, Arab American women are more active than their counterparts in the Middle East in participating in social, political, and professional work. More Arab women in the United States are teachers, engineers, lawyers, business women, doctors, and professors than in countries of their origin, yet Arab women who live in the Middle East are still encouraged to pursue work—in prestigious professions such as medicine, engineering, and law degrees rather than nursing, social work, and salaried employment.

For Westerners, one of the most controversial issues concerning Arabs is the attire of Arab women. Muslim women are expected to dress modestly, and the clothing they wear often expresses their local customs. The most common attire for Muslim women is the Hijaab commonly worn by more traditional Muslim women. The Hijaab is an traditional head cover that covers the woman's hair except the face, and in some instances a mask or veil covers the face completely. Although the majority of Arab immigrant women do not wear the Hijaab, those who do consider the Hijaab Islamic attire, prescribed by the prophet Mohammed.

Some Arab American women who wear the traditional Hijaab view themselves as protected from sexual advances by their male counterparts. They view themselves as moral and as preserving the Muslim identity. Today, the veil for some Arab women represents an Islamic revival, and university students and women who are at work wear the Hijaab as an off-limits sign, sending males the message that although they are in public, they are not to be harassed.

Although modesty is expected of both genders in the Arab society, the restrictions placed on Arab women regarding clothes do not apply to Arab men. Most Arab men wear Western clothing and are not held accountable to the Muslim norms of modesty. Yet, many Arab and Arab American progressive women view the wearing of the Muslim traditional dress as inappropriate and restrictive and are critical of the Muslim culture that encourages such practices. Some Arab women also resent the Muslim double standard of dress.

Progressive Arab American women view the woman's role in the United States as changing, and see the homemaker role as no longer practical. Thus, the dilemma of conforming to Arab traditional values or to Western values often creates strains and conflict among Arab American women.

Marriage and Divorce

Although traditional customs among Arab American Muslim families regarding marriage and divorce are changing and more Muslim families are observing Western marriage and divorce laws, such values and customs still persist among first-generation Arab American immigrants. In some Arab countries, a woman is considered a legal minor throughout her life, in need of her father's, husband's or male relative's permission to travel or to work. In some Arab countries a woman may not be entitled to be the legal guardian of her children even if her husband dies. She is considered a minor, not able to travel or to accept employment without the permission of her husband, father, or brother. Arab American women are required to follow the laws of their country of origin if they travel to Middle Eastern countries. For example, a woman traveling with her children must obtain permission from her husband to travel to Middle East if she plans to take her children along. Some Arab countries even consider a testimony of two women equal to one man (Hijab, 1988).

Among traditional Muslim families, the woman's cousin has the privilege and the right to marry her. This practice is viewed as a means of keeping the family wealth within the family. Women usually marry young. This practice may also be encouraged in the United States due to the fear many parents have about the sexual freedom given to girls in the United States. Marriage is a contract between two families. According to the Muslim culture, the groom pays the bride half of the dowry, which is to be her property. Traditionally, half of the dowry is held back to be paid in case of divorce, which acts as a financial restraint on the husband's impulse to divorce (Aswad, 1988).

Husbands have the financial obligation to support their wives for certain periods after divorce. The divorce and child custody laws may vary among Middle Eastern countries and between the Islamic religious sectarian lines. Depending on each Middle Eastern country's divorce laws, the mother may gain custody of her children from one year to several years. The impact of such laws affects Arab women in the United States who are divorced from their husbands. Often, Muslim women, divorced in the United States, who follow their Islamic tradition have custody rights that are more limited than those of their divorced counterparts in America.

Men can and do divorce their wives by simply stating, "I divorce thee" three times (Hijab, 1989). While men have the right to divorce, women have limited right to do so unless they have documented causes for divorce, such as the husband's inability to financially support his family, adultery, or sexual incompetence. Divorce laws in the Muslim world may vary and are undergoing many changes; for instance, women in Syria, Egypt, Lebanon, and Jordan are now being given more freedom to challenge divorce proceedings. Also, in some Arab countries, divorce laws are creating more restraints for men who exercise their right to divorce.

In cases of divorce, a mother usually loses custody of their children at some point (Hijab, 1989). Depending on the laws of each Arab country, and based on differences of sectarian Islamic religious laws, a woman may lose the custody of children as young as the age of two or as old as puberty.

Pregnancy and Prenatal Care

Many of the practices surrounding the period of pregnancy among Middle Eastern women reflect male/female gender relations in the Arab culture. As Unni Wikan notes, "A woman achieves self-realization through being a wife and a mother. Womanhood in fact is thought to inhere in marital status: the fundamental transformation from girl (bint) to woman (horma) is brought about by sexual experience, and the only legitimate context for this marriage. The full realization of manhood implies marriage" (Wikan, 1988, p. 452).

Customs related to pregnancy vary throughout the Middle East. Usually, healthy food habits are encouraged, and frequent visitation by the kinswomen is customary during this period.

Customs related to prenatal care also vary among Middle Easterners. However, long periods of rests, including the indulgence of the pregnant woman with food and close supervision and support by female kinswomen are common practices among Arabs. The passing of 40 days after menstruation is a cause of celebration for women in the Middle East. The pregnant woman's physical appearance, her cravings of certain foods, and her bodily changes are often thought to be indications of the sex of the unborn infant. Male children may be more desirable for some women because of the high cultural value placed on the males as breadwinners and economic supports and protectors of the family unit.

A period of forty days after childbirth is also considered a time of rest for both the mother and infant. The Arab practice of allowing the mother to rest and be fed well is a custom that ostensibly supports intimacy and bonding between the mother and the infant. Encouraging mothers to eat more frequently in order to help establish lactation is a popular belief and practiced by many Arabs in the Middle East. The 40 days are noted for the visiting that occurs from the family and friends, and their assistance with chores such as cooking and cleaning, as well as consultation and advice on raising the newborn.

The 40-day period of rest among the Middle Eastern women after delivery follows the social support model proposed by Raphael: "The common denominator for success in breast-feeding is the assurance of some degree of help from some specific person for definite period of time after childbirth . . . 'mothering the mother.' Sometimes it means doing chores like housekeeping or minding the baby so the mother can nap, but ultimately it permits the mother time to feel secure and to establish the essential rhythm of breast-feeding" (Raphael, 1973, p. 141).

Often, boys are preferred over girls, and the birth of a boy is usually more celebrated than the birth of a girl, especially if the child is the first born. Children born with a physical or mental handicap are considered a reason for shame. Often, families who have a handicapped child restrict the exposure of the child in public for fear of public ridicule and/or criticism. Children of families who are known to have given birth to handicapped children are sometimes viewed at risk for marriage opportunities for fear that they may produce handicapped children themselves.

Most customs related to pregnancy and the postpartum period are still common among Arab American women in the United States. The lack of activity after childbirth is noted among the majority of women delivering their children in American hospitals and the need of physical assistance from health care providers. Visitation by family members and close family support during the postpartum period is also very common among Arab Americans in the United States.

Fertility Patterns

Fertility rates are high among Arab American due to the high emphasis placed on the role of women as procreators and childrearers. Fertility rates in the Arab countries from which most Arab Americans emigrated range from 3.7 in Lebanon to 7.6 in North Yemen (Kuzian, 1992), with an average fertility rate of 5.98. Fertility practices of Arabs are influenced by traditional Bedouin values supporting tribal dominance, the popular beliefs that "God decides the family size" and "God provides," and the Islamic ruling regarding birth control, treatment of infertility, and abortion. High fertility rates are favored and procreation is regarded as the purpose of marriage and the means of enhancing family strength. Accordingly, Islamic jurists have ruled that the use of the "reversible" forms of birth control are considered *mukrah,* undesirable but not forbidden. These methods should be employed only in certain situations, listed in decreasing order of legitimacy: threat to mother's life, too-frequent childbearing, the risk of transmitting a genetic disease, and financial hardship. Moreover, irreversible forms of birth control such as vasectomy and tubal ligation are *haram,* or absolutely unlawful.

A report published in Jordan in 1985 indicated that among Jordanian husbands, religion and the fatalistic belief that "God decides the family size" were most often given as reasons for why contraceptives were not utilized. Contraceptives were used by 27% of the husbands, typically urbanites with high socioeconomic status. Although intrauterine devices (IUDs) and the contraceptive "pill" were most widely favored, 4.9% utilized female sterilization despite religious prohibitions (The Hashemite Kingdom of Jordan, 1988).

A survey of a random sample of 295 Arab American women in Michigan found similar results to that of the Jordanian and the Middle Eastern data. The majority (29.1%) of the respondents did not use any birth control methods because of their desire to have children, 4.3% did not use contraceptives because of their husband's disapproval, and 6% opposed using contraceptives because of religious reasons. Of the 178 respondents who used birth control methods, 33.2% used birth control pills, 12.9% had tubal ligation, and 10.7% used the IUD (Hammad, Kulwicki, & Yassine, 1996). The fertility rate was 3.2%.

Other researchers have also found religious belief to be a barrier to family planning. Kirk (1967) states that Islam has been a more effective barrier to diffusion of family planning than Catholicism. He maintains that the following reasons account for the high natality of Muslims:

- the high degree of tenacity with which old beliefs and practices are maintained by Muslims;
- conformity to religious and social practices, which are closely interwoven in Muslim life;
- the strongly patrilinear and patrilocal quality of the Muslim family, with male dominance and responsibility prescribed by the Koran; and
- the belief that the pleasures of flesh, and especially sexual intercourse, are God's given virtue to be enjoyed and a conjugal obligation to be fulfilled (celibacy is considered abnormal for men and unthinkable for able-bodied women); and the markedly subordinate place for women in Muslim society.

Although much of the published literature supporting the patriarchal attitudes and sexual satisfaction of Arab males serve as a barrier for family planning among Arabs of the Middle East, a 1996 study by Hammad, Kulwicki, and Yassine indicates that cultural and religious values towards procreation are changing among Arab American immigrants. The study indicates that only 6% of the surveyed Arab respondents viewed that religion was a major reason in not using birth control methods, and that only 4.3% of the respondents did not use birth control methods because of their husband's disapproval. A measurable percentage—31.9% of the men and 22.7% of the women—indicated that sexual gratification between spouses will remain the same with the use of contraceptives.

Childrearing Practices

The Arab family is known for its love of children. Parents indulge children in their affection and include them in all social activities. Fathers are known to be the disciplinarians, and mothers are the source of unconditional love and the peacemakers. The child's good character is always a reflection of the parent's character, and especially of the mother's successful role in the children's upbringing. Children are often praised and mothers are held responsible for the behavior of the children as well as blamed for the children's misbehavior (Kulwicki, 1996).

Children in the Arab family are taught to conform to family norms and the norms of society. A good daughter or son is an obedient child. Often boys are preferred over girls and given more opportunity and freedom to experience life. Although this practice is changing as Arab Americans become acculturated, some differences in gender rearing practices persist. A daughter's loss of virginity or sexual promiscuity is perceived as misbehavior more often than is a son's sexual experimentation. Other behaviors considered socially unacceptable are the use of drugs and disrespect to elders.

Punishment of children may include scolding or physical discipline. In rare cases, girls and sometimes boys are severely punished, or even killed, if the family honor is challenged.

ARAB AMERICAN WOMEN AT RISK

Immigrant women are often at higher risks for health related conditions than white American women. This is a result of their lower socioeconomic status, their inability to communicate with health care service providers, and their stressful living conditions.

Like other immigrant women, Arab American women may vary in their behaviors in accessing services based on their religious affiliation, socioeconomic background, country of origin, English language skills, level of acculturation, and relationship with their kin. The larger Arab social system is structured by ties of family and friendships. Cultural values play a significant role in the health care help, assistance-seeking behaviors of Arab American women. Arab culture provides security and stability to the Arab family and to women, but at the same time, some aspects of Arab culture may serve as a barrier to health and human services providers. Important concerns are the low priority the culture places on individual freedom, and the family and gender responsibilities with which Arab women are raised.

In the majority of cases, Arab women who come from higher socioeconomic backgrounds and who are exposed to Western culture are able to tap U.S. services without much difficulty. However, first-generation immigrant women with more traditional backgrounds and those who lack English language skills experience cultural barriers that impede their access to the U.S. system. For instance, the high cultural value placed on physical and social modesty as experienced and as viewed by/for females is shared as a norm of expected behavior among Arab women. The injunctions for modesty of the female body are codified in religious texts, most notably the Qur'an, and mandate that women cover their extremities (arms, legs, and in some cases the face) when they are in presence of men who are not kin (Fernea & Fernea, 1979). This sense of modesty is deeply ingrained, even among women who may not practice veiling or covering of the head. Seeking health care from male health care providers creates a serious barrier for women who find exposing their body parts to male health care providers as shameful and unacceptable by Arabic culture.

The use of health care services may therefore be lower for Arab women than their white female counterparts in the United States. For example, Arab American women are less frequently screened for breast and cervical cancer (Michigan Behavioral Risk Factor Survey, 1994). The lower rate of breast and cervical cancer screening is associated with the lower values placed on health promotion adheres to cultural values of modesty, fatalistic views toward life threatening conditions, lower education, and income. Most importantly, the cultural norms of modesty are significant factors in these lower rates of reproductive health screening behaviors. For example, the rate of breast exams among Arab women is 50.8% when compared to 71.2% for other women. The rate of mammograms among Arab women is 39.6% compared to 56.8% for the general female population. The rate of cervical pap tests is 59.9% compared to 78.5% to other women. Although, the rate of breast and cervical cancer is not yet known among Arab American immigrants, implications for early detection and treatment are important in reducing the death rate from cancer related conditions.

A study on cancer risk reduction survey of 200 low-income Arab American women indicated a low rate (51.2% when compared to 83% for other women) of mammogram screenings. Only 74% of the surveyed respondents had had a pap smear within the last three years (Hammad & Kulwicki, 1996).

Sexuality

Although customs about sexuality vary throughout the Middle East, Arab cultural values, beliefs, and expectations about sexuality and sexual relations are based on male superiority. Gender differences between men and women reflects all aspects of life, including sexuality and sexual behaviors. Sexism in the Arab culture is learned in the family and in the larger social context. In the Arab society, for example, it is not unusual to limit a girl's interactions with males so that she can maintain her innocence.

The less contact a girl has with males and the sooner she is married, the lower the risk for sexual experimentation and violation of family honor. In comparison, sexual experience for men is valued and almost a prerequisite for marriage. Sexual experience for men is believed to prepare them for adulthood and Arab manhood, while chastity for Arab women is a requisite for womanhood and motherhood. Arab women usually gain sexual knowledge through their husband by marriage. As a consequence, it is a common practice among some women to suppress their sexual desires, or place much less importance on sexual relations with their spouses. Differences in sexual expectations between married couples may result in marital conflicts that may require professional attention. However, cultural taboos placed on sexuality between males and females prevent couples from discussing their problems between themselves or with a professional. Conflicts from such cultural norms may result in men seeking sexual satisfaction outside the marriage, which may be tolerated by some spouses especially after their role as mothers has been achieved.

Arab women consequently face the risk of sexually transmitted diseases and/or HIV if their spouses practice extramarital sex. Unfortunately, as topics of sexuality for Arab men and women continue to be a taboo, so does discussion of sexually transmitted diseases. Statistics on sexually transmitted diseases (STD) among Arab Americans are unavailable. However, clinics providing STD counseling and testing have noted a higher rate of syphilis, hepatitis, and chlamydia among Arab clients.

Violence Against Women

The prevalence of domestic violence is higher and claims more lives among immigrants and minorities than in the White population in the United States. Indeed, indications are that domestic violence may be a serious health problem among women of Arab ancestry (Kulwicki, 1996). Over the past three years, sensational national media news has reported four incidents of "honor" murders in the U.S. Arab community.

There is, however, a paucity of information on domestic violence among Arabs in the Middle East and about crimes committed against women in particular. In addition, no organized system addresses the seriousness of domestic violence or violence against women in many Middle Eastern countries. "Crimes of honor" are periodically reported in Arabic newspapers, but the extent and prevalence of the phenomenon is not well known. Official estimates of domestic violence and crimes committed against women in some Middle Eastern countries are very low because of the low reporting rates of such crimes. Anecdotal evidence suggests that family members of victims consider violence committed against women to be a family matter, and they believe that cultural norms and family values dictate that legal authorities not press investigations. Hence, statistics on domestic violence may not accurately reflect the actual incidence of domestic violence. In Jordan, for example, a "hot line" for abused women, the only one in the Middle East, responded to calls from over 4,000 registered battered Jordanian women in its first year of operation.

Research on domestic violence among Arab Americans is also limited. Until recently, there was no data on cultural norms among Arab Americans that places them at higher risk for domestic violence. The first research study on domestic violence, conducted by Kulwicki in 1996, examined beliefs, attitudes, and incidences of violence against Arab women by their family members in a low-income Arab American community. Results of a select sample of low-income women indicated that almost 25% of all women interviewed had experienced some form of violence. Nearly 20% were reluctant to speak to legal authorities, citing a number of fears:

- that the family and the community would criticize them for bringing a family problem to the public;
- that they may have been the cause of the violence; that the economic situation for them and their children would worsen; and
- that the abuser would not be punished, or that they would be further abused by men.

Some of the women also voiced general acceptance of the cultural norms that men have the right to abuse women. Twenty-five percent of the women interviewed reported that they had been beaten by their spouses, 18.4% had been kicked by them and 7% reported that their husbands had used a gun or a knife on them. When asked if a man should use violence if his wife was caught having an affair with another man, 45.4% of the respondents approved of slapping their wives and 19% believed that men should kill their wives for committing acts of adultery.

Patrilineal and patriarchal values, where male authority in the household is accepted by Arab traditional values, present conflicts between Arab families in the United States. Conflicts in role expectations among more progressive Arab women in relation to the traditional role expectations of their male counterparts may lead to stresses in family relations and to the breakdown of family ties. In the same study conducted by Kulwicki (1996), 90% of the surveyed Arab men believed that men have the right to decide if their wife should go out with her friends in the evening; 82.5% of the surveyed men believed that it was important for a man to show that he is the head of the household.

STRESSES OF ACCULTURATION

Many immigrant women, regardless of their socioeconomic background, experience some levels of stress due to differences in their values and the values of the host countries. Most Middle East Arab American women are able to preserve their cultural values, norms, and customs in the United States.

However, immigrant women who lack English language skills, who come from poorer socioeconomic backgrounds, and who have minimal extended kin support may experience stresses that put them at risk for emotional disorders. A survey of low-income Arab women showed that 56.6% of the women surveyed were unable to perform their daily activities because of stress, depression, or emotional problems; 40% of the women surveyed suffered from inability to sleep; 41.9% experienced nervousness; and 35.4% suffered from fatigue (Kulwicki, 1996).

Immigrant Arab women also face tremendous stresses in parenting because of differences between the values of the Arab and the American culture. For instance, women whose children are more proficient in the English language and more aware of the American norms may be abused by their children because of their feelings of inadequacy and lower levels of self-esteem, due to their Arab heritage often viewed by American culture as inferior. Mothers, in turn, may feel inadequate in disciplining their children because of their own lack of knowledge of the American norms and behaviors and their inability to communicate in English.

Separation from kin, impoverishment and lack of support may result in an Arab woman's loss of identity, loneliness, stress, depression, anxiety attacks, and panic disorders. Negative stereotyping, prejudice, and general disrespect for Arab women by the American culture may also further the social isolation of Arab women. The factors have an impact on the Arab American woman's service utilization because they have lower expectations of respectful treatment by American professionals.

Language and Communication Barriers

One of the most serious barriers for the recent Arab American immigrant women is the inability to speak the English language. However, the ability to speak English does not ensure that Arab women will fully express themselves. There are also differences in intonation, voice, and physical expressions that may not be comprehended by the American service providers. Usually, Arab women are quieter, speak with much lower voice, and are more intimidated of the American providers than are their American counterparts.

Often, helping professionals resort to using translators and interpreters in serving Arab American clients. The most common pattern is for husbands or children to interpret the women's concerns. However, when the concerns are about marital relationships or about family, women are reluctant to express their feelings or problems while in the presence of their husbands or their children. In addition, interpreters who are family members may distort the complaints or edit the concerns for a variety of reasons, i.e., fear of exposing themselves to the public, fear of being ridiculed by the service provider or general fear of losing one's pride.

SUGGESTIONS FOR WORKING WITH WOMEN IN THIS GROUP

Arab American women, like other minority women, do not fully use the American health care system because of socio-cultural, economic, and linguistic barriers. Human service providers must examine the unique needs of this population, and develop culturally competent approaches to meeting the needs of Arab American women. Cultural competency with Arab American women requires that providers have the knowledge and ability to work with culturally diverse groups through culturally appropriate strategies in order to reduce barriers for services.

The following are recommendations to assist helping professionals in providing culturally competent services to Arab American women: Beforehand, assess your own needs and biases about the Arab culture. Learn about the Arab culture prior to working with Arab women. Try to review your information regarding the cultural, political, social, religious, national, language, immigration, and acculturation patterns of the women with whom you are working. Differentiate the values and behaviors between Arab women in general and Arab American women in particular. Be critical in choosing the resources available in gaining information about the Arab culture. Some learning resources may not be current, or may be biased and/or stereotypical towards Arab women. Understand that there may be cultural differences between and among Arab women based on their national, religious, immigration, and economic backgrounds. Explore the Arab community in your area of practice. Get firsthand information about the culture in your own community. Visit the community yourself and meet with women in the community. Develop a community resource directory to assist you in securing the resources needed to work with your clients. Assess the family unit before working with Arab women. The primary roles for traditional Arab women are of wife and mother, so asking women to be independent may be coun-terproductive. Usually, the family unit is a source of strength in helping Arab women cope with their problems. Be aware that family affairs are considered private matters and should be handled with confidentiality and respect for privacy. Thus, when issues of marital or sexual relations arise, assess the Arab woman's attitude toward sexuality before involving the spouse in counseling.

Usually, Arab American women will confide with their female friends before they consult with a service provider. Include close friends for support when working with an Arab American client. Understand gender roles and respect the Arab woman's attitude and belief toward gender differences. Helping the Arab woman to change her behavior as an Arab woman may be difficult. Be respectful of the Arab woman's modesty. Use interpreters when necessary, but make sure that the interpreters are qualified to provide the necessary information required in working with Arab women.

REFERENCES

Arberry, A. (1983). *The Koran interpreted.* New York: Oxford University Press.

Aswad, B. (1974). *Arabic speaking communities in American cities.* New York: Center for Migration Studies.

Aswad, B. (1988). The Arab American family. In I. Ahmaed & N. Adadow-Gray (Eds.), *The Arab American family: A resource manual for human service providers.* Detroit, MI: The Arab Community Center for Economic and Social Services.

Aswad, B., & Gray, N. (1996). Challenges to the Arab-American family and ACCESS. In B. Aswad & B. Bilgé (Eds.), *Family and gender among American Muslims: Issues facing Middle Eastern immigrants and their descendants* (pp. 223–240). Philadelphia: Temple University Press.

El-Badry, S. (1994, January). *The Arab American market* (pp. 22–31). American Demographics.

Fernea, E., & Fernea, R. (1979). A look behind the veil. *Human Nature, 2*(1), 68–77.

Gold, S. (1987). *Wayne County Health Department infant Mortality demonstration project:* Preliminary report. Dearborn, MI.

Hammad, A., & Kulwicki, A. (1996). *Cancer prevention and control study.* Dearborn, MI: Arab Community Center for Economic and Social Services.

Hammad, A., Kulwicki, A., & Yassine, M. (1996). *Family planning needs assessment survey.* Dearborn, MI: Arab Community Center for Economic and Social Services.

Hijab, N. (1989). *Womanpower: The Arab debate on women at work.* New York: Cambridge University Press.

Kirk, D. (1967). *Factors affecting Moslem natality.* Proceedings of the World Population Conference, Belgrade, 1965. New York: United Nations.

Kulwicki, A. (1996). *Arab domestic violence education and prevention project.* Executive Summary. Lansing, MI: Michigan Department of Community Health.

Kulwicki, A. (1996). Health issues among Arab Muslim families. In B. Aswad & B. Bilge (Eds.). *Family and gender among American Muslims: Issues facing Middle Eastern immigrants and their descendants* (pp.187–207). Philadelphia: Temple University Press.

Kuzian, G. (1992). *Encyclopedia of the Third World.* New York: Facts on File.

Naff, A. (1980). Arabs in America: A historical overview (pp. 128–136). Boston, MA: *Harvard Encyclopedia of American Ethnic Groups.*

Qur'an. Egypt: Dar Al-Kitab Al-Maszi

Raphael, D. (1973). *The tender gift: Breastfeeding.* Englewood Cliffs, NJ: Prentice Hall.

Rice, V., & Kulwicki, A. (1992). Cigarette use among Arab Americans in Detroit Metropolitan area. *Public Health Reports 107*(5), 589–594.

The Hashemite Kingdom Jordan, Department of Statistics. (1985). *Jordan's husbands' fertility survey.* Amman, Jordan. Author.

Wayne County Health Department

(1994). *Arab community in Wayne County, Michigan: Behavior risk factor survey.* East Lansing, MI: Michigan State University, Institute for Public Policy and Social Research.

Wikan, U. (1988). Bereavement and loss in two Muslim communities:

Egypt and Bali compared. *Social Science and Medicine, 27,* 451–460.

Zogby, I. (1990). *Arab America today: A demographic profile of Arab Americans.* Washington, DC: Arab American Institute.

RECOMMENDED READINGS AND RESOURCES

Abu-Lughod, L. (1986). *Veiled sentiments: Honor and poetry in a Bedouin society.* California: University of California Press.

Ahmed, L. (1992). *Women and gender in Islam.* New Haven and London: Yale University Press.

Aswad, A., & Bilge, B. (Eds.) (1996). *Family and gender among American Muslims: Issues facing middle eastern immigrants and their descendants.* Philadelphia: Temple University Press.

Goodwin, J. (1994). *Price of honor: Muslim women lift the veil of silence on Islamic world.* New York: Penguin Books, Inc.

Haddad, Y. (1991). *The Muslims of America.* New York: Oxford University Press.

Haddad, Y., & Lummis, A. T. (1987). *Islamic values in United States: A comparative study.* New York: Oxford University Press.

Mernissi, F. (1987). *Beyond the veil: Male-female dynamics in modern society.* Bloomington and Indianapolis: Indiana University Press.

Sabbagh, S. (Ed.) (1996). *Arab women: Between defiance and restraint.* New York: Olive Branch Press.

Tucker, J. E. (Ed.). (1993). *Arab women: Old boundaries, new frontiers.* Bloomington and Indianapolis: Indiana University Press.

Walther, W. (1995). *Women in Islam: From medieval to modern times.* Princeton, NJ: Princeton University Press.

GLOSSARY

divorce: a mutual agreement to dissolve a marriage wherein the wife agrees to pay a specific sum of money to the husband in return for dissolution, or a unilateral termination or repudiation of marriage by a husband repeating "I divorce thee" three times; the laws of divorce vary from one Arabic country to another; in general, men have the right to divorce, women have to petition divorce; a woman's petition for divorce must be on grounds of marital offence committed by her husband, lack of sexual relations for over four months, failure to support wife financially, desertion or cruelty; these laws may be practiced by members of the Arab American community in the United States

extended family: a family unit that incorporates more than members of a nuclear family such as grandparents, parents, uncles, aunts and children who are related through male family bloodline

honor and shame: a familial pride associated with moral behavior and compliance to social norms; honor or sharaf is sometimes related to male identity and often associated with female purity, chastity, and fidelity

Islam Religion: revealed to the prophet Muhammad and based on the concept of submission to God

Quran: the holy book of Islam; also means "recitation"

marriage: a contract between two parties: according to the Quran, the groom pays the bride a dowry; half of the dowry is held back by the groom to be paid off in case of divorce

Muslim: a believer in Islam

patrilineal: lineage through members of patriline (father); individuals born in a patrilineal system inherit through their father

polygamy: in Islam marriage is permitted to up to four wives, but only if equality between the wives can be ensured by the husband

Sharia Islamic law: considered divine and eternal; It contains a comprehensive set of rules of life

veiling: the practice of women covering the head and neck in varying degrees, sometimes including the complete covering of the face

6

Hispanic Women

H. BURGOS-OCASIO

INTRODUCTION

The presence of Hispanics in the United States has become more and more significant in recent decades. Sectors such as business, marketing, government, and the arts are realizing that Hispanics are increasingly involved in the socioeconomic and political realities of the United States. According to the United States Bureau of the Census (1991), about 22.4 million people classified as Hispanics lived in the United States in 1990, a figure which represents about 10 percent of the total population. The Hispanic population increased about 53 percent from 1980 to 1990. It is expected that by the year 2000 this group will have strong influence in the political processes of the United States. The Census Bureau indicates that between 1981 and 1991, the United States received three million immigrants from Spanish-Speaking countries (U.S. Bureau of the Census, 1993). Long-range projections indicate an estimated 140 million of Hispanics will live in the United States by the year 2080 (Nevertheless, even with current United States Census data, no one really knows how many Hispanics live in the United States. Accurate numbers are not available because of inconsistencies in demographic data collection procedures and vast numbers of illegal or temporary residents who work seasonal/migratory jobs.) Some of the reasons for the rapid growth of this ethnic group are that the average age of Hispanics is younger than that of the general population (25.6 compared to 33 years for non–Hispanics), a correspondingly high birth rate, and the constant migration of Hispanics who are in their peak childbearing years (U.S. Bureau of the Census, 1993).

Women have always been the foundation of the Hispanic family and community in the United States. However, as a result of the complex origins of this ethnic group, Hispanic women cannot be said to hold a uniform and narrow view of Hispanic culture. Nevertheless, some commonly held perceptions, values, and viewpoints are palpable among Hispanic women. The primary purpose of this chapter is to present a framework for helping professionals understand and work effectively with Hispanic women within the context of their cultural background. Also, it is intended to create awareness of some sociocultural aspects of Hispanic women to safeguard the relationship of clients and helping professionals. Today's literature points out that the use of helping models sensitive to an individual's psychological, social, and cultural aspects will improve intervention efforts.

This chapter contains several themes. The first section provides the reader with an overview of the concepts "Hispanic" and "Latinas," followed by a historical overview of the Hispanic culture. Then it discusses general similarities and differences among the Hispanic women, cultural expectations, and issues of assimilation and acculturation. It also presents family issues, personal values, and cultural traditions and beliefs that shape gender identity and roles of women in the Hispanic culture.

The chapter is written from the perspective and biases of a Hispanic woman who is herself a Puerto Rican helping professional. It covers areas that the author believes are essential in order to understand Hispanic women and provide them with adequate and relevant services.

Hispanics or Latinas?

Hispanics or Latinas? That is the question! There is confusion in the minds of many people about how to correctly address Hispanic women. Furthermore, many of the terms used to categorize the members of this ethnic group (e.g., Hispanics, Latinas, and La Raza) are rarely used among the group members and, for some of them, the terms are unknown before their arrival in the United States. Defining Hispanics is therefore a difficult task, because this group varies in its national, social, economic, and educational characteristics and backgrounds (Bean & Tienda, 1987). In general, Hispanics are identified as having common cultural values and language (Marin & Marin, 1991). The group is composed of individuals sharing a common historical, cultural, linguistic, and broad geographical background. Hispanics understand that they have a common history connecting them, also making them appear as a homogeneous group. It is a reality that among this ethnic group homogeneous characteristics are celebrated. But differences—sociopolitical, economic, and historical—are also manifested by individuals in the Hispanic population (Bean & Tienda, 1987).

In the United States, Hispanic is the term most commonly used to refer to individuals who come from Spanish-speaking countries in South and Central America and in the Caribbean region. The term "Hispanic" was created by the United States government to classify individuals who live in the United States and claim Spanish heritage (Pérez-Stable, 1987). The concept also implies the unified element of Spanish as their language (Cortés, 1991). Some political sectors argue that Brazilians, although they do not share the Spanish language, are Hispanics as a result of their geographical placement.

While the term "Hispanic" implies cultural and geographic roots, the word "Latino" is a term commonly used to refer to Spanish-speaking individuals living in the United States. The term "Latina" is used to categorize Spanish-speaking women with Spanish cultural roots and heritage, who come to the U.S. from Central and South America and the Caribbean (Cuba, the Dominican Republic, and Puerto Rico). The word emerges from the concept "Latinoamericano" (Latin American) and it earmarks those immigrants from Spanish speaking countries in the Caribbean, Central, and South America (Lederman & Sierra, 1994). Other terms, such as "La Raza," "Mestizo," and "Spanish American" are used to identify individuals of Spanish heritage who remain in these regions (Mayo, 1997). Some of the women of Spanish heritage prefer to be called Hispanics, while others like the term Latina. Others feel comfortable with either term. Yet because of their differences, it is recommended that women be identified by their country of origin (e.g., Cuban, Puerto Rican, Dominican, Salvadoran, or Colombian) (Mayo, 1997). Such an approach will give these women recognition of their particular geographical and cultural heritage and will prevent misunderstandings that sometimes create barriers between people.

The author of this chapter feels that the terms "Hispanic" and "Latina" are both appropriate and uses them interchangeably. She will use the term "Hispanics" and will basically refer to those women belonging to the three predominant Hispanic groups in the United States: Cubans, Mexicans, and Puerto Ricans. Although the census data points to an incremental increase in the number of immigrants to the United States from all of Central and South America, these three groups represent the largest cohorts among those immigrants (Rodriguez, 1994). The 1992 Census data indicates that of the total Hispanic population in the United States, 64 percent is Mexican, 11 percent Puerto Rican, and 4.7 percent Cuban (Census Bureau, 1993).

Historical Overview

In order to understand Hispanic women, their cultural environment has to be understood. Hispanics are a widely heterogeneous group and yet Hispanics can claim a common background insofar as Christopher Columbus' arrival in the New World spawned the Hispanic culture in the Western hemisphere

(Hanke, 1988). However, throughout history each of the Latin American countries developed distinctive characteristics while retaining the primary ones that gave them origin (Bean & Tienda, 1987).

At the time of Columbus, indigenous people with comprehensive economic, social, and political systems inhabited the Latin American region (Williams, 1983). Spanish colonization relied on strong initiatives lead by the Spanish crown and the Catholic Church. While Spanish royalty wanted to acquire lands and precious metals, the Roman Catholic Church argued that it wanted to save the souls of the natives. Slaves from Africa were brought in by the colonizers, particularly to Cuba and Puerto Rico, to substitute for the indigenous people who were exterminated as a result of malnutrition, hard work, battles for freedom, and illnesses brought in by the colonizers (Vivas-Maldonado, 1974).

The Spanish colonization process began in 1492 and lasted until 1898 with the Hispanic American War. At that time, Cuba and Puerto Rico, the last Spanish colonies in the New World, became a free country and a Common-wealth, respectively (Vivas-Maldonado, 1974).

Cuba had remained under Spain's control from 1511 until 1898, when it became a free country. But since the early 1800s, Cubans had strong relation-ships with Florida and New York through their import and export trades (Williams, 1983). In 1959, Fidel Castro took over political power of the country, imposing a Marxist government and consequently creating a political migration movement into the United States.

When Puerto Rico became an incorporated territory of the United States after the Spanish American War in the late 1800s, a close socioeconomical and political relationship was established between the island and the United States, and Puerto Ricans became American citizens (Vivas-Maldonado, 1974). During the early 1900s a wave of well-educated Puerto Ricans seeking employment opportunities moved to the United States (Rodriguez, 1994). Later waves of Puerto Rican migration brought displaced agricultural workers who had been impoverished by the industrialization process (Ortiz, 1996). Others came as "family helpers" for those who had migrated earlier and were working on the mainland. During the 1970s, developing industry and technology in Puerto Rico found Puerto Ricans in greater numbers at the unemployment and public assistance lines, creating yet a new wave of immigrants to the mainland (Ortiz, 1996). Currently, professional young Puerto Ricans are migrating to the United States, looking for better standards of living.

Hispanics have had a relationship with the North American continent for centuries. Spanish colonizers were in Florida in the early 1500s, and Mexicans were already established in what is now the Southwest United States before 1700. As the United States' population expanded West, conflicts emerged between the United States and Mexico. Texas, once part of Mexico, was annexed to the United States in 1845 (Williams, 1983). Conflicts between the United States and Mexico continued until the early 1900s when, like the Cubans, they fled to the United States to escape the political and economic turmoil in their homeland. Unlike the Mexicans, however, the Cuban migrants had been landowners and were generally well-educated individuals (Vivas–Maldonado, 1974).

A common history of turmoil and a common language characterize Hispanics in the United States. With the arrival of Columbus in the New World, the Spanish language was introduced and in fact imposed upon those regions that later became the Spanish colonies. Therefore, Hispanics in the United States are linked by Spanish as the single language of heritage (Cortés, 1991). Although not all Hispanics in the United States speak Spanish, most of them recognize its symbolic importance in cultural identity.

If language and some aspects of their histories link U.S. Hispanics, physical appearance is where the resemblance ends. Hispanics vary widely in appearance; with their range of skin colors, physical features, and heights, Hispanics are the result of the mixture of peoples that took place during the Spanish conquest of the new world (Banks, 1987). Particularly in Cuba and Puerto Rico, African slaves brought by the Spaniards contributed their genotypes and phenotypes to the diverging population (Vivas–Maldonado, 1974). Fewer slaves were brought to Mexico, and the integration of people of indigenous and Spanish roots resulted in a group called "mestizaje." The United States operates within a rigid system of ethnic and racial categorization, but such categories are seldom used in Latin American countries because the racial mixtures are too numerous to document (Stapples & Mirande, 1980; Ruiz & Padillo, 1977). Although Latin Americans do not experience the degree of racially based prejudice as in the United States, the racial and physical makeup of Hispanics most certainly results in discrimination against them in the United States (Ruiz & Padillo, 1977).

HISPANIC WOMEN

It has been said time out of mind that the Hispanic culture is predominantly a patriarchal one. Generally, the vision is that Hispanic women are to be protected by men (Panitz et al., 1983). Traditionally, they have been portrayed as submissive, naive, and passive, but their role in the family is a strong and important one. Indeed, if looked at carefully, women have a dominant role in Hispanic families. Women are in charge of the household and children, and in recent years, their responsibilities expanded to work outside of the home, providing financial support for the family.

Still, despite their enormously important contributions, universally held cultural values limit the roles of Hispanic women. Household tasks and child rearing practices are inherited duties (Safa, 1974; Bruce-Laporte, 1970). In many homes, the older daughters are expected to assist the mother with these duties at an early age. Girls learn these roles and develop their skills early in life, and in the absence of the mother or as a woman in the house, they perform the household tasks and duties.

The naive, uneducated, and motherly figure is the stereotype of the Hispanic woman. These women, especially those of darker skin, are also stereotyped as exotic and sensual. For instance, the Cuban "mulatta" with big breasts, buttocks, and hips, moving sensually to tropical music, is the international image of Cuban female beauty. Her beauty may be rewarded in her homeland, but that is not the case in the United States.

In the United States, Hispanic women generally live in economically disadvantaged environments (Lewis, 1998). Over 30 percent live below the poverty level and their per capita income is measurably lower than other minority groups in the United States (Miller et al., 1988). Female Hispanic immigrants typically hold low paying jobs, live in poor housing, are highly segregated, and are unemployed and underemployed (Zavala-Martinez, 1988). Making matters worse, it has been reported that fewer than half of Hispanic adolescents are completing high school in the late 20th century (Arias, 1986; Lewis, 1998). According to Bailey and Ellis (1993), Puerto Ricans who stay in the United States tend to have less education, lower participation in the labor force, and higher poverty levels than those who return to Puerto Rico.

Migration and Hispanic Women

Just as the geographical heritage patterns of Hispanics vary, so do the migration patterns. Hispanic migration to the United States has been greatly influenced by politics and the economy of their homeland; the great majority of Hispanics have come to the United States hoping to escape impoverishment and/or political persecution in their homeland (Zavala-Martinez, 1994). Historically, the migration of Hispanics to the United States has been primarily lead by males, but women and children have also participated in this process (Ortiz, 1996).

For Hispanic groups, the migration process has occurred in different ways (Bean & Tienda, 1987). The Mexicans are the largest Hispanic group to have migrated to the United Sates. With the annexation of Texas in 1845, the Mexicans who had been living there automatically became American citizens (Acuna, 1981). Many other Mexicans subsequently immigrated to the U.S., supplementing the shortages of farm, mining, and railroad workers that had resulted during World War I (Reisler, 1976). The levels of migration temporarily declined, but then, by 1924, many Mexicans were being brought in by the

United States government through the "Bracero" program. This program, which augmented the country's supply of field and farm workers, continued its employment contracts through 1964 (Reichert & Massey, 1980). In recent decades, many other Mexicans have entered the U.S. illegally at any number of locations on the United States-Mexican border (Rodriguez & De Wolf, 1990). Strong efforts have been implemented to curtail the arrival of these illegal immigrants. Among such efforts is enforcement for protection of the borders between the United States and Mexico; some essential social services now requiring proof of residence; and immigration laws applying stricter and stronger sanctions to people hiring illegal workers (Rodriguez & De Wolf, 1990).

While Mexicans are largely concentrated in the Western States, Puerto Ricans have mainly settled in New York City and other Eastern United States cities since the 19th century (Rodriguez, 1994). As explained, most Puerto Ricans often migrated in their search for a better way of life, particularly after the depression of the 1930s. Between 1900 and 1945, industrial and agricultural labor opportunities in New York and New Jersey resulted in Puerto Rican settlements, but this migration has since spread to other eastern states (Ortiz, 1996).

In what has been called "Revolving Door Migration," a phenomenon mainly occurring from 1965 to the present, many Puerto Ricans are returning to the island to retire or to raise their families in more "culturally traditional" settings (U.S. Bureau of the Census, 1991; Rodriguez, 1994). Traveling back and forth from the United States mainland to the island is a process unique to Puerto Ricans, made relatively easy by the fact that they are United States citizens and enjoy an open border between the mainland and the island (Rodriguez, 1994).

If economic opportunities drove the Puerto Rican migration, Cubans have historically migrated to the United States mainly for political reasons. Escaping the Marxist regime has been the impetus for widespread Cuban migration to the United States. Unlike Mexicans or Puerto Ricans, the first migration of Cubans assimilated into the mainstream culture at faster rates since they were generally well-educated, white, and had a strong orientation for capitalism. During the 1950s–1960s, Cubans migrated to the Miami area and later to other coastal cities, most fleeing Fidel Castro's political persecution (Vivas-Maldonado, 1974). Lately, though, many Cubans arriving in the United States, such as the "Marielitos" who came through the Mariel Port during the Carter administration in the late 1970s, have come for economic reasons. Unlike Mexicans, Cubans who arrive illegally to the United States can immediately apply for political asylum. They generally receive asylum and documentation allowing them to work legally.

Women have been key players in the migration patterns of Hispanics to the United States. They have entered the United States in a variety of ways and for many reasons, and, once in the country, they experience similar problems, including discrimination, segregation, and exploitation (Cortes, 1991; Zavala-Martinez, 1994). Although more males tend to migrate and their rate of illegal arrival to the United States is higher, women are migrating in increasing numbers (Ortiz, 1996). The tendency for men, especially Mexicans and Cubans, is to migrate illegally to the United States to work and send money to women in their country of origin who are caring for their families and children. However, because the Hispanic family is currently facing severe changes in its structure, women are also migrating to the United States in larger numbers (Ortiz, 1996). Changes in family structure are manifested in ways such as an increase of single women-headed households and women's influx in the labor force (Duncan, 1991). These phenomena have made women more aware of their need to support their families (Ortiz, 1996). Leaving the children behind to be cared by grandmothers or other relatives is often necessary as women enter the United States and get jobs as maids, factory workers, and non-skilled workers, with the intention of sending money to financially support their children and families (Vega, 1995). Some illegal migrant women even prostitute themselves or serve as drug dispatchers in order to survive.

Once in the United States, recent stringent migration laws have created difficulties for immigrant women who wish to return to their home countries to visit their children without the risk of deportation or the denial of re-entry (Rodriguez & De Wolfe, 1990). For these reasons, many Hispanic women will not see their children or families for many years. Their hope is usually to become legal citizens and to bring their children and family to the United States.

The migration patterns of Puerto Rican women differ from those of other Hispanic women (Ortiz, 1996). It is reported that Puerto Rican females have higher rates of migration to the United States and return to their country of origin than their counterparts (Bailey & Ellis, 1993). This situation owes itself to the political status of Puerto Ricans, which was explained earlier. As American citizens, Puerto Rican's have the flexibility to travel and visit families on the island, without the fear of being deported (Rodriguez, 1994). A study conducted by Bailey and Ellis (1993) about the migration patterns of Puerto Rican women from the mainland to the island indicates that a number of these women tend to return to the island for education, marriage, and childbirth.

Assimilation and Acculturation and Hispanic Women

According to Bash (1981), acculturation refers to the adoption of cultural traits and items on a piecemeal and/or formalistic basis. In other words, acculturation is the process by which members of one ethnic group adopt the behaviors and beliefs of another culture, usually the dominant one. Acculturation is evident by changes in language, attitudes, and values. Acculturation, then, is a one-dimensional process resulting in accommodation to the host culture on the part of the migrant ethnic group (Szapocznik et al., 1978). But the degree of acculturation and identification with the host culture as a reference group varies.

Bash (1981) defines assimilation as the process whereby the former cultural mores are relinquished through interaction, participation, and communication in the new society. Assimilation involves processes of psychological adjustment, cultural adaptation, and social structural integration. Migration patterns of Hispanics have varied from other immigrant groups to the U.S., including those from Europe, Africa, and Asia. Low degrees of acculturation and assimilation are reported among Hispanic women, probably the combined results of migration patterns and residential segregation or concentrations, economic status, and race and color issues (Zavala-Martinez, 1994). Hispanics, in general, have participated in a steady migration and mobility from their countries of origin. Despite the difficulties expressed earlier, the proximity of the United States mainland to Mexico, Central America, and the Caribbean allows back-and-forth commutes. This proximity also facilitates access to indigenous foods, newspapers, entertainment, and radio, allowing the Hispanic community to retain ties with its country of origin, limiting the acculturation and assimilation process.

Second, Hispanic acculturation is also measurable in terms of economic status. Some literature points out that acculturation and socioeconomic status are related. Hispanic women in the United States must follow the Anglo-American culture to gain economic, occupational, educational, or political status. However, because they continue to practice Hispanic traditions — which keep their cultural beliefs alive — they remain separated from the Anglo-American culture, rendering the acculturation process incomplete (Mayo, 1997).

Additionally, issues of race and color compound Hispanic assimilation. Unlike European immigrants, Hispanics can be members of several racial groups. Therefore, they are deemed in the United States as "others" by virtue of physical appearance. Nevertheless, given their wide-ranging racial composition, their various educational and economic backgrounds, and their political and religious views, the acculturation and assimilation rates of the Hispanic population as a whole are nearly impossible to gauge (Zavala-Martinez, 1994).

Different Hispanic groups manifest different degrees of acculturation and assimilation. For example, Mexican children are able to speak English and to deal with the social structure in the United States, although they continue to use Spanish to communicate in their household. Likewise, Mexican Americans also practice Mexican's cultural values and traditions in their communities, keeping such traditions alive (Vega et al., 1991). A study conducted by Coreil et al. (1991) regarding acculturation and smoking patterns found that Mexican American women smoked less than either Mexican American men or Anglo females. Yet as these women became more acculturated and joined the work force, their tendency was to smoke more. Some of the same findings took place in a study performed by Marksides et al. (1991) regarding young Mexican American women and drinking behaviors.

Unlike Mexican women, who have traditionally experienced difficulty and discrimination in the U.S., the first Cubans arriving in the United States were often professionals, sometimes wealthy people. As a result, many of them adopted the required demeanor—allowing them to fit in the social setting—yet they resisted assimilation by maintaining their traditional values and beliefs. The second wave of Cubans (Marielitos), who came to United States shores lacking professional or working skills, were less successful in their adaptation. Many of these migrants became recipients of public assistance and, to date, have not developed the proper skills to adapt to Anglo—American culture.

In contrast with other Hispanic migrant groups, Puerto Ricans enter the United States as citizens who can vote, serve in the armed forces, and easily travel to their homeland (Landale & Ogena, 1995). Although the sociopolitical climate that exists between the United States and Puerto Rico would seem to foster assimilation and acculturation, it is a fact that Puerto Ricans have resisted these processes. Their lack of assimilation can be judged by the fact that the current poverty rate of Puerto Ricans is higher than that for Whites, African Americans, and other Hispanics (Rodríguez, 1983; Rodriguez, 1994). Other factors thwarting adaptation of this ethnic group are biculturalism and bilingualism. Biculturalism refers to the process of integration of values and behaviors from two cultures, the ethnic and the dominant culture both characterizing an individual's identity. Bilingualism refers to an individual's ability to communicate in two languages (for our purposes, English and Spanish). Most Hispanics have evidenced a desire not to abandon their culture, language, or identity, and to become both bicultural and/or bilingual rather than assimilated.

In the United States, women in the Hispanic culture interact with social systems to a greater extent than do men (Zavala-Martinez, 1988). They are the ones who take the children to school and for health care; they are the ones who shop for essentials; they are the ones who participate more actively in church activities. Since Hispanic women must negotiate with different community systems (i.e., welfare offices, grocery stores, and pharmacies), many learn to speak English. But many others do not; Hispanics often live in segregated communities, so learning the English language is not necessary for survival. In fact, some of them rarely venture out of their own neighborhoods and never have to speak English in order to satisfy their basic personal and familial needs. In some families, the children speak English only outside of the home. In others, the parents speak only Spanish and their children respond only in English. Still others are functionally illiterate in both languages and practice their own "Spanglish" patois.

Stress and acculturation pressures also contribute to family violence, strict child rearing practices such as spanking, wife battering, socialized acceptance of male drinking and smoking behaviors, and an increase of at-risk behaviors by teens or Hispanic men. "Verguenza" (shame) and "pena" (guilt) imposed by the family discourage open discussion of what are often thought to be unacceptable behaviors.

Religion and Hispanic Women

Religion and faith have played extremely important roles in Hispanic culture, even for the nonpracticing individuals. It is hard to overstate the influence of the Spanish colonizers, and the Catholic religion was intrinsic in the origins of the Hispanic culture. Other Christian denominations are represented in some sectors, including Methodism, and the fundamentalist Jehovah's Witnesses, Pentecostal, and Baptist. Other variations of religions practiced by Hispanics include a combination of African rituals intertwined with sanctioned saints of the Catholic Church (known as "Santería"); a respect of supernatural beliefs and spiritualism (known as "Espiritismo"); and some forms of religious-focused herbal medicine (known as "Curanderismo"). Yet, Roman Catholicism is and has been for centuries the dominant dogma among Hispanics.

Home altars are an essential part of many Hispanic homes and are usually kept by the women in the family. According to Turner (1982), altars are "distinctive because they represent a personal, private, and most important, a creative source of religious experience" (p. 318). These altars display images, candles, and flowers, and sensual reminders of their religion as well as of the physical and social elements of their culture (Turner, 1982).

Within the Catholic Church, Hispanic women play another important role, constituting the primary care givers within the religious community. Women usually care for the churches, organize fund raising activities, and teach the word of God ("catecismo"). It is a fact that the number of nuns is higher than that of priests (Rodríguez, 1983). However, nuns have assumed traditional roles such as educators, social helpers, and health assistants. The role of the women in the Catholic Church is inspired by the devotion of the Virgin Mary, mother of Jesus Christ. Women see the social roles that they play as related to purity and servitude demanded of them by the Catholic Church. For example, women are expected to remain virginal until marriage and to view their chief roles as mothers and wives (Stapples & Miranda,

1990). Birth control, abortion, divorce, and the participation of women in leadership roles in church are issues of great controversy for Hispanic women.

Roles of Hispanic Women

In the Hispanic culture, gender roles are, to some extent, patterned after the ideas of "Marianismo" (the presumption that women should emulate the Virgin Mary) and "Machismo" (the high regard for distinctly "masculine" supremacy, courage and honor, and the notion that the male should be sole supporter of the family) (Becerra, 1983). Male and female Hispanic children are raised with markedly different expectations for behavior (Mayo, 1997). The female is taught to assume passive roles, to be obedient, to remain close to the family, and to guard her contact with people outside of the family. Those roles are learned through her relationship with her mother, grand-mother, and other female relatives, all of whom inculcate the assumption that women's roles are chiefly mother and wife, and that they will be unswervingly devoted to their children and their husbands. They often care for family elders during some portion of their married life (Becerra, 1983).

A double-standard does exist for males, who may be afforded certain priv-ileges or liberties related to independence, social interactions, and rites for reaching "manhood" (Mayo, 1997). The "man of the house" is an important part of the family governing structure, a role that is assumed by a son or other male relative in the absence of a patriarch figure (Sotomayor, 1991). They are encouraged to gain worldly experience outside of the home before settling down to assume the roles of husband and father. Males are taught to be the head of the household, sole financial providers, and the final authority at the time of making family decisions (Mayo, 1997).

Differences of opinion between Hispanic males and females emerge because of these conflicting roles. Women are taught that their duty to their children exceeds that owed to their husbands, while men are taught that they are husbands first and then fathers (Mayo, 1997). Conflicts inevitably arise when men demand that their wives meet their own desires before taking care of the children's needs.

It is expected for the mother to keep the infant and child very clean and well-dressed, especially little girls (Safa, 1974). Pierced ears and gold jewelry are common for very young female infants. On the other hand, children and preadolescents—especially girls—are protected from sexual information, but are exposed to adult conversations and are therefore aware of human sexuality and sensual messages early in their development. Once a young girl reaches puberty and begins menstruating, she is no longer a child and is considered a "señorita." This is a special time because she is now viewed as possessing the potential for marriage and childbearing. Her virginity is highly valued and protected by the family, and sexual experimentation is not tolerated.

An unfortunate result of such sheltered upbringing is that Hispanic women's health care has been negatively affected by their lack of knowledge about reproduction, human sexuality, and body image. Open discussion of sex-related concerns is a "taboo" subject. Hispanic women are keenly aware of general disapproval of sexual activities and childbearing before marriage (Fennelly et al., 1992) and they are expected to be virgins upon their marriage. The contradiction is that once they get married, especially during the wedding night, they are expected to be passionate lovers. This drastic transition is traumatic for many Hispanic women, often leading to sexual dysfunction. Yet sexual dysfunction is not openly discussed, even with the husband, which in many cases leads toward problems in the marriage, and sometimes in divorce.

Most of the time, the disciplinary role lies with the mother (Bryce-Laporte, 1970; Safa, 1974). Disciplining children can range from severe scoldings and threats of withholding privileges to spanking. The paternal role is framed by the assumption that the man is the "bread-winner" and "head of the family." He is seen as the firm and strict one and is consulted only for major decisions and major disciplinary issues (Szapocnick et al., 1978). Yet, all elders, and especially the females, are valued in the Hispanic culture for their knowledge. In fact, the grandmothers in Hispanic families usually have much say in the rearing of their grandchildren and are often the primary support system for the mother (Becerra, 1983). Thus, the importance of the female in Hispanic families plays itself out through several generations of family members.

Hispanic Values and Women

Cortes (1991) indicates that Hispanics' perceptions of gender and intergenerational relations tend to differ from those within the mainstream United States. He indicates that in traditional settings, men have emphasized the domain of work outside of the home and women have taken primary responsibility for "la familia" as well as for the preservation and transmission of culture (Ortiz, 1996). According to Cortes (1991), such a delineation occurs primarily because of economic demands; however, in recent decades, Hispanic women have increasingly entered every aspect of North American working life, and are becoming aware of the need of their participation in political issues and labor struggles. For example, the United States Census Bureau (1995) indicates that there was a gain in 1992 of Hispanic women's representation in local governments. The percentage of Hispanic women who were elected as local officials increased from 18.4 percent in 1987 to 22.6 percent in 1992. Nevertheless, when compared to the overall United States population,

Hispanics represented in 1992 only 1.2 percent of all local elected officials (the figure in 1987 was 1.1 percent).

The values embraced by the Hispanic culture have enormous impact in the development of Hispanic women's identity. First, work is viewed as a necessary means to a goal, but not as the most important priority in life. Rather, personal and emotional interactions are the most important aspects of life. Greater importance is also placed on the heart/emotions rather on the head/intellect (passionate display of emotions is acceptable in public), and many Hispanic women embrace a strong sense of justice for all human, personal, and social needs.

In non-Hispanic groups, punctuality is a reflection of responsibility, but responsibility means something different for Hispanic women. Responsibility is the fulfillment of the basic needs of family and friends (Panitz et al., 1983). Success is not measured by material things, but by how much family and friends can be helped. Since their identity is based on their position within their families and communities, Hispanic women focus on interpersonal ("simpatico") contacts rather than on the need for solitude or privacy. They reflect an intense awareness of the dignity ("dignidad") of each human being, regardless of social status, and a strong sense of shared responsibility for the well being of others. The "personal" for the Hispanic women comes before the "institutional," and individual needs are more important than time, work, and money.

Hispanic heritage provides women with common social values including a sense of openness towards others ("confianza"), a gregarious and amiable approach to social interaction, and a preference for simple, personal relationships and contacts rather than extreme formality (although awareness of social class status is known by all). The values of "individualismo" (individualism), "personalismo" (personalism), and "familismo" (familism) are deeply ingrained in Hispanic cultures (Mayo, 1997).

Family and Hispanic Women

As in other cultures, Hispanic families are expected to provide emotional support and the basic needs for its members. Indeed, the familial solidarity of Hispanics is a stereotype rooted in a real phenomenon (Ramirez, 1980; Ramirez & Arce, 1981). Help is sought for family members from both the nuclear and the extended family (Becerra, 1983). Outside help from nonfamily members is sought only when there is no other alternative.

The value of "familismo" (familyism) places great emphasis on the family's identity, and is a concept present in all Latin American countries (Zayas & Palleja, 1988). Familismo includes an assumption that the extended family will accommodate itself willingly to those family members in need (Zayas & Palleja, 1988). Familism serves as an adaptive function, and for women, the responsibility is that of holding the family together in times of stress. It is usually the women who will intervene first with any family member in need. Seeking professional help is a last resort.

The extended family, which in many instances includes members of the community and non-blood related family members, is also fundamental to the concept of familismo (Vega et al., 1991). Regular communication, visits, and social gatherings are common. Hispanic families are not limited by blood relations and families, and in many instances include "hijos de crianza" (son/daughters by rearing, not by birth). Children and adolescents in need of parenting or economic supports are frequently taken in by Hispanic families. These informal adoptions can be initiated by the "compadres/padrinos" (Godparents) or by aunts or uncles and others in the community (Becerra, 1983). These relationships are not often formalized through legal procedures unless enforced as requirements for guardianship.

The Spanish concept of "respeto" (respect) is manifested by deference for the needs or wishes of others. The concept is rooted in the idea that people should be valued for what they represent or contribute to the family and community. This value influences all levels of relationships and is especially recognizable in the family hierarchy. "Respeto" is demonstrated by the fact that Hispanics often avoid looking others straight in the eye. Direct eye contact is a signal of disrespect, rudeness, or violent confrontation. Yet many helping professionals misunderstand such a nonverbal code, thinking that Hispanic clients are lying when they divert their gaze.

The Hispanic family in the United States is rapidly changing, leaving some Hispanics to face what they consider the crumbling of the "familia." Single-mother households are becoming more common; these might come as a result of death, separation, abandonment, or personal choice. In such cases, women become the primary breadwinner (Ortiz, 1996). They find out that their role in traditional culture is often in conflict with Anglo-American ways and the basic requirements for living.

Health Issues Among Hispanic Women

According to Novello (1992), cancer-related deaths are twice as high for Hispanics as for non-Hispanic Whites. According to the National Cancer Institute (1994), cancer in Hispanic women is increasing faster than in other women (White or African-American). The rate of cervical cancer is reported to be double among Hispanic women than that for non-Hispanic White women. Hispanic women also have higher mortality rates and lower survival rates for breast cancer than do White women.

The National Health Interview Survey (1992) has identified several barriers that deter Hispanic women from getting mammograms. These barriers have been identified as the misconception that without symptoms there is no need for screening; lack of physician recommendation; cost and/or lack of health insurance; and lack of access to mammography facilities in their communities. Studies indicate that cultural barriers also exist, such as fear of cancer detection, difficulty with the English language, and cultural beliefs and values that do not emphasize preventive medical care.

Along with increasing cancer rates, AIDS cases are also on the rise for Hispanics. As of February 1992, Hispanics accounted for 16.2 percent of all AIDS cases in the United States, and Hispanic women represent 20.5 percent of all cases of women with AIDS. Fifty percent of the AIDS cases among Hispanic women are the result of intravenous drug use, and 39 percent can be traced to heterosexual contact with an infected partner (Novello, 1992). De La Rosa (1989) informs that a study conducted by the United States Department of Health and Human Services found that Hispanics in the United States were also at higher risk of heart disease, stroke, cirrhosis, and diabetes. Another study by Andersen et al. (1981) suggests that Hispanics residing in the southern United States have limited access to medical care, are less likely to see a doctor, rarely practice preventive medicine, are generally more dissatisfied with the medical services that they receive, and are more inclined to use the informal system (home medicines) than to seek professional medical assistance.

Fertility and Reproductive Issues The research literature suggests that the reproductive and health patterns of Hispanic women differ from those of non–Hispanic females (Smith, 1986; Humble et al., 1985; Herold et al., 1986). For example, the fertility rate is higher for Hispanics than for non–Hispanics; the average fertility rate in the United States has declined in the past decade to 1.8 births per women (Smith, 1986), but for Hispanics the fertility rate is 50 percent higher than that of non–Hispanic women. Among Hispanics, the rate for Mexican-American women is 53 percent higher than for Puerto Rican women and double the rate for Cuban American women (Ventura, 1984). According to the United States Census Bureau (1997, p. 2), "women born in Mexico comprised 30 percent of all the foreign-born women in the childbearing ages and had 48 percent of the births to these women." The Bureau (1997) also points that Mexicans had higher fertility rates than immigrant women from Asia and Europe.

The higher fertility rates of Hispanics may be the result of their general reluctance to use forms of contraception. It is known that oral contraception usage is lower among Hispanic women than non-Hispanics. Yet, among Hispanics, the responsibility of contraception relies on the women. Further, regardless of the country of origin, there is a lower rate of male sterilization and condom use; perhaps this fathering of many children is an aspect of machismo. Furthermore, many Hispanics associate condoms with clandestine sex and are infrequently used in marital sexual contacts. Oral contraceptives and the rhythm method are the most common methods of birth control. The latter, as well as other natural methods of contraception, are the only ones that the Catholic Church accepts. While oral contraceptives are not accepted by the Church, they are the most commonly used device by Hispanic women because they are easy to use and allow women to control their fertility. The decision to undergo partial or total hysterectomy or to have a tubal litigation depends on health concerns, exposure to medical care providers, and economic access to services. In many instances, these are used as permanent measures of birth control. For example, it is a fact that Puerto Rican women have a higher per capita rate of sterilization than Anglo women.

Hispanic women tend to nurse their children, and children are often breast-fed until they are two years old. Breast-feeding is culturally dictated, but is also usually practiced for economic reasons. Feeding and childcare are very carefully monitored by the elder women in the family.

Infertility is most commonly perceived as a woman's problem, and methods for increasing fertility are relatively unknown to Hispanics. Childless couples may adopt or be providers for other family members' children or younger siblings. Children are viewed as the source of companionship and help during the elderly years, and childless women are often pitied, especially in their old age. As a result, pregnancy is one of the most welcomed conditions in the Hispanic culture (Leavitt, 1974).

Once pregnant, the Hispanic woman is well cared for by all those around her. The message is that she is now a vessel carrying life, but in contrast, the Hispanic men rarely participate in the labor and birth experience. If the family has its way, the woman will not be permitted to smoke, drink alcohol, or become overly tired or hungry. Professional prenatal care is often absent, mostly because other women, particularly older women, share their expertise and care for the pregnant women. Despite the abundance of familial care she receives, the Hispanic woman often approaches childbirth with fear and misinformation, partly stemming from taboos associated with sexuality.

Once the infant arrives, the immediate family bestows much care and special treatment on the woman. Maternal postpartum care is affected by economics, time constraints, and other competing life forces. The prompt return to sexual activities is very important for most couples and closely spaced pregnancies are not uncommon.

Hispanic Women's Responses to Health Issues

Health care decisions in the Hispanic family usually become the responsibility of the "wisest" family member (usually an elder woman) who is knowledgeable about folk remedies. Traditionally, home remedies are the first choice and the women are the ones who are called to apply or administer them (Kay, 1977; Weaver, 1970). Herbal teas, special foods, periods of resting and isolation, or special massages are all methods used by women folk healers or the family's female elder. Medical attention is sought from trusted providers, usually by word of mouth (Kay, 1977).

As it is practiced in mainstream American society, preventive medicine is basically unknown to some Hispanics, and large numbers lack medical insurance (Novello, 1992; Zavala-Martinez, 1994). The avoidance of conventional allopathic preventive techniques may be related to the Hispanic tendency toward a "here and now" time orientation rather than planning for the future. Economic limitations or reliance on folk medicine could be explanations, as well. Actively seeking-out health care will greatly depend on a Hispanic individual's prior experiences with health care delivery systems, their level of acculturation, and whether they had experienced an urban or rural upbringing (Kay, 1977). Hispanic women are the ones who usually seek help for the family. However, they have a strong sense of modesty and privacy about physical exposure and emotional self-disclosure; therefore, it is very difficult for them to seek mainstream medical or mental health assistance. Exacerbating the situation is the inability of many Hispanics to speak English. For many of these women, language is an obstacle and often they rely on interpreters who may be friends, family members, or employees of the health care system. Interpreting and/or translating situations can be a cause of stress and anxiety for these women. This is problematic enough, but the complexity of the American health system is another main source of confusion and stress (Zavala-Martinez, 1994).

In instances of illness, the Hispanic family will band together to provide help at all levels (Muller et al., 1985). Such familial support is most evident at times of birth, terminal illness, or deathbed situations. When a family member becomes ill and is hospitalized, it is of concern to both the nuclear and the extended family. Assistance in child care, housework, emotional support, translating, and moral support are provided, usually by women (Muller et al., 1985). It is not uncommon for several female family members to accompany the patient to the hospital, often bringing food and other goods. Since there is still an unspoken fear of hospitals as places of death, it is expected that a family member—usually a woman—will remain in the hospital with the person at all times. This means family females take turns staying overnight with the patient, even sleeping on the floor next to the patient's bed.

Religious influences passed on from generation to generation also play a part in the response to health and illness situations. Life and death are matters controlled by God, and conscious interference with fate is considered disrespectful of God's will. In fact, for some, disease and epidemics are thought to be punishments from God. Sometimes, however, especially in mainstream U.S. culture, this fatalistic surrender to God's will is unfortunately interpreted as ignorance of current medical technologies or inertia for taking control of personal health (Guendelman, 1983).

In the case of chronic illness, the expectation in the Hispanic community is that the individual will be permitted to die with dignity. Women carry out traditional mourning rituals. These may continue for one year, characterized by public emotional displays and symbolic dress in shades of gray, white, or black.

Although they are often reluctant to seek their help, most Hispanics place great respect on health care providers (Lurie & Lawrence, 1971). Whether doctor, nurse, "curandero" (ritual healer), "santiguador" (one who lays hands/massages), or "espiritista" (spiritual guide/healer), they are all viewed as authorities by virtue of their training or education (Romano, 1985; Kay, 1977). They may also be seen as gifted with a special God-given talent. As Guendelman (1983) indicates, some of these health beliefs conflict with Western medicine, and tend to support the stereotype of Hispanics as naive or unsophisticated. This lack of awareness and appreciation for traditional systems of support creates a barrier to trust between the helping professional and the Hispanic client (Zavala-Martinez, 1994).

Folk medicine emerges from many cultures, including those of the indigenous people of Latin America, Africa, and Europe. Folk medicine in itself defines the values of Latin America. One of the innovative ways of meeting individual and community health needs is through folk medicine (Kay, 1977). In general terms, it is defined as "those health care practices which have been developed mostly out of beliefs and usage over time, and handed down from earlier generations and/or borrowed from other cultures as being in the folk medical system" (Dennis, 1985, p. 14). Folk healing serves as an important community support system for many Latin Americans suffering from mental health problems or life stressors. This practice is characterized by the belief that the mind and body must work together. It is based on the Christian belief that God can and does heal and that people with a special gift can heal in His name (Hentges et al., 1986; Ripley, 1986). Therefore, spirituality is an important component in the utilization of Hispanic folk medical practices (Sandoval, 1977).

As a result of the diversity in Latin America, several terms have emerged to classify and define folk healing. As discussed before, the most common ones are "espiritismo" (spiritism) and "curanderismo" (healing). "Espiritismo" (spiritism) for example, is known as a "syncretic religiophilosophical healing system" (Koss, 1987, p. 56). Spiritual folk healers, usually older women who inspire respect, often practice in the same community in which they live (Kay, 1977). They speak the "common day language" and do not charge exorbitant fees. "Mediums" are considered to be intermediaries between spirits and the people, and they "receive messages from the spirits or become possessed by either good or molesting spirits in order to diagnose, counsel, prescribe herbal and ritual remedies, and prognosticate" (Koss, 1987, p. 56). Hohmann et al. (1990) conclude that the establishment of such folk institutions came about as an attempt to complement the mental health system that fails to meet the needs of the Hispanic community.

Women's Problems Throughout history, Hispanic women have been key players in the development and evolution of their culture. Beginning with indigenous women, they contributed to farming, and were part of the economical, political, and social system of their communities. During the Spanish colonization, the absence of European women resulted in the mixture of races.

Hispanic women face many of the common problems of women from other ethnic groups. To comprehensively discuss all of these problems is an unrealistic task. Therefore, only those problems that seem to be most seriously affecting Hispanic women will be presented here. These problems are the lack of education, lack of employment opportunities, domestic violence, and divorce.

First, Hispanic women are usually limited in their formal education. In some rural areas, males go to school while females are informally taught at home as they learn house duties (Sullivan, 1985). For those young women who do attend school, many do not complete their education. In the United States, high school drop-out rates are very high for Hispanics: the most recent figures for Hispanic high school completion is only 53.1 percent, compared to 81.5 percent for Whites and 70.4 percent for Blacks (U.S. Bureau of the Census, 1997). It was also reported that there was a difference between gender in terms of completing 4 or more years of college. The rate was 24.8 percent for Hispanic men, compared with 19 percent for Hispanic women. On the other hand, Puerto Ricans have higher literacy rates than Cubans and Mexicans. Most Hispanic women who receive university degrees are the first generation in their families to do so.

But even if Hispanic women receive degrees, their salaries are lower than those for Anglo males and for non-Hispanic women. Career opportunities are growing, but Hispanic women have limited access to them (Zavala-Martinez, 1988). The limitations come not only from the dominant culture, but in many cases from their own culture. As it was mentioned earlier, women are taught to be mothers and wives and that they should remain at home caring for children, husband, and elders. These cultural expectations deprive women of career opportunities, even when those opportunities become available. The Hispanic culture does not allow women to put the roles of motherhood and wife aside for a career, and women who do so are viewed as selfish and even masculine. In many cases, women must choose between the family and a career (Wong & Levine, 1992). Most are inclined toward choosing the family and those who venture in a different direction are criticized and pressured to the point of losing the family ties and perhaps their marriage. Yet as a result of changes in the past decades in family and economic situations, women are increasingly forced to work outside of the home (Ortiz, 1996). They must balance the roles of mothers, wives, and outside workers, even in the face of their culture's disapproval (Wong & Levine, 1992).

Although women have had to adjust their familial and occupational roles to the reality of today's world, Hispanic male's roles have changed slowly and in many instances, have not changed at all. These incongruities in gender expectations have exacerbated incidences of domestic violence. From their young childhood, males are taught that they rule at home and that they are the ones to assume the decision-making role. Consequently, when the woman refuses to do what she is told or when she disagrees with his decision-making authority, she is often physically and/or verbally abused. Unfortunately, abusive behavior is not only condoned, but also encouraged, by the culture at large. Women are told that they must obey the husband even if he abuses alcohol, commits adultery, squanders the family's money, or fails to perform his house duties. Regardless of his transgressions, she usually stays married for the children's well-being.

Yet as Hispanic women enlarge their identities and develop their sense of personal power, perhaps as a result of their increasing presence in the workplace and their concurrent assimilation and acculturation, divorce is becoming more frequent and is creating serious problems among Hispanic families. Despite the fact that divorce is not allowed in the Catholic Church, and only in specific situations can the marriage be annulled, divorce rates are increasing among Hispanics. When the relationship between husband and wife ends, a tortuous process of diminished paternal support for the family often follows. Some divorced men even abandon the extended family altogether. Single-mother households are becoming more common to Hispanic women's reality, and divorced women become the primary bread-winner, assuming the role of both father and mother. In many instances, the divorce process is viewed as the woman's fault and their lack of understanding of their partner. Social stigma by the Hispanic community often follows divorce. Divorced women are viewed as selfish and unreliable, since they could not keep a marriage going, and often as "easy women" as well.

Although many of them understand the concept of gender equality, most Hispanic women do not embrace the tenets of feminism. In some Hispanic countries, women who have ventured to call themselves feminists have been criticized and isolated. Many Hispanic women envision a feminist as an Anglo woman of middle to upper class with very radical ideas. A large number of Hispanic women believe that, although in principle there should be equality between males and females, their differences are what make them feminine.

SUGGESTIONS FOR WORKING WITH WOMEN IN THIS GROUP

It has been well established that the term "Hispanic" demarcates individuals who share the Spanish language and a common geographical and cultural origin. Yet it is clear that these individuals differ widely one from the other, and they also differ from the mainstream U.S. population. This chapter attempted to provide some social, cultural, and historical perspectives to provide an understanding of this ethnic group. Helping professionals who work with diverse populations must understand the need for multicultural sensitivity and understanding. Professionals should also realize that they will be increasingly confronted with the challenge of working with clients of diverse ethnic backgrounds as the country's demographics shift. Sensitivity and nonjudgmental approaches need to be considered when dealing with these women. Although it is undisputed that differences exist among these women, understanding their general cultural heritage will provide a foundation for effective interactions with them. The basis for any personal or professional relationship is trust. For the helping professional to communicate effectively with Hispanic women, and for effective interventions, they must understand the social, political, economical, and cultural characteristics that partially define Hispanic women (Zavala-Martinez, 1994).

REFERENCES

Acuna, R. (1981). *Occupied America: A history of Chicanos.* New York: Harper and Row.

Andersen, R. et al. (1981). Access to medical care among Hispanic population of the Southern United States. *Journal of Health and Social Behavior, 22,* 78–79.

Arias, M. B. (1986). The context of education for Hispanics students: An overview. *American Journal of Education, 95,* 26–57.

Bailey, A. J., & Ellis, M. (1993). Going home: The migration of Puerto Rican-born women from the United States to Puerto Rico. *Professional Geographer, 45*(2), 148–158.

Banks, J. A. (1987). *Teaching strategies for ethnic studies.* Boston: Allyn & Bacon.

Bash, H. (1981). *Sociology, race, and ethnicity.* New York: Gordon and Breach.

Bean, E. D., & Tienda, M. (1987). *The Hispanic population of the United States.* New York: Russell Sage Foundation.

Becerra, R. M. (1983). The Mexican-American: Aging in a changing culture. In R. L. McNeely & J. L. Cohen (Eds.), *Aging in minority groups.* (pp. 108–118). Beverly Hills: Sage Publications.

Bryce-Laporte, R. S. (1970). Urban relocation and family adaptation in

Puerto Rico. In W. Maggie (Ed.), *Peasants in cities: Reading in the anthropology of urbanization.* Boston: Houghton-Mifflin.

Coreil, J., Ray, L .A., & Markides, K. (1991). Predictors of smoking among Mexican American: Findings from the Hispanic HANES. *Preventive Medicine, 20,* 1–10.

Cortés, C. E. (1991). Latinos/Hispanics. In *A teacher's guide to multicultural perspectives in social studies.* Boston: Houghton-Mifflin.

De La Rosa, M. (1989). Health care needs of Hispanic Americans and the responsiveness of the health care system. *Health Care and Social Work, 14*(2), 104–113.

Dennis, R. (1985). Health beliefs and practices of ethnic and religious groups. *In Removing cultural and ethnic barriers to health care* (pp. 12–28). Proceedings of a National Conference on Removing Cultural and Ethnic Barriers to Health Care. Chapel Hill: University of North Carolina.

Duncan, G. J. (1991). The economic environment of childhood. In A. C. Huston (Ed.), *Children in poverty: Child development and public policy,* (pp. 23–50). New York: Cambridge University Press.

Fennelly, K., Cornwell, G., & Casper L. (1992). A comparison of the fertility of Dominican, Puerto Rican and mainland Puerto Rican adolescents. *Family Planning Perspectives, 24*(3), 107–110.

Guendelman, S. (1983). Developing responsiveness to the health needs of Hispanic children and families. *Social Work in Health Care, 8*(4), 1–13.

Hanke, L. (1988). *Contemporary Latin America: A short story.* New Jersey: D. Van Nostrand Co.

Hentges, K., Shields, C., & Cantu, C. (1986). Folk medicine and medical practice. *Texas Medicine, 82*(10), 27–29.

Herold, J. M., Warren, C. W., Smith, J. C., Rochat, R. W., Martinez, R., & Vera M. (1986). Contraceptive use and the need for family planning in Puerto Rico. *Family Planning Perspective, 18,* 185–188.

Hohmann, A. et al. (1990). Spiritism in Puerto Rico: Results of an island-wide community study. *British Journal of Psychiatry, 156,* 328–335.

Humble, C. G., Samet, J. M., Pathak, D. R., & Skipper, B. J. (1985). Cigarette smoking and lung cancer in Hispanic whites and other whites in New Mexico. *American Journal of Public Health, 75,* 145–148.

Kay, M. A. (1977). Health illness in a Mexican–American barrio. In E. Spicer (Ed.), *Ethnic medicine in the Southwest* (pp. 97–129). Tucson: University of Arizona.

Koss, J. (1987). Expectations and outcomes for patients given mental health care or spiritists. *American Journal of Psychiatry, 144*(1), 56–61.

Landale, N. S., & Ogena, N. B. (1995). Migration and union dissolution among Puerto Rican women. *International Migration Review, 29*(3), 671–692.

Leavitt, R. R. (1974). *The Puerto Ricans: Cultural change and language deviance.* Tucson: University of Arizona Press.

Lederman, S. A., & Sierra, D. (1994). Characteristics of childbearing Hispanic women in New York city. In G. Lamberty and C. Garcia Coll (Eds.), *Puerto Rican women and children: Issues in health, growth, and development,* (pp. 85–102). New York: Plenum Press.

Lewis, A. C. (1998). Hispanic minorities. *The Educational Digest, 64*(2), 67–69.

Lurie, H. J., & Lawrence, G. L. (1971). Communication problems between rural Mexican-American patients and their physicians. *American Journal of Orthopsychiatry, 42,* 773–783.

Markides, K. S., & Lee, D. J. (1991). Predictors of health status in middle-aged and older Mexican Americans. *The Journal of Gerontology: Social Sciences, 80,* 42–46.

Marin, G., & Marin, B. (1991). *Research with Hispanics populations.* Newbury, CA: Sage.

Mayo, Y. (1997). Machismo, manhood, and men in Latino families. In E. P. Congress (Ed.), *Multicultural perspectives in working with families,* (pp. 181–197). New York: Springer Publishing Company.

Miller, S., Nicolau, S., Orr, M., Valdivieso, R., & Walker, G. (1988). *Too late to patch: Reconsidering opportunities for Hispanic and other dropouts.* Washington, DC: Hispanic Policy Development Project.

Muller, T. et al. (1985). *The fourth wave: California's newest immigrants.* Washington, DC: Urban Institute Press.

Novello, A. C. (1992). *Hispanics.* Unpublished manuscript. Columbus OH: The Ohio State University, College of Medicine.

National Cancer Institute (1994). *Hispanic American women: Breast cancer and mammography facts.* Bethesda, MD. Author.

National Health Interview (1994). *Hispanic American women: Breast cancer and mammography facts.* Bethesda, MD. Author.

Ortiz, V. (1996). Migration and marriage among Puerto Rican women. *International Migration Review, 30*(2), 460–484.

Panitz, D., McConchie, R. D., Sauber, S. R., & Fonseca, J. A. (1983). The role of Machismo and the Hispanic family in the etiology and treatment of alcoholism in Hispanic American males. *Journal of Family Therapy, 11,* 31–44.

Pérez-Stable, E. J. (1987). *Issues in Latin American care.* Newsbury, CA: Sage.

Ramirez, O. (1980). Extended family support and mental health status among Mexicans in Detroit. *La Red. 28,* 20–23.

Ramirez O., & Arce, C. (1981). In A. Barton, Jr. (Ed.), *The contemporary Chicago family: An empirical based reviewed.* New York: Praeger.

Reichert, J. S., & Massey, D. S. (1980). History and trends in the U.S. bound migration from a Mexican town. *International Migration Review, 14,* 479–591.

Reisler, M. (1976). *By the sweat of their brow: Mexican immigrant labor in the United States, 1900–1940.* New York: Greenwood Press.

Ripley, G. (1986). Mexican-American folk remedies: Their place in health care. *Texas Medicine, 82*(11), 41–44.

Rodriguez, C. E. (1994). A summary of Puerto Rican migration to the United States. In G. Lamberty & C. Garcia Coll (Eds.), *Puerto Rican women and children: Issues in health, growth, and development* (pp. 11–38). New York: Plenum Press.

Rodríguez, M. A. (1983). La discriminación de la mujer en la iglesia. *Cruz Ansata, 6,* 78.

Rodriguez, R., & DeWolfe, A. (1990). Psychological distress among Mexican-American and Mexican women and related status on the new immigration law. *Journal of Consulting and Clinical Psychology, 59*(5), 548–553.

Romano, O. (1985). Charismatic medicine, folk healing, and folk sainthood. *American Anthropologist, 67,* 1151–1173.

Ruiz, R. A., & Padilla, A. M. (1977). Counseling Latinos. *Personnel and Guidance Journal, 55,* 401–408.

Safa, H. I. (1994). From shanty town to public housing: A comparison of family structure in two urban neighborhoods in Puerto Rico. *Caribbean Studies, 4,* 3–12.

Sandoval, M. (1977). Santeria: Afrocuban concepts of disease and its treatment. *Journal of Operational Psychiatry, 8*(2), 52–65.

Smith, P. B. (1986). Sociologic aspects of adolescent fertility and child-bearing among Hispanics. *Journal of Development Behavior in Pediatric, 7,* 770–772.

Sotomayor, M. (1991). *Empowering Hispanic families: A critical issue for the 90's.* Milwaukee, WI: Family Service America.

Stapples, R., & Mirande, A. (1990). Racial and cultural variations among American families: A decennial review of the literature on minority families. *Journal of Marriage and the Family, 42,* 887–903.

Sullivan, T. A. (1985). A demographic portrait. In P. San Juan Cafferty & W. C. McCready (Eds.), *Hispanics in the United States: A new social agenda* (pp. 7–32). New Jersey: Transaction Books.

Szapocznik, J., Scopetta, M. A., & Aranalde, M. A. (1978). Theory and measurement of acculturation. *Interamerican Journal of Psychology, 12,* 113–130.

Szapocznick, J., & Truss, C. (1978). Intergenerational sources of role conflict in Cuban mothers. In M. Montiel (Ed.). *Hispanic Families.* Washington, DC: COSSHMO.

Turner, K. F. (1982). Mexican American home altars: Toward their interpretation. *Aztlan, 13,* 309–326.

U.S. Bureau of the Census. (1991). *The Hispanic population in the United States: March 1991.* (Current Population Reports, Series P-20, No. 455). Washington, DC: U.S. Government Printing Office.

U.S. Bureau of the Census. (1991). *Highlights of population profile.* http://www.census.gov./

U.S. Bureau of the Census. (1993). *The Hispanic population in the United States.* http://www.census.gov/

U.S. Bureau of the Census. (1995). *1992 census of governments: Voting age population, voting, and registration in the election of November 1992.* Washington, DC: U.S. Government Printing Office.

U.S. Bureau of the Census. (1997). Highlights of population. http://www.census.gov./

Vega, W. A. (1995). The Study of Latino families: A point of departure. In R. E. Zambrana (Ed.). *Understanding Latino families: Scholarship, policy, and practice* (pp. 3–17). London: Sage Publications.

Vega, W. A., Bohdan, K., Valle, R., & Weir, J. (1991). Social networks, social support and their relationship to depression among immigrant Mexican women. *Human Organization, 50*(2), 154–162.

Ventura, S. J. (1984, December). *Births of Hispanic parentage.* Monthly health statistics report, 33(8), *Publication PHS 85-1120.* Hyattsville, MD: Department of Health and Humans Services.

Vivas-Maldonado, J. L. (1974). *Historia de Puerto Rico.* New York: L.A. Publishing Co.

Weaver, T. (1970). Use of hypothetical situation in a study of Spanish-American illness referral systems. *Human Organization, 29,* 140–154.

Williams, M. W. (1983). The Hispanic invasion and occupation of the Western Hemisphere. In A. C. Wilgus (Ed.). *Modern Hispanic America* (pp. 23–41). Washington, DC: The George Washington University Press.

Wong, R., & Levine, R. E. (1992). The effect of household structure on women's economic activity and fertility: Evidence from recent mothers in urban Mexico. *Economic Development and Cultural Change, 41*(1), 89–102.

Zavala-Martinez, I. (1988). En la lucha: The economic socioemotional struggles of Puerto Rican women. *Women and Therapy, 6,* 3–24.

Zavala-Martinez, I. (1994). Entremundos: The psychological dialectics of Puerto Rican migration and its implication for health. In G. Lamberty & C. Garcia Coll (Eds.), *Puerto Rican women and children: Issues in health, growth, and development* (pp. 29–38). New York: Plenum Press.

Zayas, L., & Palleja, J. (1988). Puerto Rican familism: Considerations for family therapy. *Family Relations, 37*(3), 260–264.

RECOMMENDED READINGS AND RESOURCES

Amott, T., & Matthaei, J. (1991). *Race, gender, and work: A multicultural economic history of women in the United States.* Boston, MA: South End Press.

Comas-Díaz, L., & Greene, B. (1994). *Women of color: Integrating ethnic and gender identities in psychotherapy.* New York: The Guilford Press.

Cooper, E. J. (1977). Group and the Hispanic prenatal patient. *American Journal of Orthopsychiatry, 47*(4), 689–700.

De Anda, D. (1984). Informal support networks of Hispanic mothers: A comparison across age groups. *Journal of Social Service Research,* 7(3), 89–105.

Marin, G., & Vanoss-Marin B. (1991). *Research with Hispanic Populations.* CA: Sage Publications, Newbury Park.

Marks, G., Solis, J., & Richardson, J. L. (1987). Health behavior of elderly Hispanic women: Does cultural assimilation make a difference? *American Journal of Public Health,* 77, 1315–1391.

Queiro-Tajalli, I. (1989). Hispanic women's perception and use of prenatal health care services. *Affilia: Journal of Women and Social Work,* 4(2), 60–72.

Richardson, J. L., Marks, G., Solis, J. M., Collins, L. M., Birba, L., & Hisserich, J. C. (1987). Frequency and adequacy of breast cancer screening among elderly women. *Preventive Medicine, 16,* 761–774.

Rodríguez, C. (1989). *Puerto Rican born in the USA.* Wincher, MA: Unwin Hyman.

Salvo, J. J., Powers M. G., & Santana-Cooney, R. (1982). Contraceptive use and sterilization among Puerto Rican women. *Family Planning Perspectives, 24*(5), 219–223.

Vazquez, M. (1994). Latinas. In L. Comas-Diaz & B. Greene (Eds.), *Women of color: Integrating ethnic and gender identities in psychotherapy* (pp. 114–138). New York: The Guildford Press.

Weaver, H., & Wodarski, J. S. (1996). Social work practice with Latinos. In D. F. Harrison, B. A. Thyer, & J. S. Wodarski (Eds.), *Cultural diversity and social work practice* (pp. 52–86). Springfield, IL: Charles C. Thomas Publisher.

SUGGESTED VIDEOS AND FILMS

Biculturalism and Acculturation Among Latino. (1991). Studies issues of acculturation and assimilation among Hispanics in the United States. (28 minutes). New Jersey: Films for the Humanities & Sciences Company.

Chicana. (1993). 23 minutes documentary tracing the roles of Mexican/Chicana women from Pre-Colombian times to the present.

Chicano: The History of the Mexican American Civil Rights Movement. (1996). Collection of 4 videocassettes.

Hispanic Americans: One or More Cultures. (1995). Discusses the similarities and differences among Puerto Ricans, Cubans, and Mexicans. (44 minutes). New Jersey: Films for the Humanities & Sciences Company.

Hispanic Americans: The Second Generation. (1995). Examines the second generation of Hispanics in the United States and their issues of acculturation and assimilation. (44 minutes). New Jersey: Films for the Humanities & Sciences Company.

Images of Puerto Rico. (1997). Sancor, Inc. presents a film about the natural beauty of Puerto Rico and its people.

Miami-Havana. (1992). Director Estela Bravo discusses in this 52 minutes video the relationship between the United States and Cuba, and its effects on the Cuban's families.

Status of Latina Women. (1993). This 26 minutes film examines the differences between U.S. Latin woman and their counterparts in Latin America.

The Changing Role of Hispanic women. (1995). Presents the changing roles of today's Hispanic women. (44 minutes). New Jersey: Films for the Humanities & Sciences Company.

The Latino Family. (1993). Examines the changes and endurance of today's Hispanic families and the issues of keeping their culture. (28 minutes). New Jersey: Films for the Humanities & Sciences Company.

GLOSSARY

compadre (co-parent): the relationship between the parents of a child and the godparent

confianza (confidence) trust: a social value that is characterized by a sense of openness and friendliness toward others

curandero (healing) ritual healer: medicine man; an individual who heals the body, the mind, and the spirit through herbs and natural remedies

curanderismo (healer): form of religious-focused herbal medicine

dignidad (dignity): awareness of the dignity of each human being, regardless of social status

espiritismo (spiritualism) spiritism: the result of a combination of African rituals intertwined with saints of the Catholic Church; religious practice for the healing of the body, the mind, and the spirit

espiritista (spiritual guide): an individual who practices spiritualism

familismo (familism): a value that places great emphasis on the family; implies an active involvement of the nuclear and extended family, usually expanded to include non-blood related family members, in all issues and family affairs

familia (family): a social structure that is extended beyond blood-family ties; not limited to nuclear and extended relationships, it usually expands to include non-blood related individuals

hijo/hija de crianza (informal adoptions): a child usually taken in by the family or a family member for parenting or economic support; the relationship is usually not formalized by legal procedure

madrina (godmother): a female who participates in the child's baptism and/or confirmation ceremony and makes a commitment to help raise the child (financially and spiritually)

machismo: high regards for masculine abilities; a determinant in the allocation of hierarchical roles within the family; implies that men must take charge, be strong, supportive, controlling, and a good provider for the family

marianismo (marianism): the sanctification of women; women are viewed and expected to act with the same sanctity as the Virgin Mary; women are attributed characteristics of purity, devotion, and gentleness

marielito: second waive of Cuban immigrants that came to the U.S. through the Port of Mariel in the late 1970's

mestizo: individuals born from a mix of native Indians and Spaniards

mulatto: males born from a mix of African slaves and Spaniards

mulatta: women born from a mix of African slaves and Spaniards

padrino (godfather): a male who participates in the child's baptism and/or confirmation ceremony and makes a commitment to help raise the child (financially and spiritually)

padrinos (godparents): those who participates in the child's baptism and/or confirmation ceremony and make a commitment to help raise the child (financially and spiritually)

pena (guilt): pressures by the family that discourage the discussion of certain topics such as sex, drugs, and teen pregnancy

personalismo (personalism): a gregarious and amiable regard for social interaction, personal relationship, and contact rather than formality

Raza (race): a concept that establishes that a mixing of races and ideologies occurred, producing what today are known as Hispanics/Latinos

respeto (respect): the deference to the needs or wishes of others rather than those of oneself

santería (ritual healing): a religious practice that combines the African rituals intertwined with saints of the Catholic Church; it is used to for the healing and/or "cleaning" of the body, the mind, and the spirit

santiguador (healer): an individual who uses massages, herbs, and prayer to heal

señorita (young lady): term used to refer to girls when they reach puberty; term used to refer to young women who have begun to menstruate and are no longer considered a child

simpático: congenial; pleasant; nice; agreeable; interpersonal contacts in the Hispanic culture are valued more than extreme imposed rules of privacy

spanglish: a mixture of the Spanish and English languages, used by a number of Hispanics in the United States as a way to communicate

verguenza (shame): disgrace; dishonor; discourages the discussion of topics such as sex and teen pregnancy

7

Women's Issues and Jewish Halacha

D. SPERO

INTRODUCTION

Jews operate in two separate contexts. Within the larger society in which they happen to be living, Jews function according to the rules and mores of that society, depending on the extent to which that society permits them to do so; that is, Jews living in America live as Americans, Jews living in North Africa live as North Africans, Jews living in Australia live as Australians. Within those larger, dominant societies, Jews also operate within their Judaism according to rules defined by the *halacha*. The *halacha,* a Hebrew word which means "the way," is a comprehensive set of rules defining what the Jew must do or may not do. For the most part, the Jew who wishes to live both in a society, especially a free society like the United States, and practice as a Jew, can do both. The behaviors outlined by the *halacha* usually do not impinge an individual's functioning within society. In fact, using economics for an example, the behavior suggested by the *halacha* is to follow the rules of the society. In situations where there might be a religious conflict, such as when one's boss insists that an individual work on the Sabbath, the recommended behavior is for the individual to follow the *halacha*.

If we place these two "living" contexts on opposite ends of a continuum, each Jew places himself or herself somewhere on that line. The more "religious" Jew would tend to skew his or her behavior toward the *halacha,* while more "assimilated" Jews would tend to skew their behavior toward that of the culture in which they reside. In the example cited previously, the religious Jew would give up the job and struggle in poverty rather than compromise the *halacha.* The "assimilated" Jew would adjust his or her behavior to fit the society and would choose to violate the Sabbath in order to keep the job.[1]

Prior to World War II, it was much more difficult than it is today for "religious" Jews to practice their Judaism according to the *halacha.* The Reform and Conservative Jewish communities arising in this country during those years accommodated their religion to the society. In other words, where there was a conflict between their religion and the demands of the society around them, the Reform and Conservative Jew would most likely give up a particular religious duty. Yet after World War II and following the Holocaust, a large influx of devoutly religious European Jews came to the United States. In Europe they had structured their lives according to the *halacha* and were not prepared to veer from their strict observation of Judaism. At this time, we also saw the beginnings of the Civil Rights Movement and an increasing tolerance of diversity in the marketplace. These events made it easier for Jews to practice their religion according to the *halacha,* and larger numbers of religious Jews became visible in the United States.

This spectrum of religious behavior also exists with respect to women's issues. The *halacha* has a great deal to say about the behavior of Jewish men and women in the areas delineated by marriage and divorce. Premarital sex, homosexuality, birth control, abortion, and numerous other issues confronting men and women in our society are all dealt with in the *halacha.* When questions arise that are nominally different from questions that have arisen in the past, it is those who have studied the *halacha,* the seminary-trained Rabbis, who are qualified to address questions. The rabbis usually do sympathize with women and try to find pathways within the *halacha* to accommodate the needs of the individual. The more religious Jewish woman will consult these Rabbis and abide by their decisions, while the assimilated Jewish woman will tend to follow the path most accepted by the society around them.

To understand the religious Jewish response to women's issues is to understand the ways in which the *halacha* has historically responded to these questions. Yet even an outline of the *halacha* in the area of women's issues would fill many volumes and is beyond this writer's capability. Nevertheless, in this chapter I will introduce some general guidelines of how women are viewed in the *halacha.* I will then focus on Jewish marriage, which occupies a central place within the *halacha*. From the vantage point of marriage according to *halacha,* we can also understand premarriage and post-marriage (divorce).

As our society has advanced and opened itself to discussion of moral and ethical issues and even changes in practice, it is the religious Jews who have come to be heard as they respond to issues which are being addressed by many segments of our society. As each opinion is heard, it is important to understand the origin of that opinion, and indeed, the purpose of this chapter is to explore such origins within the Jewish communities. To that end, the process by which the *halacha* was established will be set out. The goal is to help the reader develop a sense of the sophistication and wisdom that under-lies the *halacha*. After a brief historiographical introduction we will examine the process of *halacha* in detail with respect to women. Before addressing these issues, however, the author would like to place herself within the context of the discussion to clarify any biases in the discourse that follows.

BACKGROUND

I approach the writing of this chapter from the vantage point of both a professionally trained nurse and childbirth educator, as well as a practicing religious Jew, observant of the *halacha*. I was born in St. Louis, as were my mother and father. My paternal and maternal grandparents were born in Eastern Europe and came to the United States as adults. I have two younger siblings. We are all married and among us we have ten children. Five of these children are married. In terms of the "assimilation" scale described in the previous page, my paternal grandparents were intensely religious. My paternal grandfather was in fact brought to St. Louis as a religious functionary; he was a *shochet*[2] and a *mohel*.[3] My maternal grandparents were much more secular. My mother is the only religious member of her family.

While my grandparents had all been educated in Jewish schools in Europe, my parents did not have the benefit of an extensive Jewish education. There were not many Jewish schools in the United States in the twenties and thirties. My father studied briefly in a rabbinical seminary in Chicago, but the Depression put a quick end to that opportunity.

By the forties and fifties, Jewish education in the United States began to change. The large influx of religious Jews into the United States after the Second World War created a demand for more intensive Jewish religious education than was previously available. Jewish schools began to develop all over the United States. My siblings and I attended such Jewish schools, as did my husband and his siblings. My children have all been well educated in Jewish schools and have spent time in Israel. Prior to the Second World War, the majority of the Jews in this country were not religious and of those who were, most were not necessarily well educated in their religion. With the forties and fifties, a change occurred, so that today there are many more religious Jews who are well educated in the tenets of their faith.

The secular openness that has characterized our society over the last several decades has also made Jewish religious practices, as they reflect women's issues, more visible. These religious practices, while only recently becoming visible to the society as a whole, date from the beginnings of the present structure of traditional Judaism.

Historiography

The starting point for understanding the *halacha* and the halachic process is to develop some understanding of Jewish historiography. The starting point is the Bible itself, in particular the Five Books of Moses called in Greek the Pentateuch. Tradition ascribes the authorship of the Pentateuch to Moses, verbatim, as dictated by God. These books were given to the Jewish people prior to the death of Moses, which took place around the year 1240 BCE.

While God dictated the specific wording of the books, a larger body of material, an elaboration of many of the observances mentioned in the Pentateuch, was transmitted by God to Moses and taught to the Jewish people. This oral tradition was carefully preserved and passed down from generation to generation. With the various Exiles it became more and more difficult to maintain this tradition in oral form and various leaders and scholars among the Rabbis began to write down parts of it. These notes were finally edited by Rabbi Judah the Prince into a text called the Mishnah in the year 210 CE.

The Mishnah represented the Oral Tradition in outline form, which was sufficient at that time. The Mishnah was used in schools and seminaries to teach the Oral Tradition. As time passed controversy arose as to the meaning of parts of the Mishnah. Teachers began to make notes regarding their interpretations of the Mishnah, and in the year 390, the notes were edited in Palestine into what has become known as the Jerusalem Talmud. In the year 499, in Babylonia, the texts were again edited in what has become known as the Babylonian Talmud.

The Babylonian Talmud, the explication of the Oral Tradition delivered to Moses by God, forms the basis for the *halacha,* the traditional Jewish practice that continues today. Practicing Jews believe that within these pages—some 64 volumes—guidelines and precedents can be found for all behavior. Every situation that we might possibly encounter can be addressed by those who are well versed in this literature.

The next milestone is the year 1180 when Rabbi Moses, the son of Maimon, known as Maimonides, published his Mishneh Torah, an organized encyclopedia of the laws set forth in both of the Talmuds. The Mishneh Torah

continues even today as a major resource for the *halacha*. A second encyclopedia, also very much in use today, is the Shulchan Aruch published in 1564 by
Rabbi Joseph Caro.

The Babylonian and Jerusalem Talmuds, the Mishnah Torah, and the
Shulchan Aruch have been intensively studied over the centuries. These
volumes have become the basis for a massive body of literature of case law,
which has been used to establish precedents for every imaginable situation
that Jews anywhere in the world might encounter. Admittedly, because it is
interpreted by human beings who themselves are products of their time and
their environments, the corpus has taken on nuances of time and place. Yet
there is a clear continuity between the practices outlined in the two Talmuds
and Jewish religious practice today.

The following discussion highlights the critical role that the Talmud
and its interpretations play in the lives of women in Jewish society. The
starting point will be the status of women in the *halacha* in areas of civil and
criminal law.

Jewish Women in Civil and Criminal Law   The *halacha* observes no
difference between men and women in Jewish civil or criminal law. This is
explicitly stated in the Talmud in the tractate Baba Kama (p. 15a),[4] where
women are subject to the law of Torts:

In the Mishnah, women are explicitly included as equals as in the laws of
torts (damages). However, the following question is raised: *From where in the*
Bible *is this notion of equality under the law derived?* Three answers are given,
each of which establishes the equality of men and women in this area.

> Rab Judah said on behalf of Rab, and so was it also taught at the
> school of R. Ishmael: Scripture states, When a man or woman shall
> commit any sin (5:6) Scripture has thus made woman and man equal
> regarding all the penalties of the Law.
>
> In the School of Eleazar it was taught: Now these are the ordinances
> which thou shalt set before them (Exodus 21:19). Scripture has thus
> made woman and man equal regarding all the judgments of the Law
> (Exodus 21:1).
>
> The School of Hezekiah and Jose the Galilean taught: Scripture
> says. It hath killed a man or a woman. Scripture has thus made woman
> and man equal regarding all the laws of manslaughter in the Torah.

The next paragraph is especially interesting in that it explains why the above
mentioned three schools felt that it was necessary to cite three sources.

> Had only the first inference been drawn, [I might have said that] the
> Divine Law exercised mercy towards her so that she should also have the
> advantage of atonement, whereas judgments which concern as a rule man

who is engaged in business, should not include woman. Again, were only the inference regarding judgments to have been made, we might perhaps have said that woman should also not be deprived of a livelihood, whereas the law of atonement should be confined to man, as it is he who is subject to all commandments, but should not include woman, since she is not subject to all the commandments. Moreover, were even these two inferences to have been available, [we might have said that] the one is on account of atonement and the other on account of livelihood, whereas regarding manslaughter [it might have been thought that] it is only in the case of man, who is subject to all commandments, that compensation for the loss of life must be made, but this should not be the case with woman. Again, were the inference only made in the case of compensation for manslaughter, [it might have been thought to apply] only where there is loss of human life, whereas in the other two cases, where no loss of human life is involved, I might have said that man and woman are not on the same footing. The independent inferences were thus essential.

Women are excused from being witnesses in civil and criminal cases. The *halacha* provides a broad range of commandments from which women are excused, all stemming from the fact that their duties in the home take precedence.

Another civil area in which women's rights differ is in the area of inheritance. While sons have priority over daughters in the settling of an estate, the laws of inheritance provide very generously for the maintenance of the women in the family.

Marriage

The very first commandment to Adam and Eve is to procreate and extend life. As it says in the Book of Genesis: Be fruitful and multiply (Genesis I, 28). This mandate is the focus of a good part of the *halacha* approach to marriage. In order to provide a framework within which life can be extended to the next generation, the *halacha* has sanctioned marriage, a well-defined relationship between two parties, the husband and the wife. The *halacha* has defined marriage in terms of the rights of each of the parties. The rights of the wife are explicitly stated in the marriage document, or *ketubah,* which is given to the wife at the time the marriage takes place.

In the Mishneh Torah, Laws of Marriage, Maimonides (Yad, Ishut, 12:2) lists the ten obligations that a husband accepts with respect to his wife: to supply sustenance and maintenance, to supply clothing and lodging, to provide conjugal relations, to provide the funds mentioned in the *ketubah* in the event of a divorce or death, to procure for his wife medical care, to ransom her if she is taken captive, to provide her with a suitable burial, to provide her sustenance from his estate in the event of his death, and to ensure her right to live in his house, to provide for the maintenance of her daughters after his death, and to provide that her sons will inherit the funds mentioned in the *ketubah* if she dies. While many of these points have more relevance to different times and places, most of the obligations they insist upon are relevant today. There is a framework within the *halacha* for the woman to assert her own financial independence should she so wish it, if she has her own resources. The *halacha* also lists the four obligations of the wife to the husband and discusses at length which of these obligations can be abrogated and under what circumstances:

1. to relinquish her earnings to her husband;
2. to give her husband anything she may happen to find;
3. during her lifetime, to turn over profits from her property to her husband for the benefit of the household, while she retains ownership of the property itself; and
4. to acknowledge her husband's right to her estate after she dies.

The **Shulchan Aruch** suggests that the primary reason for the existence of the husband's ten obligations is to provide security for his wife. The wife's four obligations were instituted to maintain goodwill between husband and wife by compensating the husband to some extent for the cost of some of his obligations.

The *halacha* discusses what should occur if the wife decides not to fulfill some of her obligations to her husband. For example, if she wants to retain her earnings so that she can be more financially independent, she may do so, because her earnings were only instituted for goodwill as mentioned in the above paragraph. On the other hand, the husband is not permitted to stop supporting his wife because that would threaten her security and the foundation of the home.

Because marriage is so important in Judaism, the *halacha* stresses that the preparation for marriage is equally important. Premarital sex is prohibited, and there is a strong familial and societal bias against those who violate this prohibition. Modesty in dress and behavior is the norm. Jewish schools tend to separate the sexes at a very early age, a practice that today is finding increasing acceptance in education in general.

A woman cannot be forced into marriage. That is clearly stated in the Babylonian Talmud (Tractate Kiddushin, 2b) and restated both in Maimonides' Mishneh Torah Code (Yad Hachazakah, Ishut 4:1) and in the Rabbi Joseph Caro's Shulchan Aruch (Even Haezer 42:1). There is no ambivalence about this point. Historically, there have been instances where there have been abuses. For example, if the larger society in which the Jews were residing condoned arranged marriages, it was not unheard of for Jewish fathers to arrange marriages for their young daughters. In another instance, Jewish history documents a number of cases in which Jewish girls of marriageable age were forced to marry non-Jewish men. As a reaction to this custom, the Rabbis permitted fathers to arrange a marriage.

Within marriage, modesty is maintained and the *halacha* suggests an entire body of laws under the rubric, "Purity of the Family." In particular, and this has Biblical origin, the husband and wife refrain from sex while the wife has her period and for one week afterwards. Understandably, this period can be very difficult for both the husband and the wife. Modest behavior on the part of both parties helps the couple observe these rules. At the end of this period of abstention, the wife performs an immersion in a *mikveh,* and marital relations resume.

One of the most discussed issues in modern society is that of birth control. Modern technology has offered quite a few alternatives, and discussions of these technologies have taken place among the experts in the *halacha*. While birth control is discouraged, it is recognized that there are circumstances under which it might be undertaken. When that is the case, according to the *halacha,* it is the woman who exercises birth control technologies. For example, medical reasons, including reasons of mental health, might justify the use of birth control. A diaphragm or birth control pills might be permitted. (A rabbi must be consulted, because this is a question of halacha.) There are some halachic authorities who permit birth control—by the woman—if the couple have a boy and girl (others insist on two boys and two girls). The appropriate authorities must decide upon each situation.

Divorce

Because of the importance of marriage, the Rabbis will go to great lengths to make peace between husband and wife in order to prevent a divorce. To illustrate the importance, of preventing divorce, there is a story told in the Jerusalem Talmud (quoted in Michael Kaufman's *The Woman in Jewish Law and Tradition,* pages 181–182) concerning Rabbi Meir who lived during the second century. Every Friday evening Rabbi Meir would lecture in the synagogue at Hamat (near Tiberias in present day Israel). One Friday evening, his lecture ended later than usual. A woman who had attended the lecture returned home late. When she explained to her husband that she was late because the lecture had lasted longer than was expected, her husband did not believe her and banished her from the house. She could not return, he said, until she spat in the great rabbi's eye. Rabbi Meir learned of the husband's condition for reconciliation, and when he saw the distraught wife at his next lecture he invited her to the podium at the conclusion of the lecture. Before the remaining audience, he explained to her that his eye was troubling him and it could only be relived if someone would spit in it. He invited her, before witnesses, to spit in his eye. When she hesitated, he insisted explaining that if she would spit in his eye seven times, he knew that he would be fully healed. The woman finally did as he asked, and Rabbi Meir, who was now "cured," told the wife to tell her husband that she had not only spit once, but seven times.

Rabbi Meir's students were very critical of their teacher's behavior. They felt that the dignity of the Bible, as represented by the Rabbi, had been compromised by his behavior. They would have forced the jealous husband to come before the congregation and shamed him for his behavior to his wife. Rabbi Meir responded to their criticisms: "and is my name greater than that of the Creator? If the Holy Name of God, written in holiness, may be erased in order to bring peace between man and wife *(sotah)*, surely Rabbi Meir's honor may be diminished for the sake of this vital task of promoting peace between husband and wife.[5]"

Thus, reconciliation is the first recourse. Nevertheless, the *halacha* recognizes that some marriages are unworkable. Because the social climate is more tolerant of divorce than it once was, divorce within halachic Judaism is now more prevalent than it was years ago. Rabbis are more accepting of divorce as a solution to marital problems than they were years ago.

The bill of divorce, the document that formally dissolves the marriage, is called a *get piturin,* or "get" for short. The get is prepared by the husband or his agent and is then delivered by the husband or his agent to his wife. The get itself must be written in Aramaic by an authorized scribe or *sofer,* and it must be written especially for this couple, that is, it cannot be on a preprinted or a filled-in form. There are many detailed and exacting rules and most rabbis are not qualified to handle divorces, so the couple is referred to recognized authorities. This procedure serves the purpose of giving the couple as much time as possible to consider the ramifications of what they are about to do. There is another purpose as well.

Children born of an adulterous relationship have the status of a *mamzer.* A Jewish man or woman cannot marry anyone with the status of a *mamzer.* This being the case, the rabbis have to be sure that a marriage has been legally dissolved according to the most stringent rules. Otherwise, the children of subsequent marriages of the divorced woman also might be labeled with the status of *mamzer.*

Another important concept related to divorce is the concept of Agunah, which can be loosely translated as "anchored woman," is the term for a wife whose husband has left her or is missing (as in a wartime situation), and who is prevented from remarrying, either because she cannot obtain a divorce or there is no confirmation that her husband is dead. The problem of *agunah* arises because of the particular structure of marriage demanded in the *halacha*. In order to formalize marriage, it is the man who executes an agreement with the woman which leads to marriage in the first place *(ketubah)*, even though both must agree to the marriage. Consequently, since it was the man who entered into the agreement, it must be the man who dissolves the agreement (the *get*), even though both parties must agree to the divorce. Thus, situations may arise, either by accident or by intent, in which the man does not give permission for the divorce, circumstances that leave the woman an *agunah*. Because the structure of the *halacha* is so fundamental to Judaism, such contingents have unfortunate consequences for the Jewish women who are subject to such conditions.

Times of war when soldiers may be declared missing in action, or when vast upheavals of population and mass killings occur, as during the Holocaust, may lead to frequent cases of *agunah*. In these situations, the *halacha* becomes as lenient as possible (while still remaining consistent). In these cases, the Jewish courts accept hearsay and documentary evidence where they normally will not, such as single-witness testimony, testimony of those who are otherwise considered legally incompetent as witnesses, and even overheard conversations among non-Jews. In such times, all such tactics are acceptable and there is no cross-examination. This approach is not new and dates back to Talmudic times when such cases did occur. Every avenue is explored to help release the woman from her status as *agunah,* but the resolution must ultimately be within the constraints of the *halacha*.

In more recent times, another situation has arisen. According to the *halacha,* when a wife has grounds for divorce, she may compel the husband to divorce her. In order for the woman to be divorced, the husband must prepare a *get* for her. Some husbands, in order to blackmail their wives, have gone into hiding or simply refused to give the *get*. In such cases, it is not unknown for the wife to hire "enforcers" who will "persuade" her husband to grant her the get. In Israel, where the secular court system recognizes *halacha,* the woman can have the court attach his resources and even place him in jail. *Agunah* is acknowledged to be a difficult problem and substantial resources are being devoted to finding solutions, both for each individual case and globally.

The Case of Women and Abortion

I would like to examine in some detail the issue of abortion as it has appeared in the case law of *halacha*. Abortion deals with a number of important issues. These include the status of the fetus while it is in the mother's womb and the abortion process itself.

Chapter 7 of the volume of Mishnah called Oholoth (paragraph 6) cites:

> If a woman is in travail when giving birth [and it is feared that she may die] one may sever the fetus from her womb and remove it, [even if necessary], limb by limb, for her life takes precedence over its life. Once most of the fetus has exited, one may not touch it for one may not put aside one life for another.

The famous medieval commentary Rabbi Yitzchak ben Aizik, known as RASHI,[6] comments:

> So long as it has not emerged into the air of the world it is not a human being and it is permitted to kill it in order to save the mother's life. However, once the head has come out one must not kill it, for it is considered as if born.

Is there a Biblical basis for not considering the fetus to be a human being? Actually there is, and this is an excellent illustration of the subtlety of the Bible, on one hand, and the brilliance of the Rabbis, on the other. In the Book of Exodus in the Pentateuch, Chapter 21, sentences 22 and 23, in describing an injury to a pregnant woman as the incidental result of an argument between two people, we read the following:

> If men fight and hurt a pregnant woman so that her unborn children depart, but no harm [fatality] results, he shall be fined in accordance with the demand of the woman's husband, and he shall pay as the judges determine. If, however, harm [fatality] results, then you must give life for life (Exodus, XXI, 22 and 23).

In discussing the damages to be paid arising from inflicting bodily damages, the Talmud in the tractate Baba Kamma (p. 42a) identifies the harm of fatality referred to above as alluding to the woman and not to the fetus. In such a situation, if the fight causes the woman to miscarry, she is only entitled to a monetary compensation. Killing the fetus is considered a transgression but not a homicide. The reason for this decision is that until the fetus is delivered it has the legal status of being part of the mother's body. This is the point made in various different contexts in a number of places in the Babylonian Talmud.

Having established the principle that killing the fetus is not homicide, what is the attitude of Jewish people towards abortion? There are a number of references in the Talmud and its contemporary literature which define the attitude towards abortion. In discussing those laws applying to all mankind, a quote from Zohar[7] (Exodus 3b) and the Talmud in the tractate Sanhedrin (57b) reads:

There are three persons who drive away the Divine Presence from the
world making it impossible for the Holy One, Blessed be He, to
fix His abode in the universe, and causing prayer to be unanswered . . .
[The third is] the one who causes a fetus to be destroyed in the womb,
for he desecrates that which was created by the Holy One and His
craftsmanship. . . . For these abominations the Spirit of
Holiness weeps.

The Babylonian Talmud, in discussing those laws which apply to all
mankind states:

On the authority of Rabbi Ishmael it was said: A man is executed
even for the murder of an embryo. What is Rabbi Ishmael's reason?
Because it is written, "Whoever sheds the blood of man within
[another] man, shall his blood be shed." What is a man within
another man? An embryo in his mother's womb (Tractate
Sanhedrin, p. 57b).

Reviewing the various sources we have mentioned, while it appears that
aborting a fetus accidentally is not considered homicide, abortion as such is
prohibited. Returning to the original Mishnah quoted in this section, what is
the justification for performing an abortion in the case cited? The mother
may die if she delivers.

The Babylonian Talmud addresses this issue in the tractate Sanhedrin, and
labels the fetus in this situation, in which abortion is not only permitted but
mandatory, a "rodef." A "rodef" is essentially a stalker who has a homicidal
intent. Because the fetus (unintentionally) is in the process of killing its
mother, it may be dealt with as one deals with a "rodef," that is, the "rodef"
can itself be murdered (Tractate Sanhedrin, p. 72b). Notice that the Mishnah
qualifies the abortion as being permitted only so long as the head has not
been delivered. At that point, the fetus gains the status of a human being and
the label of "rodef" cannot be applied because the child has the same right to
life as the mother.

The preceding principles, established in Biblical times and iterated
formally in the Talmud almost two thousand years ago, are the principles with
which the Rabbis of today must deal when working with women. As
situations arise, these must be addressed within the context of principles
already established. This is the basis of the halacha and is the framework within
which the observant Jew addresses gender issues.

Questions do arise, however, such as the dilemma when the mother has
a serious medical problem but the fetus is not a "rodef," that is, the fetus
in itself is not a threat to the mother's life. If the fetus is not a "rodef,"
the abortion is not justified; on the other hand, if the pregnancy is

not aborted, the mother will die. More recent gender issues and questions have arisen with the advent of ultrasound and amniocentesis. Are women permitted to abort a fetus that has been diagnosed with a mental or physical defect such as Tay-Sach's disease, Down's syndrome, or AIDS? While most rabbis do not permit abortions in such cases, a twentieth-century accepted rabbinical authority, Rabbi Eliezer Waldenberg, did permit the abortion during the first three months of pregnancy if the mother had as yet not felt the fetus move. The discussion of this Jewish authority is highly technical and beyond the scope of this presentation; it is sufficient to say that it is based on precedents dating back to the original Talmudic citations mentioned above.

The question of what is considered a threat to the mother's health is being discussed as well. The mental health of the mother is included in these considerations and abortions have been permitted when there is a serious threat to the mother's mental health, but also with restrictions and qualifications within the context of the case law.

The *halacha* has also considered cases of conception that results from rape or adulterous or incestuous relations. Since every situation is different, a reliable rabbi well versed in the *halacha* must be consulted. The rabbi plays a critical role in many of the situations that are addressed today. It is the consistency of the *halacha's* decisions concerning women that must be addressed by the rabbi.

As a concluding note, I offer the following paragraph from Michael Kaufman's (1995) book, *The Woman in Jewish Law and Tradition* which summarizes the approach of the observant Jewish woman and her family to the issues raised:

> Abortion at will, or abortion without valid reason, because a baby is unwanted, or to limit the size of the family, or to avoid the travail of childbirth, or for economic reasons, is condemned in Judaism as a serious transgression. . . . When a mother's life or health is endangered, rabbis allow abortion as an extraordinary procedure on the basis of the Jewish view of the reverence of life. Abortion is a last resort, and must be performed *only after consultation with a competent halachic authority.* (Italics, mine) (pp. 168–169).

SUMMARY

The objective of this chapter has been to try to identify those essential characteristics within Judaism differentiating the attitudes toward women and women's issues from the positions more commonly found in society today.

These characteristics are encompassed in the *halacha,* the framework of laws followed by traditional Jewish men and women. While individual adherence to the *halacha* might vary within the Jewish population, those committed to observance of the Law will follow the dictates of the *halacha*. The *halacha* addresses virtually every facet of life from birth to death and does not only address religious behavior but also ethical, civil, and criminal behavior as well. As a result of the upsurge in religious observance among the younger population, understanding the *halacha* and its importance to the observant Jew has become increasingly important in recent years, particularly for understanding the Jewish woman.

SUGGESTIONS FOR WORKING WITH WOMEN IN THIS GROUP

Working with Jewish women, especially those who follow the *halacha,* should not be any different than working with anyone from a different culture. Being aware of the role that the *halacha* plays in the lives of Jewish women will certainly help overcome awkward moments. For example, Jewish women may have unusual constraints on time, like an early Friday schedule in order to get home for the Sabbath, or unusual social constraints, like a reluctance to eat out because of dietary restrictions. While it is difficult to differentiate between religious needs and personal needs, or even personality quirks, demanding behavior, bigotry, or general nastiness is definitely not meant to be part of any Jewish practice and is certainly not in the *halacha*.

ENDNOTES

1. The reader may have heard about different sects of Judaism such as Chasidic, Orthodox, Conservative, and Reform. There are theological differences between the Orthodox, Conservative, and the Reform; however, they all agree that any individual born of a Jewish mother is, according to the *halacha,* Jewish. In this essay we will be focusing on the practice of Judaism according to the *halacha*. In that context the Conservative Jew and the Reform Jew would be considered more assimilated and would be less likely to follow the *halacha* while the Chasidic and Orthodox Jews would be more likely to follow the *halacha*. In fact, the extent to which any Jew follows the *halacha* determines their place on the above spectrum. Chasidic Jews are Orthodox Jews who identify very strongly with a particular religious leader. This identification includes modalities of dress and other behaviors which help identify them as belonging to their particular group.

2. A shochet is an individual trained to slaughter animals, both fowl and cattle, according to a prescribed procedure making the slaughtered animal permissible to be eaten. The shochet is also trained to identify a diseased animal that cannot be eaten even if it is slaughtered according to the rules.

3. A mohel is an individual trained to perform ritual circumcisions.

4. The following discussion is taken from Schottenstein edition of the Babylonian Talmud, tractate Baba Kama, Messiah Publications, Ltd., Brooklyn, New York, 1997.

5. In the Pentateuch, if a woman is suspected of an adulterous relationship, she is brought before the high priest, who makes her drink a potion in which the secret name of God has been dissolved. If she is innocent nothing happens and she returns to her husband without any recriminations. If she is guilty she suffers death by poisoning from the potion she drank.

6. A common practice for Jewish commentators on the Bible and Talmud is to refer to them using acronym based on the first letters of their name.

7. The Zohar was first published in the 11th century but it purported to be based on much earlier sources. It is designed as a commentary on the Bible.

ACKNOWLEDGMENTS

Since I do not have rabbinic training I have had to consult others in the preparation of this manuscript. In particular, my husband, Dr. Samuel Spero, who has had rabbinic training and is familiar with both the methodology of the *halacha* and the sources quoted, was especially helpful both in developing the direction I have taken in this chapter as well as the integration of the sources. For this and other things I express to him my thanks and love.

REFERENCES

Bleich, J. (1977). *Contemporary halakhic problems*. New York: Yeshiva University Press, Ktav Publishing House, Inc.

Bleich, J. (1983). *Contemporary halakhic problems* (Vol. II). New York: Yeshiva University Press, Ktav Publishing House, Inc.

Bleich, J. (1989). *Contemporary halakhic problems* (Vol. III). New York: Yeshiva University Press, Ktav Publishing House, Inc.

Kaufman, M. (1995). *The woman in Jewish law and tradition*. Northvale, NJ: Jason Aronson, Inc.

Relevant articles in the *Encyclopedia Judaica* (Keter, Jerusalem, 1971) which is indexed.

RECOMMENDED READINGS
AND RESOURCES

Aiken, L. (1993). *To be a Jewish woman.* Northvale, NJ: Jason Aronson, Inc.

Biale, R. (1995). *Women and Jewish law: The essential texts, their history, and their relevance for today.* New York: Schocken Books.

Feldman, D. (1968). *Birth control in Jewish law: Marital relations, contraception, and abortion as set forth in the classic texts of Jewish law.*

New York: New York University Press.

Finkelstein, B., & Finkelstein, M. (1993). *B'Sha'ah Tovah: The Jewish woman's guide to pregnancy and childbirth.* New York: Feldheim Publishers.

Trepp, L. (1980). *The complete book of Jewish observance: A practical manual for the modern Jew.* New York: Behrman House.

The best introduction to the Talmud and its importance that I have read is the book by Adin Steinsaltz entitled, *The Essential Talmud* (Basic Books, 1984).

The Responsa Literature (Jewish Publication Society, 1955) and its companion volume, *A Treasury of Responsa* (Jewish Publication Society, 1962), both by Solomon Freehof, provide an excellent introduction to the process of *halacha*.

Rabbi Bleich's three volumes on *Contemporary Halakhic Problems* cited in the Reference section contain many detailed analyses of issues relevant to this chapter.

Michael Kaufman's book mentioned in the references is still the best work I have encountered for providing a comprehensive introduction to women's issues from a *halachic* point of view.

GLOSSARY

agunah: "Anchored woman," a woman who cannot obtain a divorce because her husband is missing, or because uncertainty exists whether her husband is alive, or because he refuses to cooperate by granting her a legal Jewish divorce; this is a problem that is currently receiving a great deal of attention from the rabbis

bar kayama: Viable, in particular a viable human being; the *ubar*

(fetus) is not considered a *bar kayama* until 30 days after birth

Bar/Bat mitzvah: literally, "son/daughter of the commandment," that is, under obligation to fulfill the commandments; a term denoting both religious majority and the occasion at which this status is formally assumed, age thirteen years and one day for boys, and twelve years and one day for girls

Bet Din: Rabbinic court; in

ancient times, a court of law; in modern times, an ecclesiastic court dealing primarily with religious matters such as *kashrut* and divorce

get (get piturin): the Jewish bill of divorce

Halacha: Jewish law; literally, "the way"

Halitzah: a Biblically prescribed ritual (Deuteronomy 25:9–10) conducted between a childless widow and her late husband's brother, which obviates the necessity for levirate marriage; levirate marriage is a custom dating back to Biblical times; if a man dies with no children, his brother is required to marry his widow; if the brother refuses to marry the widow, he performs the *halitzah* ceremony

hatan: groom

herem: excommunication; this is used as a tool to force a reluctant husband to give a *get*

kallah: bride

ketubah: literally, "her writ" the marriage document containing the husband's obligations and guarantees to his wife presented at the marriage ceremony

kiddushin: literally, "sanctification"; marriage betrothal; the first part of the Jewish marriage ceremony

mamzer: the offspring of certain prohibited adulterous or incestuous relationships

mazal tov: the expression used to wish "good luck"

mikveh: ritual bath

moch: contraceptive tampon, mentioned in the Talmud

negia: physical contact between men and women; prohibited before marriage

niddah: menstruant; the status of the woman from the onset of her menstrual period until her immersion in a *mikveh*

onah: literally, "season"; the husband's obligation for marital relations with his wife

rodef: pursuer; mentioned in the discussion of abortion and the *halacha*

shalom bayit: the peaceful home; harmony between husband and wife

shadchan: matchmaker, marriage broker

sofer: scribe of Hebrew books and documents like a *get* or *ketubah*

taharat hamishpachah: purity of family life; the laws and the way of life that govern marital relations between husband and wife, especially those relating to *niddah* and *mikveh*

tevilah: immersion in a *mikveh*

tzeniut: modesty

ubar: fetus

8

Native American Women

B. NEAL

INTRODUCTION

My ancestry is Miami. My affiliation is with the Miami Tribe of Oklahoma. As a cultural anthropologist, my studies have focused on the woodland peoples who were or still are indigenous to the Great Lakes Region, with emphasis on the Miami, Ottawa, and Shawnee. Of major interest is Indian identity in Northeastern Oklahoma, headquarters of the Miami, Ottawa, Shawnee, and other Indian nations. Most of my studies have been conducted in this region.

Giving a generalized overview of how ethnic and gender socialization occurs and how this socialization affects women of Native American ancestry and affiliation is problematic. According to the federal government's Native American Consultation Database, April 1, 1998 there are "771 Federally recognized Indian tribes (including Alaskan Native villages), Alaskan Native corporations, and Native Hawaiian organizations." There are over 350 federally recognized tribes in the continental United States. These tribes represent different geographic environments, different language families, different economic and political structures, different kinship systems, and different histories relative to interaction with the conquering and dominant non-Native society. In other words, these Native Nations each have distinct individual histories and cultures. Perhaps the real value, the most beneficial contribution of this chapter will be increased awareness about the complex diversity found among and between the peoples who are indigenous to what is now the United States.

The historic relationship of Native Peoples with the government of the United States is unique. This relationship, begun hundreds of years ago with the coming of European explorers to this continent, continues to be relevant in the everyday lives of contemporary Native Americans, who are the only conquered peoples residing within the borders of the United States. Indigenous people occupied this land, living, farming, hunting, raising families, and burying their dead here. When Europeans came to the continent, Native rights to their land diminished. The right to hunt and fish as they had been accustomed, their freedom of movement, and the sovereignty of their governments were either diminished or entirely usurped. These nations occupied what is now the United States, and our government took from these nations their traditional lands and traditional rights.

The idea that these separate "groups" of Native Peoples were, and still are, recognized as independent nations is difficult to comprehend. However, prior to the rise of the United States and continuing today, they are sovereign nations. The legal status is nations within a nation. This status is supported by hundreds of years of treaties made first between Native nations and European governments and later with the United States. The United States government made treaties with Native nations from 1778 to 1871, with the U.S. Senate ratifying 370 Indian treaties during that time. Just as the North American Treaty Organization (NATO) or free trade agreements are legally binding, treaties between Native nations and the U.S. government are documents between entities whose rights and authority over certain territories and practices are recognized by both or all parties participating. These treaties are the basis of Federal Indian Law that binds the Federal government and contemporary Indian nations together. For Native Americans, the rights provided by treaty surmount rights provided by the Constitution of the United States (Utter, 1993, pp. 45–54).

One might think, because no treaties have been ratified since 1871, that they are a thing of the past, having no real bearing on Native Americans today. This is not the case. Treaties are still being argued before the courts, as is evidenced by the recent ruling by the 8th U.S. Circuit Court of Appeals stating eight Chippewa Bands have the right to hunt and fish without state regulation in East-Central Minnesota (American Indian Bureau Report, 1997). Although many land claims by Natives against the federal government have been settled as a result of the U.S. Indian Lands Claims Commission of 1978, the issue of land ownership remains litigious. Tribes are still in the legal process of trying to regain former lands, clarify land rights issues, and/or receive reparations for land taken without compensation. Treaties not only allow American Indians rights regarding hunting and fishing that are separate from non–Natives, but treaties also provide specific rights for education and educational benefits, a separate health care system (Indian Health Service), separate laws regarding Indian child welfare, and legal statuses associated with Indian land. These provisions and federal government responsibilities apply and are accessible only to American Indians.

Determining who is an "Indian" and therefore eligible to use Indian Health Service or receive educational benefits through the various education acts is not clear-cut. One might suppose, since Indian nations are to be viewed as sovereign powers, the right to determine citizenship would rest with tribal governments. Neither France, nor Great Britain, nor Italy, would allow the United States to dictate who can and who cannot be considered French, British, or Italian. But in the instance of American Indian nations, the United States government does decide what constitutes "Indian." The criteria for being Indian vary from act to act and department to department. To gain access to some benefits, a person must be of one-quarter blood ancestry. For others, self-identification (checking the appropriate box on a form) is all that is required (Bureau of Indian Affairs, 1987, p. 24). Tribes have their own policies for enrolled member status, but even that must be checked and cleared by the Bureau of Indian Affairs. Even the most fundamental right of determining who is eligible for citizenship in an Indian nation is controlled or interfered with by the Federal government. The treaties and acts, while providing for education, health care, and child welfare also impinge upon, if not negate entirely, Indian self-determination.

Prior to conquest and domination, Indian nations had their own ways of providing education, health care, caring for the welfare of children, and maintaining order and social control. But with subordination of their freedoms Native Peoples lost their ability to administer their own "programs" as they saw fit. The United States government paternalistically decided what was best for the Indians and formulated programs to meet its goals. A brief look at the history of education programs for American Indians documents the force of this paternalistic attitude.

From forced removal of children from their parents, families, homes, geographic locale to Federal boarding schools, beginning in 1879, to the Indian Education Act of 1972, the U.S. government has guided Indian education. The boarding school policy was nothing short of forced assimilation. Young children were taken away from their homes and placed in institutional settings with other Native children. Often children from the West were taken East to distance them from their families. Children from many language groups were put together so they could not understand each other's Native languages and would be forced to learn and use a common language in which to communicate. The language, of course, was English. They were forbidden to speak their Native language and were punished, sometimes quite severely, if they refused to comply. Hair was cut. Customary clothing was replaced with uniforms reflecting the dominant culture's concept of appropriate attire. Parental visitation and student vacations were restricted. Indian boys were taught trades and the girls were taught domestic skills. It is difficult to imagine the trauma felt by young children as they were forcibly removed from their home and family.

> So somebody knocked on the door, my uncle was a Peoria, and he said, "Will, answer that." So my Daddy got up and went to the door and lo and behold it was the superintendent of the Quapaw Nation—soldiers and a hack driver. Said, "We've been informed by the government" . . . this government man said, the superintendent of schools said—"We've been informed that you've got two girls here that needs to be in school." Course it kinda' dumbfounded my Dad and he said, "Well, now I have two little girls and they need to be in school, but I didn't think it was any concern of the government." He said, "It never was where I come from and they went to school every day." Well, we never got to finish our dinner. They picked us up and took us off. (Interview of Miami woman who was 83 years old at the time, Tyner, 1968).

Many Native Americans who were forced to participate in the Indian boarding schools system found themselves in two very different worlds, belonging in neither. Upon returning to their homes they could no longer communicate in their Native language and had adopted many non-Native ways. Yet, when they tried to succeed in the white world, they were still considered Indian and looked upon with prejudice. It is not surprising many of these boarding school educated Indians did not teach their own children to speak their Native language or about their Indian culture. Given their own experiences, they would not want their children to suffer punishment and discrimination for embracing and expressing their Indian heritage (Lesiak, 1998). The result has been subsequent generations that know little of the Native language and cultural heritage. The history of forced assimilation through education is an issue that is still on the front burner for many Native Peoples and will be covered more fully when the discussion turns to cultural pressures. However, let it be said, the education received by Native American children, whether in a boarding school or in a mainstream elementary, secondary, or post secondary setting leaves the unmistakable imprint of white, Anglo-Saxon, Protestant, male values and historical perspective. This historical perspective includes the mission of the boarding schools, as articulated by Henry Pratt, the founder of the first off-reservation school at Carlisle, Pennsylvania. "Kill the Indian and save the man." Education is but one cause of death decreasing the Indian population in the United States.

At the time of European contact, the indigenous population was approximately 1.2 million. By the early part of this century, only 250,000 individuals were counted as Indian. More deadly than bullets were the diseases brought to this continent by Europeans. Native Peoples had no immunity to smallpox, measles, whooping cough, chicken pox, bubonic plague, and other contagious diseases that were introduced by Europeans. Single epidemics often reduced the size of a tribe by half and in some instances nearly decimated the tribe entirely. In 1837, a smallpox epidemic among the 1600-member Mandan tribe killed all but 31 people (Utter, 1993, p. 19). Tribes having the greatest exposure to the newly introduced diseases finally developed some resistance by the late 17th century. In addition to epidemics and warfare, contributors to Native mortality rates included starvation, malnutrition, and mistreatment. Forced relocations, the rounding-up of thousands of Indians, moving and restricting them to confined areas, inadequate supplies for these forced marches, as well as for the reservations, resulted in many deaths.

The 1990 census reflects a much different picture from the 1900 data, with almost two million individuals identifying themselves as Indian. Estimated projections by the Census Bureau forecast a population of about 2.2 million in 1999 and 4.3 million by the year 2050. The Census Bureau states the rise in population cannot be attributed only to "natural increase," but must include improvements in the census questions, counting methods, and the use of self-identification (1998).

Most American Indians do not live on reservations or within TJSA (Tribal Jurisdiction Statistical Areas which are former reservation areas in Oklahoma). About 22% of the Indian population live on legally designated reservations; a little over 10% live within TJSA; another 2.7% live outside Oklahoma on former reservation areas; leaving over 62% of the total population living outside any officially designated area. Sixty two percent of the population lives in cities, towns, suburbs, rural areas as does the rest of the population of the United States. Four states have Native populations of over 100,000 — Oklahoma, California, Arizona, and New Mexico. The populations of these four states represent 42% of the total Native population. One-half of the total population lives west of the Mississippi River.

By conservative estimates, over 300 languages were spoken by the indigenous populations of what is now the United States prior to European contact. Two hundred and fifty of those languages are still associated with Native Americans. However, less than 100 of those languages are actually still spoken and only about 1/3 of the Native population speaks any of their Native language. With the passing of each generation, fluent speakers disappear. Exposure to all English speaking schools, television, and other media makes English the first language of most Native Americans and places Native languages in a subordinate category, if they are spoken at all (Utter, 1993).

The Miami, with whom I am most familiar, are in the process of reintegrating the Native language into the lives of members. Linguists have been documenting the language for the past ten years and have developed programs to reintroduce Miamis to their Native tongue. It has been through this language learning process that knowledge about traditional kinship systems, sacred plants, and our colors representing the four directions are being relearned. In other words, it is the reintroduction of language that will revitalize Miami culture. The Miami are not unique in their process of relearning language. However, there are some nations who have maintained language and traditions to a large extent. Nations who have been able to remain together have retained many more of their traditional ceremonies, traditions, and their Native language. The Federal government has played a major role in determining contiguity for some tribes and the loss of it for others.

It is important to keep in mind the United States government did not give land rights to Native Peoples. Native Peoples gave the United States land rights. The land rights term with which we are most familiar is "reservation." A reservation is an area of land set aside for occupation and use by an Indian band, village, or tribe(s). Initially the Bureau of Indian Affairs held the reservation land in trust for the band, village, or tribe(s). Subsequent policies have allowed individual ownership of lands within the reservations. The largest reservation in the U.S. is the Navajo Reservation, covering about 14.5 million acres. One of the smallest reservations is the Sheep Ranch Rancharia in California with less than one acre (Utter, 1998). With the passage of the Dawes Act in 1887, the Federal government sought to break up large land holdings by tribes and granted allotments to individual men and families. Incentive to break from the Native's traditional concept of land usage was enhanced by the offer of citizenship. If a man received clear title to land, he could become a citizen of the United States. Men who opted to break away from their tribes and adopt "white" ways could also gain citizenship. Prior to 1924, the only way a Native woman could be a citizen was if she married a non-Native and adopted his cultural ways. All Indians did not become official citizens until 1924, and it wasn't until 1948 that all states allowed Indians to vote (Oswalt & Neely, 1996). Interestingly, since Indians were not citizens when World War I began, they could not be inducted into the armed forces. However, those who wished to serve were allowed to do so and became citizens by acts of Congress. About 8000 Native men served in World War I. The Bureau of Indian Affairs estimates that 25% of adult Indian men are veterans (1987).

The GI Bill has had an affect on the Native population's education levels, as it has upon outside Native population. The percentages of Native Americans and Alaska Natives over the age of 25 who have completed 12 or more years of schooling vary by region of the country and by sex. In metropolitan areas, 61.4% of males have more than 12 years of schooling, with 60.8% of females reporting more than 12 years of education. In non-metropolitan areas, the percentages are males 49.8 and females 48.5. Off reservation, 61.8% of males and females and 55.7% of females have completed 12 years of education. On or near reservations, 56.3% of the men have 12 or more years of education compared to 52.9% of females. The Bureau of the Census also reports statistics on the probabilities of Native Peoples completing four or more years of post secondary education. Again, there are regional differences represented and I have simplified the statistics by averaging the numbers in each category. For males in a metropolitan area (the category with the highest probability rate) the probability of completing four or more years of post secondary school is .173; for females, the probability is .132. For males living on or near a reservation (the category with the lowest rate of probability) the numbers are lower with a .130 probability of males completing four or more years of post secondary education and only .10 probability of females achieving such completion. In each instance, and regardless of geographic area, we observe the statistics reflect higher education levels for Native males than Native females. There has recently been an increase in educational level attainment. In 1970, 3.8% of the American Indian/Alaska Native population had four or more years of college, compared with 4.4% of the Black population, and 11.3% of the White population. In 1980, 7.7 % of the Native population had four or more years of College, compared with 8.4% of the Black population, and 17.1% of the White population (Bureau of the Census, 1991).

Higher education levels among Native Americans are not directly reflected in improvement in socioeconomic status. Higher levels of education and more years of schooling do not translate into higher and better employment figures for the population.

The statistics from the Census Bureau (1991) regarding employment require a brief explanation. "Unemployed" refers to those who have been actively looking for work within the last four weeks. "Not in the work force" refers to those who have been without work for longer than four weeks and are not considered to be actively looking for work. The 1980 statistics reflect the following. Five point eight percent of white males were unemployed; 16.3% of Black males were unemployed; and 17.3% of Native males were unemployed. This same set of statistics reflects a seemingly better picture for Native women: 5.7% of white females were unemployed; 11.6% of white females were unemployed; and 12.4% of Native females were unemployed. The figures for those not participating in the labor force are higher in all cases: 23.9% of white males, 33.3% of Black males, and 30.4% of Native males are not in the labor force. For females: 50.6% of white females, 46.7% of Black females, and 51.9% of Native females are not part of the labor force. This last group of statistics represents males and females aged 16 and over. Not detailed in these statistics are those unable to work as a result of age, illness, or disability. Underemployment issues are also not reflected in these numbers. Such statistics can give the reader a general idea as to where Native women fall in comparison with non-Native women and Native and non-Native men, but fall short of representing the complexities relative to employment issues affecting Native Americans.

Native American families are the poorest socioeconomic group in the United States. The Census Bureau figures present a grim picture. The 1990 data records an increase in the poverty rate for Native individuals and families (1991). Twenty seven percent of Indian families fell into the poverty category with a median family income of $21,750, compared with the median family income of others of $35,225. Fifty percent of the Indian families with female heads-of-households fell below the poverty line with a median income of $10,742, compared with a median income of $17,414 among the other 31% of minority women heads-of-households. Native American families, especially those with no husband present, are the most impoverished in our country.

The United States government's policy "of divide and conquer" has had irreparable impact on Native Americans. In its educational policy, children were divided from their families, and ultimately their culture. In its citizenship policies, men gained citizen status if they divided themselves from their tribes, as did women who divided themselves from their relatives and traditions. Communally held land was divided into individual parcels, further neutralizing identity and the assets of the Indians. One further division has had great impact on Native families. In the early 1950s, the Federal government enacted legislation that was aimed towards ending Federal responsibility to Indians (House Concurrent Resolution 108, 1997). The government decided it no longer wanted to maintain responsibility for services to American Indians such as schools, welfare, and law enforcement, even though these responsibilities were provided for via treaties. In implementing this Resolution, many tribes were "terminated"—they lost federal recognition and thereby lost access or right to federal services. Accompanying this policy was an urban relocation program encouraging Indians to move from their reservations and homelands to urban/metropolitan areas. It is estimated that by the 1970s about 10,000 Indians were annually leaving the reservation for the cities. The government provided a bus ticket and a job-training voucher and relocated Indians to the cities. This development accounts for much of the Lakota population in Columbus, Ohio, the large Chippewa population in Springfield, Missouri, and so on. This modern-day removal has further decreased the connection between tribal families, their lands, and traditions.

Despite the removals, terminations, and assimilation policies in most tribal communities, whether city, country, or reservation, there is still a reliance on extended family. Extended families are not confined to "blood" relationships.

In many traditional societies elder women will be referred to as "grandmother" and elder men as "grandfather." These are terms of respect and honor, indicating the elder's wisdom and knowledge, and they are respected simply for having survived to an old age. For a child to be cared for or reprimanded by a woman other than her/his own biological mother, grandmother, aunt is commonplace. The most basic part of traditional life for a Native woman is a natural, built-in support system centered in the family. So many of the government's policies have threatened this basic element of Native life. We hear from college counselors about the tendency of Native youth to come to a college or university to further their education and, upon completing their degree, returning to their home area. Often, employment opportunities are scarce in these home regions. But, the pull back to the community is strong. The community is a place where no explanations are necessary and where special events and activities support individuals. The community is a place of understanding and acceptance.

Native American men and women have been affected by the coming of explorers and traders, the colonization and settlement by non-Native on Native lands, and by the founding and continuation of the United States government, and the U.S. government's policies dealing with Indians. One could perhaps examine "traditional" (before European contact and influence) roles for Native men and women and conclude men's roles have experienced the greatest change. The stereotype of Indian males as warriors—those who participate in and fight wars—and the fact that the opportunity for raiding neighboring tribes or infringing settlers no longer exists would appear to make this conclusion about the degree of change appropriate. Combine this logic with the majority of ethnographic and historic data placing Native women as homemakers, child-care givers—supporters of the males and the conclusion's accuracy seems quite positive. Native women have traditionally been the caregivers, the homemakers, in addition to influencing political and social life. For many women this has not changed. However, nearly everything else has changed! As mentioned above, the extended family support system has deteriorated, if not disappeared. Self-sufficiency no longer means being able to count on a male to provide meat while the woman plants, tends, and harvests from nature and the garden. It may mean the woman must seek work away from her home and even her village, leaving her to find adequate child-care outside the traditional norm. If a woman's husband dies, the system of kinship that provided a new husband for her no longer is in tact. What a Native mother must teach her children in order for them to survive in this world has certainly changed. Too often, we are confronted with over-simplifications directly related to stereotypes and a lack of information and understanding about the importance of women and their roles within their traditional societies. It is important to remind the reader, once again, of the diversity among the customs and cultures of Native Americans. The roles of women varied from tribe to tribe, geographic region to geographic region.

It is for this reason that I have chosen to present a range of behaviors and attitudes, common to Native American women, without citing tribal tradition or custom as causation. This is not an attempt to embrace Pan-Indianism— advancing the mistaken idea all Native American cultures are the same or similar. Rather, because of the great diversity of customs, roles, responsibilities, I choose not to cite specific tribal examples, but to give a range of behaviors, problems, and attitudes. It would be an error for readers to assume my examples are representative of the entire female Native American population. The examples I present do not adequately portray the differences that are present within and among specific tribes. However, apparent in all my examples will be this impulse toward home and community and the sense of aloneness that emerges in the absence of community.

Historically, we are probably most familiar with the roles of Native women of the Iroquois. The story of the Clan Mothers of the Iroquois seems to be a favorite of movies, history, and anthropology books. No important decisions were made without consultation with this wise women's group. They had the final say on who would lead and could stop wars. Because this example is used so frequently, readers may come to think the Clan Mothers of the Iroquois are unique among Native Cultures. This assumption is incorrect. I have heard many tribal leaders make a statement very similar to the following: "It might have been a bunch of men sitting around those council fires making decisions, but behind them were women with very long, sharp poles." The inference is, the women might not have been "out front" but they were still influencing the decisions.

Today, many Native American women are "out front" leading their people. Wilma Mankiller became the Principal Chief of the Cherokee Nation of Oklahoma in 1985. While living in California she was active in Native American rights activities, including the occupation of Alcatraz Island (Mankiller, 1993). As her personal troubles increased combining with a growing desire to help her people, she decided to move herself and her children back to Mankiller Flats, her ancestral land, in Oklahoma (Mankiller, 1993). Here is an example of a very strong woman who stood against tradition and the odds to take the top leadership position of the second largest Indian Nation in the United States. Her autobiography, *Mankiller*, makes it clear she hopes her success will inspire a new generation of Cherokee females to become actively and openly involved in Tribal Government. While Mankiller feels she has put the question of gender in leadership to rest, her ties to the land of her immediate ancestors and to her community remain. Her desire and need to be with other Indian people and give back to this community is evident in her writings.

Other Indian Nations have women Chairpersons, or First Chiefs. Tribal governments have changed and so have the acceptable roles of women within those governments. The Indian Reorganization Act of 1934 forced the majority of Native Nations to write and adopt constitutions modeled after the U.S. Constitution. Many tribes elect business committees as governing bodies, composed of a chief, second chief, secretary, treasurer, and council persons. In order for women to influence decisions, the long, sharp pole has been replaced by the poling place and getting enough votes to win an election. The mandate still originates with the people, but the "form" is very different from earlier historic times. However, the roles are still based on respect and political savvy, just as they were in earlier times.

Not all nations relinquished traditional roles. There are tribes who kept their council of women elders. In some cases the council of women have total control over the ceremonial life of the tribe and the business committee runs the business portion of tribal life. In other instances, women do not hold the top leadership position, but serve as members of the business committee, or whatever the governing council is termed, and serve on other committees supporting their interests within their Nation.

Women have always played important and influential roles within their Nations and we should not be surprised to find when one form changes, others are affected. Yet to link the changes in women's roles within Native American Nations to feminism would be an oversimplification. Certainly the range of behaviors present in this group contains feminists — women who have been and are active in the women's movement as we know it in the general population of the United States. However, we cannot overlook the evolution of cultures, the changes in organizational structure, as cause for role changes. Native women have always been "heard" in their communities, and their concerns, desires, and ideas seriously considered. But, times have changed. No longer do messengers run from village to village carrying the news. Members of specific Nations no longer occupy bounded territories. Messages are not retained through memory. Global communications, mobility, and technology have affected Native Nations, just as they have affected the majority population. The point is, the role of Native women today is in large part an adaptation to the changes that have occurred in our world.

The changes mentioned, as well as the example of Wilma Mankiller, do not mean all Native women believe it is their place to be the spokesperson for their nation. Many Native women would still not run for chief, nor would they vote for a woman who was running for chief. Some women feel quite comfortable sitting around the drum at ceremonies and pow wows (traditionally a male-only role) and others would never consider doing such a thing. Some women will enter a dance circle in pants and others will not. Some women would publicly disagree with a male leader and others would use more traditional forms of expressing their opinions (gossip, rumors, and telling someone else your opinion, knowing it will eventually get to the person for whom it was intended). In my experience, these attitudes have little do to with age. The way in which a woman has been raised seems to be the greatest contributing factor. For most of history and for many Native women today, the phrase, *separate but equal*, could exemplify the feelings about male/female importance in Native societies. Combining this phrase with extreme respect and acknowledgment that Native women are the caregivers, the backbones of the nations, perhaps exemplifies the attitudes of Native men.

Historically, in most tribes, women owned all the household goods as well as the "house." A man's only possessions were his weapons and clothing and horses. In many Nations, women owned the land and herd animals and it was through the female line these things were passed. In times past when a woman wanted a divorce, often all that was required was setting the man's meager belongings outside the house. That was it. Customs were in place to ensure a woman with children was cared for. Often when a man died, leaving a widow and children, the deceased man's brother would marry the widow. If a mother passed on, leaving children, quite often the deceased woman's sister would take her place. This is truly Indian child welfare! The tribes took care of their responsibilities to women and children. They did not require the imposition of an outside government or outside law enforcement. Today, with the current status of nation within a nation, The Bureau of Indian Affairs and the United States Congress set the laws and policies for Indian Child Welfare. Professionals interacting in Native communities or in metropolitan areas, or with Native Peoples anywhere must become familiar with federal Indian Child Welfare policies and laws. They are not the same as for other minorities. Again, we have this distinction. For instance: If a child is either an official member or eligible for enrollment in a federally recognized tribe and is being removed from his/her home, the tribe must be notified. In some cases the tribe can actually take custody of the child and make determinations as to foster care and adoption. Federal law has replaced tribal care. But, we are able to see with the special caveats within the law, Native Nations have not given up their rights nor responsibilities to children.

Some things have not changed. The emphasis on hospitality, ensuring everyone present has what they need in the way of food and other necessities and comforts still exists. For non-Natives it is often frustrating to deal with Native women because much must be done before business is conducted. Courtesy, concern for well being, visiting—all these come before business transactions or serious discussions. The pace is different from the norm of non-Native society. When a visitor is told, "We are on Indian time," it means things will happen when they happen. Many times I've heard a visitor in Indian Country ask when some evening activity will begin, only to be told "dark thirty"—no set time, just "approximately." And, "approximately" may be too definite a word!

Hospitality and courtesy to visitors and strangers may give the uninformed a wrong impression. They may feel acceptance and agreement for their positions. However, rarely will a stranger be trusted, accepted immediately, or given decisions on the spot. What normally occurs is discussion after the stranger leaves. This decision-making process may take days, weeks, or years. This process applies to deciding whether a person will be accepted and trusted, and it also applies to business activities. Deciding these matters usually takes place in a group context. If not, there is at least some consultation going on somewhere. This process exemplifies the emphasis on the well being of the community rather than individual achievement.

Native Americans are confronted daily with a lack of comprehension about their history, culture, and current circumstances. An Indian child who has been reared to work for group excellence and harmony has a difficult time in United States classrooms where the emphasis is on personal excellence. In tribal life, often the emphasis is on helping each other and standing together. In most of our classrooms, the emphasis is on helping oneself and standing apart and above the others. If an Indian child, who has been taught to put the group first, is singled out, the child may take steps to insure their mediocrity and position back within the group. In this same classroom setting Indian students of all ages are faced, as are other minorities, with history presented from the conqueror's viewpoint. Most of the time, no effort is made to bring Indians out of this biased history and into the present. Does the second grade teacher—upon completing the section on early American history and telling about Indians living in tepees, riding horses, using tomahawks and wearing war bonnets—not realize seven and eight year-old children do not make 200 year leaps on their own? Non-Native children have fewer reference points for Indians than for their own cultures. They may be able to understand Abraham Lincoln lived in a log cabin and studied by the light of the fire and today we live in other types of houses and have light bulbs. But their frame of reference for Indian heritage is not as complete. If teachers fail to include additional materials explaining the changes in Indian culture and way of life, Indians get left in their European created historical contact.

In 1992, myself, another Indian woman, and several young people gave a presentation about American Indians to five different groups of second graders. Some of us were dressed in our dance regalia and some in street clothing. After our presentation we asked if there were questions. The questions were unsettling. How did you get here? Did you ride a horse? What kind of house do you live in? Is it a tepee? Do you still have wars? Why are you speaking English? The questions were particularly unsettling because the teachers had just finished their units on Indian history. Guess where the teachers left the

Indians? This example is truly representative of many of the presentations to children and adults I've made over the years. There is a lack of comprehension that Indians are still around. If that comprehension exists, then the lack comes in understanding that we have changed with the times just as the majority population has. Compounding the perception problem is the lack of adequate descriptions of Native women's lives and contributions in even the most well-intentioned texts and presentations. For Indian people this comprehension has led to stereotyping and lack of awareness. Indians are still alive and well and just might be sitting next to you in the classroom or in the office.

An additional part of the problem is phenotype—a person's physical appearance. Even prior to European contact and intermarriage, The First Peoples of this land embodied many different characteristics. The Plains people with which we are most familiar—high cheek bones, long straight noses, very dark hair—differed greatly from the Zuni of the Southwest with their much lighter skin. They also differed significantly from the Woodland Peoples of the Northeast who were shorter, lighter skinned, and had more rounded facial features. With the mixing of blood between Natives and between Natives and non-Natives, we have even greater phenotypic variation. One of the Indian women I have worked closely with over the past few years told me, "When I lived in northeastern Oklahoma everyone knew I was Indian. When we moved to Memphis people thought I was Black. When we lived in San Antonio they thought I was Hispanic and when we vacationed in Hawaii, they thought I was a Native Hawaiian." There must be something different in the way this woman looks, something different from the majority of the population that places her within the category of the most predominant minority in a particular community. With stereotypes come certain expectations of behaviors and attitudes. What happens when you cannot tell by looking? Perhaps, in the case of Native Americans, it has aided the tendency to forget Indians are still present.

Indian women have been portrayed in literature as near slaves performing only the most menial tasks. In anthropology, women in general have not been included as fully participating and important components of cultures until the past few decades. Certainly with Indian women, the details of their lives have mostly been confined to gathering vegetation, child-rearing, preparing food, and making clothing. Very little attention has been given to the influence of the women on the overall lifestyle of a tribe. The literature we have relative to Indian women comes mainly in the form of biography rather than their lives being shown as an integral part of the cultural whole. In Hollywood films and on television Indian women have been portrayed by non-Indian women (Donna Reed as Sacagawea and Audrey Hepburn in "The Unforgiven," for example). Indian women have been portrayed as reaching their potential when they give up their traditions for European-based traditions (voting and Pocahontas). Indian people in general live within a nation that is unaware of the offensive nature of some representations of Native Peoples. Chief Wahoo, the

logo for the Cleveland Indians, is probably the most infamous of the representations, but others like the logo for Land-O-Lakes butter and Chief Illiniwek,
the mascot for the University of Illinois sports teams, exist. Very few non–Black
parents would consider allowing their children to dress up as an African Zulu
warrior for Halloween. Scoutmasters would not permit young Anglo boys to
blacken their faces and don clothing representative of an historic African nature and parade through town on the Fourth of July. But, these same parents
and Scoutmasters do allow their non–Native children to dress up like Indians
and participate in all manners of public functions. Unfortunately, most non-
Natives do not think they are offending anyone because Indians are thought to
be a thing of the past. This lack of awareness does set Native American margin-
alization apart from most of the other minorities in the United States. All
minorities are affected by the White, Anglo-Saxon, Protestant, male historical
perspective, by power resting with and reflecting the dominant culture's values,
and the resultant dominance of English. However, I can think of no other minority that continues to have its history, spirituality, clothing, and the names of
its nations co-opted by the majority population and flaunted in its face. Maintaining tribal and personal Indian identity is becoming increasingly difficult.

Misunderstood identity, being relegated to history, changes in geographic
location by forced removal or incentives to move from traditional lands to
metropolitan areas; isolation from the supportive community; forced changes
in traditional ways of dealing with death, education, welfare of women and
children; poverty; lack of opportunity—all affect the well being of and place
pressure upon Native American Women. The responses to the pressures are
varied and many, reflecting the diversity within and between Native nations.
The source of the strength does not seem varied. The strength is in the family,
the biological family and extended tribal and community family. The strength
also lies in ancestral homelands—the traditional spiritual landscape. What
maintains that strength is strong women caring for their children, families,
relatives, nation, and land. The manifestations of that caring form a broad
spectrum of behaviors, but the caring remains and will surely see the Indian
Nations of the United States well into the future.

REFERENCES

American Indian Bureau Report.
(July 1997). In Melissa L.
Gedachian (Ed.), *In Court* (p. 7).
Washington, DC: Author.

Bureau of Indian Affairs (1987).
*American Indians Today: Answers to
Your Questions.* Washington, DC:

U.S. Department of Interior.
Author.

Gedachian, M. (Ed.). (July, 1997). In
Court, in *American Indian
Quarterly.* Fairfax, VA: Falmouth
Institute.

Mankiller, W., & Wallis, M. (1993).

Mankiller. New York: St. Martin's Press.

Native American Consultation Data Base (1998). Washington, DC: National Park Service. http://www.cr.nps.gov/aad/nacd

Oswalt, W. H., & Neely, S. (1996). *This Land Was Theirs.* London: Mayfield Publishing.

Tyner, J. W. (1968). *Interview of Rose Carver, Miami woman.* Transcribed by Monette Coombes. Miami, OK.

United States Bureau of the Census (1991). *American Indian and Alaska Native Areas: 1990.* Racial Statistics Branch. Washington, DC: Author.

United States Bureau of the Census. (1998). *The American Indian, Eskimo, and Aleut Populations.* Washington, DC: Author.

United States Department of the Interior (1998). Bureau of Indian Affairs Home Page. Washington, D.C.: http://www.doi.gov/bureau-indian-affairs.html

Utter, J. (1993). *American Indians, Answers to Today Questions.* Lake Ann, MI: National Woodlands Publishing.

RECOMMENDED READINGS
AND RESOURCES

Bataille, G. M., & Sands, K. M. (1984). *American Indian Women.* Lincoln: University of Nebraska Press.

Beck, P. V., & Walaters, A. L. (1988). *The sacred ways of knowledge: Sources of life.* Tsaile (Navajo Nation), AZ: Navajo Community College Press.

Brown, J. E. (1982). *The spiritual legacy of the American Indian.* New York: Crossroad.

Campbell, D. (1993). *Native American Art and Folklore.* Avenel, NJ: Crescent/Random House.

Cruikshank, J. (1990). *Life Lived Like a Story.* Nebraska: University of Nebraska Press.

Deloria, P. J. (1998). *Playing Indian.* Boston: Yale Historical Publications.

Deloria, V. Jr. (1969). *Custer Died for Your Sins.* New York: Macmillan Publishing.

Deloria, V. Jr. (1992). American Indians. In *Multiculturalism in the United States* (pp. 31–52). New York: Greenwood Press.

Deloria, V. Jr. (1997). *Red Earth White Lies.* Colorado: Fulcrum Publishing.

Deloria, V. Jr., & Lytle, C. M. (1983). *American Indians, American Justice.* Austin: University of Texas Press.

Dippie, B. W. (1982). *White attitudes and U.S. Indian policy.* Middletown, CT: Wesleyan University Press.

Erboes, E. (Ed.). (1984). *American Indian myths and legends.* New York: Rantheon.

Ferrero, P. ((Producer & Director). *Songs of the Fourth World.* New York: New Day Films.

Foster, D. V. (1992, February). *Treatment issues with American Indians.* NOFSW Newsletter, pp. 4–5.

Foulkrod, P. (Producer & Director). *Tribes of the Southeast: Persistent Cultures of Resilient People.* Atlanta: Educational Video Network, TBS Productions.

Francis, L., & Bruchac, J. (Eds.). (1996). *Reclaiming the Vision.* New York: Greenfield Review Press.

Grant, M. (Producer) & Foulkrod, P. (Director). *Nations of the Northeast: Strength and Wisdom of the Confederacies.* Educational Video Network, TBS Production.

Green, M. K. (Ed). (1995). *Issues in Native American cultural identity.* New York: Peter Lag Publishing.

Green, R. (1975). The Pocahontas perplex: The image of Indian women in popular culture. *Massachusetts Review, 16,* 698–714.

Green, Rayna. (1981). *Native American women: A bibliography.* Wichita Falls, TX: Ohoyo Resource Center.

Guerrero, J. A. M. (1996). Academic Apartheid: American Indian Studies and "Multiculturalism." In Gordon & Newfield (Eds.), *Mapping multiculturalism* (pp. 49–63). Minneapolis: University of Minnesota Press.

Hirschfelder, A., & Molin, P. (1992). *The encyclopedia of Native American religions.* New York: Facts on File.

Kohn, R., & Montell, W. (Eds.). (1997). *Always a people.* Indianapolis: Indiana University Press.

Lesiak, C. (Producer & Director). *In the White man's image.* Washington DC: PBS video.

Medicine, B. (1978). *The Native American woman: A perspective.* Austin: National Educational Laboratory Publishers.

Mihesuah, D. (1998). Commonality of difference: American Indian women and history. In D. Mihesuah (Ed.), *Natives and academics* (pp. 37–54). Lincoln: University of Nebraska Press.

Montana Indian Children. Scarsdale, NY: Campus District Video. Presents women interacting with children in different settings.

Moses, L. G., & Wilson, R. (Eds). (1993). *Indian lives.* New Mexico: University of New Mexico Press.

Norelli, G. (Producer & Director). *Sunrise dance.* New York: Filmakers Library.

Reyhner, Dr. Jon. (1988). *Teaching the Indian child.* Montana: Eastern Montana College.

Simeone, W. E. (1995). *Rifles, blankets, and beads.* Oklahoma: University of Oklahoma Press.

Snipp, C. M. (1989). *American Indians.* New York: Russell Foundation.

Waldman, C. (1984). *Atlas of the North American Indian.* New York: Facts on File.

Wilson, A. (1998). Grandmother to granddaughter: Generations of oral history in a Dakota family. In D. Mihesuah (Ed.), *Natives and academics* (pp. 27–36). Lincoln: University of Nebraska Press.

GLOSSARY

Bureau of Indian Affairs: housed in the Department of the Interior, the Bureau of Indian Affairs (BIA) is the federal department charged with providing services to American Indians, Alaska Natives, and Native Hawaiians

clan: a descent group in which relatives are traced primarily along the male or female line to a presumed common ancestor

dance circle: (see pow wow definition) during traditional and social gatherings, using a southern tradition, a drum will be placed in the center of an open area; the singers (those who do the drumming) have been traditionally men, but in some regions this is changing to include women, are seated around the drum with women standing behind; around this drum those participation in the ceremony or gathering will dance; if the gathering is using a northern tradition the drum may be to the outside of the circle

elders: those people who have reached an older age and are respected for their having lived a longer life and for their wisdom

federally recognized tribe: "recognition" is a legal term meaning that the United States recognizes a government-to-government relationship with the tribe and that a tribe exists politically in a "domestic dependent nation status"; a federally recognized tribe is one that was in existence, or evolved as a successor to a tribe at the time of original contact with non-Indians

kinship system: the way in which ancestry is traced: matrilineal is through the female; patrilineal is through the male; unilineal is through either female or male; bilineal is through both female and male; the kinship system could determine rights of inheritance, provide for surrogate parents, and also define familia relationships

nation: tribes who are federally recognized (see definition for Federally Recognized Tribe) under Article 1, Section 8 of the Constitution of the United States vests the federal government the authority to engage in relations with the tribes; tribes possess a nationhood status and retain inherent powers of self-government

Native Americans: this term is somewhat interchangeable with American Indian and refers to the first people inhabiting what is now America; native populations in Alaska and Hawaii are referred to as Alaska Natives and Native Hawaiians; as a general principle an Indian person is of some degree Indian blood and is recognized as an Indian by a tribe and/or the United States; no single federal or tribal criterion establishes a person's identity as an Indian

Pow Wow: a Narraganset word originally referring to the activities of shamans; presently used to refer to a public Indian gathering focusing on feasting, dancing, other performances, and the sale of Indian craft items; also, a time of reunion

reservation territories reserved as permanent tribal homelands: some were created through treaties while others were created by statutes, or executive orders

treaties: "contracts among nations", representing the supreme law of the land; between 1777 and 1871 United States relations with individual Indian nations were conducted through treaty negotiations

tribe: a group of indigenous people, bound together by blood ties, who were socially, politically, and religiously organized according to the tenets of their own culture, who lived together, occupying a definite territory, and who spoke a common language; the usage in today's terms would indicate ancestors of the people who met the above guidelines

9

Southeast Asian-American
Women

A. ZAHARLICK

INTRODUCTION

The primary focus of this chapter is on Southeast Asian women, a subset of one of the newer ethnic groups in the United States. Most Southeast Asian women arrive in the United States as refugees and subsequently undergo dramatic changes in their lives. In order to understand these women, it is important to know where they have come from, what they have experienced, and what challenges they are confronting in this country. They need to be viewed within the larger historical and sociocultural context that has shaped their lives and within their former and present circumstances, which set the parameters for how they respond to the challenges they are facing today.

Since the early 1980s, I have conducted anthropological research in the Southeast Asian refugee communities of central Ohio. Specifically, my research has focused on the changing health and mental health beliefs and practices of Vietnamese, Lao, and Cambodian refugees, the fertility transition of the ethnic Lao, and family violence and intergenerational conflicts. I have served as a consultant to hospitals, schools, mutual assistance associations, social service agencies, and advocacy groups. I am neither Southeast Asian nor a refugee.

To provide this context and enough specific information to facilitate understanding, I have organized the chapter into several sections. First, I provide some descriptive and general demographic information about the major groups of Southeast Asians now living in the United States—to both define the populations considered here and to note the diversity within them. I follow this discussion with an historical overview of the circumstances that have resulted in many Southeast Asians becoming refugees. The refugee experience has had a profound effect on Southeast Asians, particularly on the lives of women. The next section describes some of the major values and norms shared by the five Southeast Asian groups I discuss. Particular emphasis is placed on the value of the family. It is beyond the limits of this chapter to describe the tremendous diversity among Southeast Asian ethnic groups or the women within them. Therefore, in order to provide some specific information on women, I focus in the next two sections on one Southeast Asian group in particular: the ethnic Lao. The ethnic Lao are placed in their historical context in Southeast Asia, and their traditional culture is described.

Later in this chapter, I document how the refugee experience has disrupted the lives and families of Southeast Asian women and how they have struggled in the United States to bring coherence and stability back to family life. To ground the description of changes and continuities that have occurred, the experiences of the ethnic Lao in the United States are scrutinized. Finally, the chapter focuses on some common problems Southeast Asian women and their families face living in the United States.

SOUTHEAST ASIAN-
AMERICAN POPULATION

Over one million Southeast Asian refugees have been resettled in the United States since 1975. Most of these refugees came in two major waves, one in 1975 and the other in 1980–1981. The Southeast Asian population includes the children subsequently born in the United States to these refugees, those persons from Vietnam, Laos, and Cambodia already in the United States in 1975, and those who have arrived in recent years as immigrants rather than legally defined refugees (Haines, 1989). The category "Southeast Asian refugee" is a tenuous one. Better, though still inadequate to describe the diversity of this population, is the commonly used division of these groups into five distinct "ethnic" populations: ethnic Chinese (mostly from Vietnam), Hmong, Khmer, ethnic (lowland) Lao, and Vietnamese, though there are other, smaller populations as well.

With an estimated population of 800,000, the largest Southeast Asian refugee/immigrant group currently in the United States is the Vietnamese.

Cambodians (Khmer), with an estimated population of 150,000, and Lao or Laotian and Hmong, with an estimated population of 250,000, are the next most sizable groups. Each of these groups not only have distinctive cultural, social, and linguistic backgrounds, but also clear differences in pre-arrival history and experience in the early years of residence in the United States.

Southeast Asians are now a significant and rapidly growing minority population in this country and comprise a major element within the general Asian American population. Although they are scattered widely throughout the United States, many have settled in kin and ethnic group enclaves that range from a few dozen to tens of thousands of individuals (Zaharlick & Brainard, 1987). The Southeast Asian refugee population is internally diverse and has been so since the earliest arrivals in 1975. Elderly Southeast Asian refugees and newer immigrants tend to adhere to traditional folkways, whereas families who have lived in the United States for a longer time tend to be more acculturated. Except for the effects of the presence, among the 1975 arrivals, of an important segment of the well—educated Southeast Asian population, the average educational level for Southeast Asians in the United States remains in the range of seven to seven and a half years (Haines, 1989). Data on the ability to speak "good" English also shows a break between initial arrivals and later ones. This outcome has been less demonstrable after 1980, reflecting the effects of English language training at the processing centers in Southeast Asia through which most refugees passed after that time.

Available demographic data shows that the Vietnamese are the best educated, the most fluent in English, and the most experienced in professional and technical occupations prior to coming to this country. This is true for men and particularly so for women. The Chinese are closest to the Vietnamese in these characteristics, despite the fact that many more of them come from urban areas. These two groups appear to have the lowest fertility, smallest households, and least extensive aftereffects of exodus, including smaller loss of kin and shorter periods in refugee camps. On the other hand, the Hmong are the most rural, the least educated, and spent the most time in refugee camps. They also have the largest households and the highest fertility rates (Zaharlick & Brainard, 1987). The Khmer and the Lao occupy the region between these two poles. Each group has significant urban and rural components, each averaged a little over two years in refugee camps, and the members of each average about five years of formal education. Sizable numbers of people with no education tend to balance out those with extensive education. Each group also has an occupational profile that shows significant proportions of both white collar and farming/fishing occupations. As a result of the atrocities of the Pol Pot regime that took power in 1975 and of the warfare resulting from the Vietnamese invasion in 1978, the Khmer experienced a greater loss of relatives and friends, per capita, than did the other four ethnic groups. These factors figure prominently in the psychological problems experienced by many Khmer refugees.

Historical Background

Most people are now quite familiar with the dimensions of the Southeast Asian refugee diaspora. With the collapse of American-supported governments in 1975, millions of people fled, or tried to flee, from Cambodia, Laos, and Vietnam. Facing fear, danger, and the possibility of death, they sought asylum in frequently indifferent or hostile neighboring countries. Many died. Those who survived often languished for many years in refugee camps in the initial asylum countries. Some survivors were ultimately repatriated, while others eventually moved on to third countries for resettlement. Many of those who resettled were abruptly placed in a new, strange, unpredictable society and were faced with an often bewildering reception in their new homes. (For examples in the United States, see Freeman, 1989; Kelly, 1977; Nguyen-Hong-Nhiem, Halpern, & Halpern, 1989; Rutledge, 1992; Tenhula, 1991).

This history has resulted in a number of major transitions for Southeast Asian refugees. First were the transitions within their own societies caused by political upheaval and resulting in conditions that led them to flee their homes: war, fear, the death of family and loved ones, persecution by hostile authorities, and loss of homes, livelihoods, status, and a future. Refugees also experienced difficult transitions associated with flight from a home country to life in a foreign land.

Before becoming refugees, however, Southeast Asians had experienced lives in which there was peace and stability, a home and enough food to eat, a place in society, and a future for themselves and their children. When they chose to migrate across national and cultural borders and became refugees, they did not give up their understandings of what various individual and family social behaviors meant. Once the refugees resettled in a new country such as the United States, they began the transition of gradually merging into the evolving mosaic of racial, ethnic, and economic relations within the larger system of the new country.

The majority of refugees worldwide are female. Women refugees generally suffer more dramatic changes in role and status than do their male counterparts (Davison, 1981). Women are traditionally disadvantaged in Southeast Asia, and such disadvantage tends to be intensified in a refugee situation. Women are highly vulnerable to risks of sexual abuse, and they frequently experienced poor nutrition and difficulties in caring for children in camp conditions. During the resettlement phase, women refugees cope with a host of new problems. They are expected to care for their families and contribute to their new lives in a productive way. Yet many are poorly equipped to do so, as they typically have low levels of formal education and few transferable skills. Further, family strain associated with international migration, including marital and intergenerational conflicts, and general pressure on family cohesion and unity, tend to be exacerbated by the refugee and resettlement experience.

Less recognized is the special strength many refugee women possess. In some cases, they have been found to cope better than men during the resettlement period because women may be more willing than men to accept any employment available, thus increasing the family's income. For example, Vietnamese women have been less concerned than men about "status inconsistency" and downward socioeconomic movement because their occupational status in Vietnam was generally below that of men. These women's entire upbringing had prepared them for radical and difficult change later in life, that is, marriage and adjustment to the demands of the husband's family. Thus, it is important to acknowledge the strengths of women refugees and the important contributions these women make to their families as well as the disadvantages they face.

Southeast Asian Values and Norms

Although there is much diversity among Southeast Asian ethnic populations, several values and norms are common among them. Some of these values and norms derive from the eastern religions of Confucianism, Buddhism, and Taoism. Behaviors such as diligence and a willingness to make sacrifices, together with relatively high educational levels and median incomes and low utilization of mental health resources have led many to think of Southeast Asians, along with other Asians, as a "model minority." The common interrelated values emphasized in this chapter, those most central to understanding Southeast Asian women, are family continuity, filial piety, avoidance of shame, and self-control.

Family is of central importance to Southeast Asians. The family links individuals with their ancient forebears and ensures the perpetuation of the family's good name. In keeping with these goals, families tend to be hierarchical, male dominated, and highly structured. Although the nuclear family is the primary unit of residence and function, it is intimately located within the extended family. A large family is considered a source of happiness (Hopkins, 1994; Muir, 1988). There is also an economic factor for valuing the family, for in Southeast Asia, more children meant more hands to till the fields and harvest the crops. The individual derives his or her identity from membership in the family, and ancestors continue to play a part in family life. Major holidays throughout the year commemorate the family as an eternal unit. Spirits of departed relatives are celebrated, living family members are reunited, and one is reminded of his or her place within the larger context of the perpetual family lineage.

The husband or father is accepted as the head of the household and has primary responsibility for making major family decisions. Wives or mothers dominate in the domestic sphere and are responsible for maintaining financial matters and promoting family unity. Children are obligated to exhibit filial piety; that is, they are to be respectful and deferential, to unquestioningly obey their parents and the elderly, and to be loyal to their families. Obligations within a family extend primarily to the closest family members. Females are expected to defer to males, and the young are expected to defer to their elders. Children are supposed to share with, play with, and care for siblings. Parents should love their children, and children are, likewise, expected to love each other and their parents. Southeast Asians place high value on love, togetherness, happiness, hospitality, generosity, respect, and honor. The family represents love and the fulfillment of its members' physical and emotional needs. Conflict within the family unit is to be avoided at all cost. Love for parents and grandparents is taken seriously and expressed by treating them with the utmost respect and unwavering obedience, and by supporting and caring for them in their old age. Above all, family members must avoid shaming the family, the welfare of which supersedes the pursuit of individual goals. Southeast Asians are sensitive to appearances; and if personal problems or behaviors that are discrepant with family and community expectations come to be known to others, the person and family feel shame and lose face. Therefore, families expect members to control their emotions and avoid antisocial behavior. Subscribing to these values is regarded as a sign of maturity, and restraint is viewed as a resource that promotes self-discipline, patience, and diligence.

LAO IN SOUTHEAST ASIA

Laos is one of the Indochinese countries that border Cambodia, Thailand, and Vietnam. It has a population of about five million people. There are estimated to be 68 different ethnic groups within the borders of Laos, not counting resident foreigners. With respect to ethnicity, Laos is divided vertically, reflecting the fact that the more powerful groups inhabit the more fertile river valleys while other tribal groups inhabit the harsher altitudes. The Lao people are usually classified into three major divisions according to altitude. The low-land Lao groups, which include the politically and socially dominant ethnic Lao, comprise only 45%–50% of the population. The Lao Theung ("of the mountain slopes") are the oldest inhabitants of the area. They were driven out of the valleys approximately a millennium ago. The Lao Soung ("of the mountain summits"), including the Hmong, live at the highest altitudes, only moving into the region from China about 200 years ago.

Customs, traditions, and languages differentiate each tribe or group. Some differences are minor, with groups speaking almost identical dialects, while in other cases the differences are much greater. Such incredible ethnic diversity poses problems in speaking about "the culture of Laos," for there are in fact over 60 cultures. The discussion that follows is about the largest of these groups, the ethnic Lao.

The Lao have lived through 30 years of war, from roughly 1945 while under French control until the final victory of the Communist Pathet Lao in 1975. U.S. bombing and other military action, dislocation of the population, recruitment into various armies, propaganda, and infusion of foreign capital transformed Laotian society, particularly between 1960–1975 (Ireson & Ireson, 1989). For its own geopolitical reasons, the United States spent huge amounts of money on direct military aid and other economic assistance to Laos (Barber, 1979). Internal refugees from fighting and U.S. bombing from 1963–1973 disrupted the rural economy and expanded urban populations. Massive sociocultural change occurred for most Lao refugees well before they left their country.

Beginning in 1975, the military, political, and commercial elite began their flights from the country. Peasant farmers and the majority of the educated and skilled work force followed, avoiding collectivization under the new regime (Ireson & Ireson, 1989). The policies of the new regime, "reeducation" of the individuals who had served in the Royal Lao Government or military, and a perceived lack of opportunity resulted in a large flow of refugees to Thai refugee camps and ultimately to the U.S. and other countries. By 1985, about 350,000 people, or close to 10 percent of the population, had fled. About half of these came to the United States (Van Esterik, 1985).

Traditional Lao Culture

Most Lao were traditionally peasant farmers growing paddy rice in the river valleys of their country. This enterprise is highly labor intensive, requiring short periods of work by a large labor force (Barber, 1979; Hanks, 1972). Most of the labor was provided by "domestic groups of the extended-family type" (Keyes, 1975). In traditional Lao society, the nuclear family was firmly situated in the wife's parents' extended family which, in turn, was ensconced in the larger network of friends and relatives who made up a village. Requirements for more help with labor were solved by the Lao through informal work exchange networks, primarily among kin (Barber, 1979). Large families were valued because of the labor contributions of children and because children were insurance for one's care in old age. Many women also engaged in outside activities to earn additional cash by selling crafts or vegetables at market.

The dominant religion of the Lao is Theravada Buddhism, which originated in India, but incorporates animistic elements in its Lao version. Ninety-five percent of the population is Buddhist. One cannot understand Lao culture without a thorough grounding in Theravada Buddhism. Theravada Buddhism is a state religion that provides educational and ideological support for the political system and pervades all areas of traditional Lao village life (Tambiah, 1970; Van Esterik, 1985). Social hierarchy is also a critical component of traditional Lao Buddhist culture. Yet within Theravada Buddhism, there exists the concept that while one's place in the order of things is determined by *karma,* individuals are capable of creating their own *karma* (Keyes, 1977).

In conventional readings of Buddhist texts, women are seen as "inherently lower in status than men, and women are barred by sex from aspiring to the roles to which the greatest virtue attaches" (Keyes, 1977, p. 161). Laotian men are, ideologically, superior to women. Women are associated with nurturing and attachment, while men are esteemed by virtue of their ostensible detachment from worldly things and supramundane power. This perception results in low status for women culturally. They cannot become monks, which is a critical route to spiritual attainment for men. Yet paradoxically women have a measure of spiritual and economic autonomy. They are often the most active and devout of participants in temple activities. As elsewhere in Southeast Asia, women in Laos have traditionally participated in market trading and entrepreneurial activities as well as in the domestic sphere (Van Esterik, 1982).

Therevada Buddhism strictly dictates the behavior of monks, or *bonzes,* who live at the temple, or *wat,* while the general laity are expected to live their lives according to a few general virtues. The notion that one's behavior determines good fortune or trouble in later lives demands that Buddhists must strive to "make merit." The Law of Karma stipulates that humans can reduce suffering by performing meritorious acts, or they can perpetuate their misery by demeritous acts. Thus, merit-making is a fundamental premise of village life in Laos, and it can be observed in daily food offerings to local monks and in the laity's support of the local temple. Merit-making embraces ideals of nonviolence, charity, and humility, and essentially living life as properly as one can.[1]

Opportunities for education beyond the primary school level were extremely limited, especially for women. The educational system in Laos was set up by the French and consisted of a primary school system, after which students could progress to "college" (secondary school), temple training, or other vocational training. Most of the rural population had access to

---

[1]Christianity has been known in Laos only since the period of French colonialism, and it is not very widespread. Only about 10 percent of the Lao population identify as Christian.

the first three primary grades at best. The basic method of instruction was lecture and rote memorization. A student did not progress automatically from grade to grade as in the American system, but often spent several years in one grade. Children did not begin school until around the age of seven or eight.

The Buddhist temple itself serves several important functions in the village. Traditionally, boys and men are expected to spend some time at the temple as novices. Usually the time period for such novitiates is three months and constitutes the only formal education available in the village. While only males are able to become novices, females can become nuns, though this choice was usually made only by elderly women. The many ceremonies held throughout the year in the temple provided a source of entertainment for all villagers. Young women of courting age contributed to *wat* affairs by sewing and embroidering cloth items for the temple. In addition to their role as religious teachers, *bonzes* might also serve as healers and judges, and were highly respected members of the community.

While Buddhism provides the longer-term philosophical structure to understanding life, spirit cults provide immediate relief from daily problems. According to Buddhist teaching, one cannot hope to change troubles in the present life, but in reality the Lao do try to manipulate the spirits, or *phi,* which they believe cause troubles and illness in the present. There are *phi* for places and elements in the environment as well as 32 souls that guard the 32 organs of the human body. These spirits leave the body at death and recombine to form a new person. Any spirits that do not come to be reincarnated in this way, as happens in the instances of violent deaths or death at childbirth, can cause trouble. Spirits are appeased through certain rituals and offerings, which are conducted upon any significant occasion in a person's life, such as birth, marriage, important holidays, embarking on a journey, or recovery from illness. In the ritual known as *BaSi* (also spelled *Baci*), strings are tied into a knot around the wrist of the honoree for whom the ceremony is held. This ritual is accompanied by many good wishes. The knot ensures that spirits cannot undo the blessings.

Traditionally, marriage partners were found within the village or at least in the same district (Tambiah, 1970). The ability of a woman to choose her mate and the requirement that men find a mate in order to gain access to land gave women real "power and authority" in Laos (Rynearson & DeVoe, 1984). Given the right of women to divorce their husbands, a man's formal authority within a village depended on his wife's continuing consent. Ideally, the husband was older than the wife and was able to pay an appropriate bride-price. While adequate survey information is unavailable, one ethnographic study of a Thai-Lao village reported the average age of marriage to be 24 for men and 19 for women (Mizuno, 1971). When a couple decided to marry, they went through a traditional ceremony, which included negotiation between the families and approval of the couple's choice of mates. Although "love marriages" were common, premarital contacts between the sexes were controlled and limited, and serious interest in a member of the opposite sex was expected to result in marriage (Klausner, 1983; Levy, 1963). Reliable data on marriage and divorce rates are not available, either from Laos or for Lao refugees in the United States. One problem is that marriages and divorces both in Laos and in American Lao communities are frequently not recorded in official records.

Traditionally, men were permitted to take multiple wives as long as they could support all of the families. In cases where this occurred, usually among the more well-to-do, the first wife was always to be treated with more respect. Women were not permitted to have multiple husbands.

Traditionally childbirth took place in the home with the help of female relatives and sometimes a midwife. After birth the mother was placed on a hot bed (a bed under which a warm fire is kept burning) and cleansed. She was treated with the hot bed and special foods for a varying length of time according to her preferences. A few women delivered their babies in clinics or hospitals.

While living in Southeast Asia, the Lao desired large families. Like farmers elsewhere in the world, children were seen as a measure of status and wealth, for the larger the family, the more hands available to work the land. Children helped in production activities, transplanted rice, cared for animals, brought food to parents in the fields, helped with household chores, and cared for younger siblings (Zaharlick & Brainard, 1987).

The Lao have historically viewed their nation as underpopulated, with access to labor rather than access to land as a limiting factor in production (Evans, 1990). This pronatalist cultural value has been expressed in several modern governmental policies that applied to both rural and urban populations. For instance, under the Royal Lao Government, civil servant wages were tied to family size, thus providing economic incentives for births among the elite. Further, contraception was outlawed for the first 12 years of the Communist regime (Ireson & Ireson, 1989), encouraging high fertility among all segments of the population.

THE REFUGEE EXPERIENCE

When they fled their homelands, most refugees left behind families and many lost family members to death or involuntary separation. During the time spent in camps in asylum countries, refugees attempted to locate lost members and reunite their families. Others formed new families, either through marriages or the incorporation of others from their home countries. Problems arose for many of these families while being considered for resettlement by the U.S. Immigration Service. Refugees were recognized in terms of family units, but in a restricted sense. "Family" was defined either as parents or husband, wife, and children, which meant that a man was forced to choose between declaring either his elderly parents or his wife and children as relatives.

Other problems arose because children who had turned 21 years old or who had married were suddenly no longer considered children. Under the U.S. Immigration and Nationality Act, "the term 'child' means an unmarried person under 21 years of age." Therefore, such newly emancipated family members were left behind in camps to seek resettlement on their own. Similarly today, families face the same problem when they locate missing sons or daughters and try to bring them into the United States (Hopkins, 1994). Immigration may be denied because, in the time that has elapsed since the families entered the United States, the child may have turned 21 or married.

A similar dilemma exists for polygamous, or multiple-spouse, families. War and the political upheavals in their homelands profoundly affected marriages and family structure. Husbands and wives were very often separated from each other and told that the other was dead. In some cases, a spouse was sent to a different region of the country for a significant time. Thus, people might have remarried without ever knowing the fate of a previous spouse. After the war, or in the camps, these former families were sometimes reunited with a former spouse and his or her new family. Often, men continued to feel love, loyalty, and some obligation to care for and support both families. U.S. law permits polygamous families to immigrate, but once they arrive in the United States, marriage laws make polygamy illegal. Therefore, a man must claim only one wife. The choice has serious consequences for the wife not chosen, for she is not entitled to any legal or economic benefits, such as an inheritance, that may accrue from her husband.

Southeast Asian-American women worry constantly about their families in the United States as well as in their home countries. In the process of being incorporated into American society, many have experienced culture shock and may also suffer from an identity crisis. These problems have been aggravated by social and economic concerns, which frequently cause frustration and instability in the family. The women also worry about their ability to maintain traditional family values in the context of their new lives and about how their children are growing up in the United States. Upon arrival in their new homeland, one of the first priorities of Southeast Asian-American women has been to reestablish their families. For most, this has meant finding a safe, secure place to live; bringing members of their families together; becoming participants in the larger society through work and schooling; sharing hospitality and meals; restoring order and continuity to life; and providing a sense of security for family members. Drawing upon the cultural knowledge they bring with them, Southeast Asian–American women, along with their husbands, attempt to reestablish a familiar context so they can take control of their lives and begin the demanding process of adapting to a new culture.

Lao in the United States

In the United States, Buddhism remains a strong component of Lao ethnic identity. Likewise, the *BaSi* continues to be an important ceremony for marking recovery from illness, childbirth, leaving for a journey, or any other important event in a person's life. Most Lao in the present generation of adults are quite interested in maintaining the traditional culture and community, although they recognize the need to speak English and to acquire skills to secure and keep a decent job. Adults generally want their children to learn to speak, and in some cases to read and write, Lao and to learn to "be Lao" (Muir, 1988). This generation of adults has little interest in assimilating into American society. In fact, many Lao prefer to consider themselves apart from Americans. The next generation, however, shows a shift in its goals. The children like American clothes, music, and food, and many are adopting increasingly non-Lao-like behaviors and manners. Some Lao children even refuse to eat traditional foods.

In the United States, Lao women are the source and protectors of Lao tradition. They continue their traditional roles of managing household and production activities, rearing children, and cooking. They encourage communal activities and traditional caretaking and nurturing attitudes on the part of older children toward younger children. They also maintain the traditional Lao home into which men may retreat.

To the Lao, food means hospitality, and hospitality means being Lao (Muir, 1988). Food and eating are enjoyable pastimes. Women provide the traditional accoutrements of hospitality—the food, the drink, and the warmth of welcome. While Lao women are expected to be slender, they do not pretend to be full when they are not nor do they say they are dieting and therefore cannot eat. Women regularly gather at one woman's house to help with cooking, which is often a cooperative effort. Generally, they eat together in the kitchen, talking and laughing, while preparing and serving food to the men sitting in the living room. The women are free to sit with the men and eat, but many prefer what they consider more interesting conversation and company in the kitchen. After dinner, the family visits with other families, or friends may drop by (Muir, 1988). Adults will sit and talk, men with men and women with women, while children play in the home or outside.

Children are, and have always been, desired by the Lao. Everyone loves a baby. Children of both sexes continue to be desired, although men tend to want male offspring. Both boys and girls must help around the house. Girls, however, are required to continue such tasks until they marry. Usually the youngest daughter and her husband inherit the family wealth and, in turn, care for their aging parents.

While breast-feeding is the traditional source of nourishment for Lao babies, bottle-feeding is rapidly replacing it in the United States. The Lao do not regard the breast as primarily sexual in nature, but rather as a source of food for the baby. Anytime or anywhere the baby wants to nurse is the right time and place. Whether using the bottle or breast, a Lao mother feeds her child whenever he or she appears dissatisfied or hungry. Babies who fuss, children who are unhappy, and adults who are sad are all offered food, which is seen as an appropriate antidote to emotional trauma. Children are not put to bed, but sleep whenever they are tired. Excretory functions and toilet training are dealt with in a similarly relaxed manner.

The youngest child usually stays close to the mother or father until around three years of age (Muir, 1988). At this time, the child switches to greater association with peers. If another sibling arrives before this time, the child will gravitate to the peer group at an earlier age. Other children, especially girls, are supposed to entertain the babies so adults may work and talk. Should the baby become upset, he or she is returned to the mother or father. The parents will frequently offer sympathy and comfort to an angry child. Older children function within a group of peers, are responsible for themselves, and are largely independent of adults.

As it was in the past, discipline continues to be verbal and more by example than by direction (LeBar & Suddard, 1967). As previously noted, Lao adults believe children should be respected. Adults prefer to give children encouragement and provide examples of good behavior, rather than to directly instruct or force compliance. When unacceptable behavior is witnessed, parents talk to their children or try to distract very young children into a more acceptable activity. If they become very upset with the children, they might speak loudly to them—an action they usually consider rude and wrong. However, many of the younger parents who had not experienced the often troublesome years of toddlerhood parenting in their traditional society may use more physical means of discipline such as spanking (Muir, 1988). The more acculturated Lao often feel compelled to make their children conform to American expectations, which may include physical punishment.

The Lao in the United States clearly recognize that education and the acquisition of employment skills are central to their children's future. Education is viewed as a child's primary duty. Parents generally do not participate in their children's education, in part due to their perception that formal education is best accomplished between the child and the school. They also feel they lack the necessary educational skills to help their children. Most Lao would never openly question the wisdom of an educator or a school policy, although they might have some private doubts. For example, some older Lao have informally expressed concern over the anatomy lessons taught in schools to children, especially daughters, believing that such lessons are for doctors, not children.

The question of dating is a major point of contention between the generations. Most Lao parents are not comfortable with the American system, especially for daughters. Boys may date, but if they want to date American style, they find American dates. Since Lao males are fairly free to do much as they please, there has been little conflict between parents and sons over the issue of dating. A Lao girl, on the other hand, is faced with either waiting for a Lao boy who is interested in a traditional courtship or with defying her parent's authority. If a daughter chooses to date against her parents' wishes, she risks ostracism by the family.

Although change is occurring, many single Lao men ready for marriage still prefer a Lao wife. When men are interested in marriage, they are introduced to appropriate Lao women by friends and relatives and proceed with a traditional courtship of visiting. A man calls on a woman and her family to talk, and after a period of months, a mutual friend will approach the woman's family about the possibility of a union after the couple has decided that marriage is what they both want. Assuming the arrangements are agreeable to all, a traditional ceremony is held.

While many Lao continue to prefer traditional marriage ceremonies, others choose American civil or religious ceremonies, and still others use a combination of traditional and American ceremonies. Some Lao couples live together without any formal marriage contract. Lao parents no longer necessarily approve the choice of marriage partner in advance nor do they always negotiate a marriage settlement, in fact, traditional bride-price customs are often reinterpreted in Western economic terms. Young U.S. Lao women can now be heard insisting that they do not want to be "sold like property" or have their family receive a "down payment" from the groom to be married, although they may still desire a "traditional" wedding ceremony (Zaharlick, Jabrack, & Calip-DuBois, 1993).

When asked, Lao women characterize the ideal man as liking to work and provide for the family. Women should stay home and men should not have to do housework. Generally, men do not assist much with the housework anyway, even if they are unemployed and the wife works. Men should be polite, quiet, and strong. As explained earlier, husbands should be older than their wives for it is believed that a more mature male helps to ensure a harmonious marriage. It is also believed that an older husband will be wiser than a younger man, and therefore respected by his wife (Muir, 1988).

Lao men describe the ideal woman as being pretty and polite. She should stay home and cook, do housework, and help raise the children. Women should dress nicely, but not wear too much makeup. Because Lao women provide the necessary hospitality and maintain the traditions, they are regarded as the strongest part of the family (Muir, 1988).

Public interaction between husbands and wives, and men and women in general, is controlled, polite, respectful, and somewhat distant. Physical and verbal interaction is minimal. One stoops to avoid walking upright in another's line of vision. Eye contact is indirect and politeness and respect maintained. In all-female gatherings, however, the atmosphere is quite different. Talk is noisier, people are not as conscientious about stooping when walking in front of others, and most eye contact is direct. There is much joking and laughing, and things are generally more relaxed. Although physical interaction between genders in public is taboo, women frequently touch and habitually greet each other with a hug. In many ways it seems that the bond between women is stronger than that between women and husbands; certainly, their interactions are more affectionate and reciprocal.

Pregnancy for many Lao women is regarded as a time of illness, although little data exists on this point. Throughout their pregnancies, most women visit a doctor or clinic, often accompanied by social service providers, sponsors, or friends. Since coming to the United States, women most often give birth in hospitals. Usually the husband, and a bilingual companion if the husband does not speak English, accompanies the woman to the hospital but does not attend the birth itself.

There is a later start on marriage and family-building for Lao refugees in the United States than in Laos. In Laos, men desired to marry earlier in order to establish themselves economically and, consequently, obtain preferred young brides. As rights to the control of land were held by couples, from a young man's point of view early marriage meant access to land (Keyes, 1975). This traditional motivation for early marriage has changed for Lao men living in the United States, who primarily earn their living through wage labor. Today, more men desire to be economically self-sufficient before marrying because gaining economic power through marriage is no longer an option. The expense of establishing a separate household, the Lao's preferred form of residency after marriage, is considered a major reason for later marriage. U.S. compulsory education, which requires school attendance to a later age than was common for young women in Laos, is another significant reason offered by Lao for their later marriage pattern. Some Lao also have difficulty finding suitable mates in the small ethnic communities in which they live in the United States (Zaharlick & Brainard, 1987).

As a result of economic concerns, a growing tendency for Lao women in the United States is limiting the number of their offspring. More and more families are living in nuclear rather than extended family units, as children are no longer important for perpetuation of the domestic agricultural group. The economic value of children as producers is seen to be extremely limited and in the United States children are seen as economic liabilities. Women's work outside the home is also cited as another conscious factor in a woman's decision to limit family size. In addition, the change in household structure toward isolated nuclear families and the geographical separation of kin create a childcare problem when both parents are employed outside the home, for day care is expensive (Zaharlick, Jobrack, & Calip-DuBois, 1993).

The sociocultural and economic constraints on family size for the Lao has also coincided with increased availability of Western birth control technology. Lao women seem to have accepted Western contraceptive methods relatively quickly compared to other ethnic groups (Chongvatana & Lavely, 1984). Yet this recent use of contraceptives does not necessarily imply a move away from all traditional beliefs and values. Some fundamental Lao traditional attitudes may promote individual acceptance of Western contraceptive methods under the new conditions of life in America. As Buddhists, the Lao tend to place responsibility for choice, including reproductive choice, on the individual. Although some older Lao believe that contraception is immoral, they also believe that it would not be appropriate, for example, to impose their views on a daughter facing economic constraints in the United States. This approach speaks to the relative autonomy traditionally exercised by Lao women. Although ideally both spouses should agree on family planning goals, most Lao believe that women should make the final decisions regarding use of contraceptives.

Many Lao women have opted for surgical sterilization following the birth of a child, while others have had abortions since coming to the United States. Most women who have had abortions have told their husbands, who have not objected. Because marriage tends to occur later, Lao women have their first child at a later age today than in the past. In addition, a growing number of Lao women are unmarried for portions of their lives as a result of the increasing frequency of divorce. For all these reasons, Lao women have fewer children during their lifetime in the United States than their counterparts in Laos.

While divorce was easier in Laos than in many other traditional societies and could be initiated by either partner, it is much rarer among Laotians in their homeland than it is among Lao in the United States. One reason is that Lao women in the United States are not as dependent on men for the financial support of their families. Generally, women have access to a network of friends and relatives who can assist them if they want to leave their spouse. The reasons for divorce are economics (in which case the husband is considered an ineffective provider), faithlessness, interference from relatives, or no-fault (the couple simply does not get along). With government public assistance programs and with their own abilities to earn incomes, many Lao women no longer feel they must stay with husbands who abuse or neglect them or who have extramarital affairs.

Some Lao women believe that Lao husbands are becoming more "respectful" of their wives in the United States, a situation they attribute to the fact that polygamy is illegal in the United States. They also believe that Lao men have come to realize that their wives generally will not tolerate their husband's extramarital affairs or abusive behavior (Zaharlick, Jobrack, & Calip-DuBois, 1993), an outcome of assimilation.

Because Lao women have been involved traditionally in marketing and entrepreneurial endeavors, they have been able to make the shift to involvement in the host economy rather successfully. In fact, the addition of wage labor for Lao women does not yet seem to have altered their roles in the family to any significant extent. Further, women's experience in the market and the general economic activity of Laos has permitted Lao women to enter the labor force here in the United States with little resistance from Lao men.

Yet the path to assimilation has had its problems. Because the Lao were admitted to the United States as nuclear family groups, without parents or siblings, they were stripped overnight of the traditional support of their extended families. Women, more than men, seem to feel this loss, which is not surprising because it was usually the Lao woman's family of birth that made up the household group they left. In Laos, a woman could turn to sisters for help with household duties and to parents for security. Childcare was given automatically. There were always friendly hands to make a task easier and enjoyable (Muir, 1988).

In the United States, Lao women are faced with the same responsibilities but lack the methods of meeting them. Worst of all, they are alone. Their mothers and sisters are gone. Yet the women must still cope with the tasks of childcare, food preparation, housework, managing finances, and maintaining the health and identity of the Lao family, often in addition to work at full- or part-time jobs. This means delegating traditional duties to others and a new responsibility for providing or contributing financial support for . . . the family.

The use of American patron networks, whether public assistance programs or institutions such as churches, has been one answer to meeting some of these responsibilities, particularly those of an economic nature. Public assistance programs provide Lao families with cash, food, and health care. Churches and American sponsors supply food and money as well as job leads. Some churches assist with the daycare needs of working Lao mothers. Most mothers, however, prefer that their children stay in the care of Lao friends because they are perceived as undeniably trustworthy and better able to understand the children's needs.

To a large extent, Lao women have been successful in replacing their extended families and friends, lost to the refugee experience, with new social networks. Lao women are more task-oriented than Lao men and will work toward a goal without worrying if the process is absolutely correct (Muir, 1988). They create networks to accomplish everyday tasks communally. As such, these relationships do not focus on patron-client relationships, power, or competition, but rather on cooperation. Lao women's networks are useful for information dissemination as well. For example, they are used to pass through the community and to other communities news of jobs and assistance programs, sources of potential mates and traditional curing specialists, and other scarce commodities. The women's networks help to draw new people into the community as well as provide for needs that public assistance programs do not recognize, such as access to traditional foods and clothes and to the networks that make everyday living bearable and fulfilling. These networks also give the Lao mobility because one can always find a relative or "cousin" to live with upon moving to a new community.

If a person is lucky enough to have relatives in the United States, they would form the core of his or her social group. Proximity is an important factor in forming and joining networks, particularly for women, who often lack transportation. In some ways, proximity has replaced kinship in determining everyday interactions. Women find it convenient to interact with their women neighbors, whom they regard as "sisters." Thus, there is a tendency for Lao women to seek replacements for lost kin ties with other refugees and to accord these replacements with kin status.

Lao women have also attempted to address the challenge of their new responsibilities through the formation of women's organizations. The tradition of women participating in social or political action, although restricted in the public sphere, was not altogether lacking in Laos before refugee resettlement. But only a few women had the boldness, education, and elite status to have their ideas publicly heard and accepted (Krulfeld, 1997). Some factors that may be responsible for women more recently becoming politically active in their communities are: growing community concerns, particularly about problems facing Lao youth; a view that female concerns are being overlooked; a need for women to take up women's causes; and a lack of action by male-run Lao organizations in solving community problems.

Non-Lao American women are only rarely included in Lao women's networks. Lao men are excluded. Lao men demonstrate more concern about formalities and ceremony than women, are more individualistic and competitive, and tend to form networks around patron-client systems. Lao patrons act for the community in most important dealings with outside organizations and interests. Men strive for leadership roles and participate extensively in networks they can control. Such activities often result in factionalism (Muir, 1988).

Women's networks operate within the Lao community and cut across male political factions. The wife of one patron may socialize regularly with the wife of a rival patron. Patrons do not socialize, and interact very little. Lao women, then, serve to integrate a community that may otherwise be fragmented by political factionalism.

PROBLEMS LIVING IN
THE UNITED STATES

One of the first difficulties that refugees face is finding adequate housing, especially for larger families. Most refugees resettle in the poorest, most dangerous neighborhoods, usually in small, low-rent, subsidized apartments in large complexes that are often noisy and rundown. Neighbors are often unfriendly, and violence is routine. Under these conditions parents find it difficult to provide a sense of security and protection for their children, children find it difficult to have respect and confidence that their parents are in control, and Lao community leaders recognize that such environments do not provide the kind of model circumstances that they wish for their youth.

In interacting with the larger society, refugees face many bewildering restrictions and opposition to their lives and family values (Hopkins, 1994). The most damaging result is the breakdown of traditional family structure caused by the isolation and reduction of status of the old, the struggle of the middle generation to survive economically, and the rapid Americanization of youth. Because most Southeast Asian refugees arrive lacking adequate English, education, and urban job skills, it is difficult for refugee parents to find work to provide financial security for their families. Also, lacking knowledge of American society and education, Southeast Asian parents find that their children have more knowledge and control over everyday life than they do. For these reasons, they fear that children no longer respect them and that they can no longer manage their families with confidence and authority.

Many Southeast Asian parents view the school system as problematic because it conveys values that work against those they promote in their homes. Schools find it difficult to support refugee values, such as the importance of the family over the individual, group over individual decision-making, and an authoritative parenting style requiring obedience of children rather than negotiation between parents and children. Often, educators are openly critical when families keep children home to help with childcare or translation. In schools in their home countries, children worked closely together and older siblings helped younger ones. Individuals worked hard to bring pride to the family, not to themselves, so cooperation in classwork and homework was encouraged and rewarded by both the school and the family. By contrast, children in U.S. classrooms are told to do their "own work," and siblings are encouraged to surpass one another. Children also have problems in school because their politeness (smiling and nodding agreement) is frequently interpreted by American teachers as comprehension, when, in actuality, the opposite may often be true. Moreover, their cultural backgrounds ill-equip Southeast Asian students to deal with learning situations where they are expected to discuss and debate issues with teachers. For Southeast Asian children, learning is listening rather than participating (Hopkins, 1994; Muir, 1988).

Southeast Asian parents believe that the U.S. legal system, including child abuse laws and the juvenile justice system, undermines their authority. When problems arise, parents want to resolve them within the family, in part, because it is so important not to lose face within the Southeast Asian community. For this reason, parents may hesitate to call police, even in dire situations, because they fear their neighbors, seeing the police arrive in uniform with lights flashing, will think less of the family. Children are encouraged to bring their problems to their parents, but parents do not share their problems with the children. Extended family members, especially family elders, and close friends may be consulted in some instances. If a problem exceeds the capacities of family and close friends, community leaders may be called in for guidance. Only as a last resort will problems be reported to officials.

The concept of "problem" among Southeast Asians is usually defined in terms of the outward display of trouble, rather than what most Americans might see as the root of the problem. For instance, the differences in lifestyles that might cause confrontations between a husband and wife, such as when a woman adopts modern American values while her husband wants her to retain her more traditional mindset, are not considered as much of a problem as the loud arguing and beatings that result from their disagreements. The American construct called "problem-solving" is absent in the traditional method of resolving conflict in Southeast Asia, for as long as outward behavior conforms to cultural norms, all is well. Differences in perspectives and desires do not "count."

Instead of resolution, Laotians often try to manage their conflicts. This process usually takes the form of first attempting to ignore the conflict and encouraging proper role behavior. If this tactic is unsuccessful, then violent punishment may be meted out. Lastly, one party may be alienated from the other, even if this means breaking up a family. Americans might view Southeast Asians as handling problems primarily by avoidance. In fact, tolerance is extremely limited. Repeated criminal offenses have traditionally been punished by death, dismemberment, or life imprisonment, regardless of the severity of the crime. Generally, people are expected to try to mediate differences only two or three times before resorting to the extreme of alienation. When action is deemed necessary, it is swift and decisive. For example, in the case of rape or molestation, the two families involved are traditionally expected to fight each other. The majority of disputes in the United States do not come to this level of violence, however. Talking is the preferred method of managing disputes, and parties often achieve satisfactory solutions on the first try.

In the matter of deeply personal problems, people are expected to keep their concerns to themselves. Domestic violence toward women and children exists in both traditional Lao society and in Lao communities in the United States. Although stresses have undoubtedly increased for the Lao, as for other refugees and immigrants, cultural alternatives to violence do exist. Specifically, an abused wife, or child, may use her social network and mobility to leave the abusive situation. This action mirrors traditional patterns of conflict avoidance. Leaving also minimizes the likelihood of intervention by law enforcement authorities, which could have unpleasant ramifications. In the instance of rape, women rarely tell anyone what has occurred. When disclosure is made, one is usually advised to forget about it and get on with life. The rationale for such advice hinges upon the need to uphold the reputation of the family despite one individual's personal troubles.

What seems to matter more than the act of violence is who bears the blame for it. Thus, the initial step in mediating most conflicts is to determine who is at fault, then proceed with the traditionally prescribed action. When situations become so desperate that the police must be called, Southeast Asians expect to explain their side of the story and have the police begin an investigation on the spot. Action is to be taken based solely on who is at fault, with little allowance for extenuating circumstances. If an individual is guilty, it is expected that this person will be punished, not given probation or reduced sentences. Such practices in the American legal system are perceived as ineffective.

If the victim or survivor is considered to have brought the violence on him or herself by disobedience, then no reprisal or action is considered necessary. Though people will feel sorry for the helpless and blameless survivor, little is done except to encourage stoicism. As long as amends have been made between the families, there is little more that can be done to address the needs of the individual survivor. Again, the primary concern is maintaining the face of the family.

There are a number of issues in the Southeast Asian-American community that non-Southeast Asian-Americans consider problematic. Some of these problems are identified by the Southeast Asian community as a source of concern, while others are seen as perfectly normal. Among the issues identified as problematic by the Southeast Asian community are the rapid acculturation of youth and their identification with negative aspects of American culture. Issues of concern to non-Southeast Asian-Americans and mainstream institutions include physical abuse of children, child neglect, and spousal battery. While these forms of violence exist within the Southeast Asian community, they are considered to be well within the tolerance limits of the cultures, and thus are not a source of worry to the community as a whole. Generally, issues of violence or neglect only concern the Southeast Asian population to the extent that these activities are illegal and have caused conflict with the American legal system and protective service agencies. Individually, however, Southeast Asian survivors of these forms of violence are as traumatized as are other American trauma survivors.

One of the most common problems Southeast Asian families face in the United States is the lack of discipline among their children. Southeast Asian youth frequently reject their parents' culture and language and have great difficulty reconciling their parents' traditional values to those they are learning in school, from their peers, and through the media. This rejection too often becomes manifested in dysfunctional behaviors such as running away from home, skipping or dropping out of school, unapproved dating, sexual promiscuity, abusing drugs and alcohol, joining gangs, engaging in criminal activity, and general rebellion against parental as well as institutional authority. Parents are frustrated because U.S. laws do not permit them to discipline unruly children as they did before—usually through beatings or tying them up. If, and when, they resort to calling the authorities for help, they find that the authorities treat the case as a first offense despite the long history of unreported events. Thus, if the case is pursued, there begins a long process of officials issuing warnings and handing out lenient treatment—a process that gives the impression to adults and children that the American system is ineffective at disciplining children. In contrast, when allegations of abuse are leveled at parents, either by children or by teachers, the official response is swift and decisive. Children use this knowledge to threaten their parents.

Because the Southeast Asian family is such a tightly closed unit, intervening in family matters is strictly prohibited except in extreme and desperate cases. When some type of conflict develops within the Southeast Asian community, it is first addressed at the level of the family. Even problems that appear to involve only two individuals, such as a husband and wife, necessitate the involvement of both families, especially the elder generations. Such is the case in situations of rape, which requires that the family of the perpetrator pay reparations to the family of the victim. What matters most in conflict situations is making sure that the family does not lose face, because there is no way that their standing in the community can be restored.

Thus, conflicts within families must be kept strictly within the nuclear unit, meaning that family members are expected to ignore problems and live with their differences. If family members cannot live with the problem, a hierarchy of authority figures is called into action, beginning with the parents of the two who are at odds. In the vast majority of cases in the traditional cultures, the parents are able to resolve the conflict by reminding both parties of their duties, obligations, and proper role behavior. Brothers, sisters, aunts, uncles, or cousins are then approached for help. In those few cases where family members still have disputes, elders in the extended family or community leaders (such as the village head in the past or a community leader here in the United States) will be called in. The advice given by these people will be much the same in content as what parents have said, but the words carry more weight by virtue of the more respected status of the individual. Age and authority are two very critical characteristics necessary to individuals who will act as counselors or advisors to Southeast Asian families, whether members of the community or not.

Typically, advice and criticism flow from those of higher status to those of lower status, as measured by generation, age, and gender. Communication in this direction is permitted to be more direct and forward when limited to the family. One is expected to confide problems and troubles to those of higher status. Children, therefore, are traditionally not permitted to speak back to their parents, or to interfere in their parents' business, but are expected to give full and complete answers when parents question them. Historically, the only recourse to children mistreated by parents was refusal to care for them in their old age. The child's viewpoint is given no credibility, so children are not permitted to provide input into family matters. Parents, for their part, cannot confide or even acknowledge problems to children. Financial worries, personal hardships, health concerns, and marital difficulties are kept from the children, despite the fact that issues of this kind will affect their home life.

In practice, though, children often avoid confiding in their parents and choose to disobey family rules despite giving the appearance of listening when being lectured. One area of special concern is the sexual activity of Southeast Asian youth. Southeast Asians have a conservative orientation toward sex. Premarital sex is disparaged, especially for women. Discussion of sex is taboo, as well as any expression of sexual feelings, again, particularly for women. Affection between men and women is not displayed in any company, including in the presence of the children, so rules governing intimate relationships are unclear to youth. Consequently, there is virtually no preparation in the home for the experiences encountered in dating. Because many parents are aware of the comparative sexual freedom and emphasis placed upon sex in American society, the issue of dating causes great conflict in families and may easily erupt in violence. The lack of practical sex education renders Southeast Asian females particularly vulnerable to sexual violence.

A very close friend may serve as a confidant, though there are strict limitations on the degree to which he or she can help or intervene with a problem. "Good" friends are those who counsel others to keep their family or marriage together, to forget the problem and try to get along. Neighbors may witness violent conflicts or instances of neglect, but have no right to intervene except in the case of neglect of an elder and must have the permission of the family for such intervention. Friends and neighbors are obliged to respect the family's need for privacy. Thus, even when friends and neighbors know of trouble, they will often take no action because their roles do not allow them to do so.

Relationships outside the family are based on reciprocal exchanges. When help is asked, one must offer the help or the relationship will be negated. Institutional help offered by American social service agencies is unthinkable to most Southeast Asians. Institutions are seen by many as interference, weakening the family rather than strengthening or supporting it. Many simply will not discuss family business in front of strangers. Typically, people do not seek help or become familiar with available services until after conflict has arisen. Before this time, there is no acknowledgment of the potential for trouble. When someone outside the family provides assistance, the person is repaid with loyalty and favors. Exchanges of favors and goods, therefore, constitute the helping relationship in Southeast Asian cultures. Referrals, promises, or spoken words do not count as a form of help with these communities. Assistance is measured in terms of immediate, concrete results.

CONCLUSION

Having survived the trauma of flight, asylum, and initial resettlement, Southeast Asian-Americans strive to reunite and reestablish their families in new cultural contexts, using the knowledge, values, and traditions they brought with them from their homelands. However, their attempts to achieve viability and coherence in their lives are often frustrated by the rapid assimilation of their children into American culture and by the attempts of U.S. institutions to mold them to conform to American definitions, values, attitudes, and behaviors. Much to their credit, Southeast Asian-American women are finding ways to use their own resources to improve their families' lives rather than to rely on increasingly strained or unavailable federal, state, and local resources.

As Southeast Asian-American women draw upon both their traditional knowledge and values and the new skills they are acquiring as part of adapting to their new lives in the United States, they are empowering themselves. When and where this occurs, it has far-reaching consequences for self-esteem, self-determination, access to status and resources, and autonomy in general

(Krulfeld, 1997) Many serious problems continue to plague their communities and need to be solved. It will not be easy, for there are challenges to face not only within the Lao communities but also vis-à-vis the larger, mainstream American society. So far, Southeast Asian-American women have endured, grown, and above all, preserved the family. The future appears hopeful.

REFERENCES

Barber, M. J. P. (1979). *Migrants and modernization: A study of change in Lao society.* Unpublished doctoral dissertation, University of Hull, Hull, UK.

Chongvatana, N., & Lavely, W. R. (1984). *Knowledge and practice of contraception in two Indochinese camps.* (University of Michigan Population Studies Research Report No. 61). Ann Arbor: University of Michigan.

Evans, G. (1990). *Lao peasants under socialism.* New Haven, CT: Yale University Press.

Freeman, J. A. (1989). *Hearts of sorrow: Vietnamese-American lives.* Stanford, CA: Stanford University Press.

Hackett, B. N. (1996). *Pray God and keep walking: Stories of women refugees.* Jefferson, NC: McFarland and Company.

Haines, D. W. (1989). Introduction. In D. Haines (Ed.), *Refugees as immigrants: Cambodians, Laotians, and Vietnamese in America* (pp. 1–23). Totowa, NJ: Rowman and Littlefield.

Hanks, L. (1972). *Rice and man: Agricultural ecology in Southeast Asia.* Chicago: Aldine Atherton.

Hopkins, M. (1994). Thwarting "family values": American culture vs. Cambodian refugee families in the United States. In A. Zaharlick & J. L. MacDonald (Eds.), *Selected Papers on Refugee Issues: III* (pp. 132–149). Washington, DC: American Anthropological Association.

Ireson, W. R., & Ireson, C. J. (1989). Laos: Marxism in a subsistence rural economy. *Bulletin of Concerned Asian Scholars, 21*(2–4), 59–75.

Kelly, G. P. (1977). *From Vietnam to America.* Boulder, CO: Westview Press.

Keyes, C. F. (1975). Kin groups in a Thai-Lao community. In G. W. Skinner & T. Kirsch (Eds.), *Change and persistence in Thai society* (pp. 274–297). Ithaca, NY: Cornell University Press.

Keyes, C. F. (1977). *The Golden Peninsula.* New York: Macmillan.

Klausner, W. J. (1983). *Reflections on Thai culture: Collected writings of William J. Klausner* (2nd ed.). Bangkok, Thailand: The Siam Society.

Krulfeld, R. M. (1997). When the powerless take control: Self-empowerment through organization-building among Lao refugee women. In D. Baxter & R. Krulfeld (Eds.), *Selected Papers on*

Refugees and Immigrants: V (pp. 99–121). Washington, DC: American Anthropological Association.

LeBar, F., & Suddard, A. (Eds.). (1967). *Laos: Its people, its society, its culture* (Rev. ed., 3rd printing). New Haven, CT: HRAF Press.

Levy, B. P. (1963). Yesterday and today in Laos: A girl's autobiographical notes. In B. Ward (Ed.), *Women in the new Asia* (pp. 224–265). Amsterdam: UNESCO.

Mizuno, K. (1971). *Social system of Don Daeng village: A community study in northeast Thailand.* (Discussion Paper 12–22). Kyoto, Japan: Kyoto University.

Muir, K. (1988). *The strongest part of the family: A study of Lao refugee women in Columbus, Ohio.* New York: AMS Press.

Nguyen-Hong, N., Halpern, L., & Halpern, J. (Eds.). (1989). *The Far East comes near.* Amherst: University of Massachusetts Press.

Rutledge, P. J. (1992). *The Vietnamese experience in America.* Bloomington: Indiana University Press.

Rynearson, A. M., & DeVoe, P. A. (1984). Refugee women in a vertical village: Lowland Laotians in St. Louis. *Social Thought,* 33–48.

Tambiah, S. J. (1970). *Buddhism and the spirit cults of northern Thailand.* Cambridge, UK: Cambridge University Press.

Tenhula, J. (1991). *Voices from Southeast Asia: The refugee experience in the United States.* New York: Holmes and Meier.

Van Esterik, P. (1982). Introduction. In P. Van Esterik (Ed.), *Women of Southeast Asia.* (Northern Illinois University Center for Southeast Asian Studies Occasional Paper No. 9, pp. 1–15). DeKalb, IL: Northern Illinois University.

Van Esterik, J. (1985). The Lao. In D. W. Haines (Ed.), *Refugees in the United States: A reference handbook* (pp. 149–165). Westport, CT: Greenwood Press.

Zaharlick, A., & Brainard, J. (1987). Demographic characteristics, ethnicity and the resettlement of Southeast Asian refugees in the United States. *Urban Anthropology, 16*(3–4), 327–373.

Zaharlick, A., Jobrack, S., & Calip-DuBois, T. (1993). Economic and sociocultural influences on the fertility transition of Lao refugees. In M. Hopkins & N. Donnelly (Eds.), *Selected Papers on Refugee Issues: II* (pp. 177–194). Washington, DC: American Anthropological Association.

RECOMMENDED READINGS AND RESOURCES

Cornellier, R. (Producer). (1990). *Women at risk* [Videotape]. (Available from Filmakers Library, 124 East 40th Street, New York, NY 10016 and info@filmakers.com)

Davison, L. (1981). Women refugees: Special needs and programs.

Journal of Refugee Resettlement,
1(3), 16–26.

Evans, G. (1990). *Lao peasants under socialism.* New Haven, CT: Yale University Press.

Fadiman, A. (1997). *The spirit catches you and you fall down: A Hmong child, her American doctors, and the collision of two cultures.* New York: Farrar, Straus and Giroux.

Freeman, J. A. (1989). *Hearts of sorrow: Vietnamese-American lives.* Stanford, CA: Stanford University Press.

Hackett, B. N. (1996). *Pray God and keep walking: Stories of women refugees.* Jefferson, NC: McFarland and Company.

Haines, D. W. (1989). Introduction. In D. Haines (Ed.), *Refugees as immigrants: Cambodians, Laotians, and Vietnamese in America* (pp. 1–23). Totowa, NJ: Rowman and Littlefield.

Hayes, Tom (Writer, Producer & Director). (1981). *Refugee Road* [Videotape]. (Available from Arkansas Humanities Council, 10816 Executive Center Drive, Suite 310, Little Rock, AR 72211–4383 and http://www.arkhums.org/)

Kelly, G. P. (1977). *From Vietnam to America.* Boulder, CO: Westview Press.

Keyes, C. F. (1977). *The Golden Peninsula.* New York: Macmillan.

Kwan, P., & Iger, A. (Co-writers & Co-directors), & Lundahl, P. (Co-producer). (1993). *Anatomy of a springroll* [Videotape]. (Available from Filmakers Library, 124 East 40th Street, New York, NY 10016 and info@filmakers.com)

LeBar, F., & Suddard, A. (Eds.). (1967).

Laos: Its people, its society, its culture (Rev. ed., 3rd printing). New Haven, CT: HRAF Press.

Muir, K. (1988). *The strongest part of the family: A study of Lao refugee women in Columbus, Ohio.* New York: AMS Press.

Rynearson, A. M., & DeVoe, P. A. (1984). Refugee women in a vertical village: Lowland Laotians in St. Louis. *Social Thought, 33*–48.

Siegel, T. (Producer). (1988). *Blue Collar and Buddha* [Videotape]. (Available from Filmakers Library, 124 East 40th Street, New York, NY 10016 and info@filmakers.com)

Siegel, T., & Conquergood, D. (Co-producers). (1986). *Between two worlds: The Hmong shaman in America* [Videotape]. (Available from Filmakers Library, 124 East 40th Street, New York, NY 10016 and info@filmakers.com)

Tenhula, J. (1991). *Voices from Southeast Asia: The refugee experience in the United States.* New York: Holmes and Meier.

UNICEF. (1979). *Remember Me* [Film short]. (Available from AFSC Video & Film Library, 2161 Massachusetts Ave., Cambridge, MA 02140)

Velazquez, E. (Producer & Director). (1990). *Moving mountains: The story of the Yiu Mien* [Videotape]. (Available from Filmakers Library, 124 East 40th Street, New York, NY 10016 and info@filmakers.com)

Zaharlick, A., & Brainard, J. (1987). Demographic characteristics, ethnicity and the resettlement of Southeast Asian refugees in the United States. *Urban Anthropology, 16*(3–4), 327–373.

GLOSSARY

BaSi: a ritual accompanied by good wishes in which strings are tied into a knot around the wrist of the honoree to ensure that the spirits cannot undo the blessing

bonzes: Buddhist monks

karma: Buddhist philosophy that the sum of one's acts, words, and deeds decides one's fate in each stage of existence

phi: according to Buddhist belief, spirits who can cause trouble and illness in the present

wat: Buddhist temple

10

Conclusion

The Systemic Interface of Religion and Gender

S. RATLIFF

INTRODUCTION

In the preceding chapters we can discern the often vivid and sometimes more subtle systems and subsystems that coalesce to create the cognitive and affective environments in which gender identity emerges within ethnicity. The purpose of this final chapter is not to summarize the various systems discussed, but to delve more deeply into one common theme that runs through the majority of the cultural systems as a structural concept, religion.

Most of us have been socialized to revere religion (at least in principle) as an ennobling and edifying foundation of civilization without which, some believe, morality and civility would decay into social chaos. At its best, religion offers answers to the unanswerable, hope for the ineffable, and a guided pathway to spirituality. At its not-so-best, religion degenerates into an oppressive rationalization for male supremacy, racial hegemony, and political fanaticism. In the previous chapters we have witnessed an intertwining of these threads. Often it seems that women tolerate the "not-so-best" outcomes in order to preserve the "best."

At the core of most of the ethnic groups considered, religion exercises a dominant defining and regulative function. Biological imperatives have been encoded and sacralized in myths and scriptures serving to define women and their roles for all time. The resulting dogma circumscribes the context within which the kaleidoscopic interplay of sexuality, family, economics, education, politics, and self-determination must occur. To more fully appreciate the power of this critical aspect of culture, we may benefit from a more focused examination of the roots of the major religions and their rationalizations of women's "place" and "function." We can also observe some of the dynamic contemporary efforts being launched by courageous women from many cultures to re-define themselves within the very contexts constraining them.

Concerning these constraints and their apparent ties to religious beliefs, there are implications for care providers. First, not all behaviors and attitudes are indicators of religious beliefs. Some are just part of the culture as such. Thus, Islam will appear differently in more conservative countries than in liberal ones. In the United States, for example, Muslim women run the spectrum of "covering," with some choosing modest Western clothing and others covering all but their eyes. It is suggested that clinicians ask whether a behavior is based on the religion itself or is part of national culture. Further, even if an individual or family believes that a behavior is mandated by the religion, this may not always be the case. An example of this presented in the emergency department of a large metropolitan pediatric hospital where a Muslim family brought their four-year-old daughter to have her stomach pumped because she had eaten a piece of pork bologna. The resident physician refused to perform the procedure and the family threatened to sue him. The family may have truly believed that the child had committed a grievous sin. However, Islam is not so cruel or insensitive as to expect a young child to know that (1) bologna may have pork in it, or (2) that eating pork is disallowed by Islam. It is also possible that the parents merely wanted to make a strong impression on the child with the painful procedure. In such cases, the provider is urged to check with knowledgeable religious specialists before assuming the validity of these claims.

There are six major world belief systems in the world today. The three Abrahamic religions originated in the region commonly referred to as the Middle East and trace their roots back to the covenant between Abraham and his god. Judaism, Christianity, and Islam constitute this triad. Hinduism and Buddhism arose on the subcontinent of India, although Buddhism has a scant number of followers there now. Confucianism and Taoism are indigenous to China, although both philosophies have significantly influenced virtually all of East Asia. We turn first to a brief exploration of the interplay of the systems of religion and gender identity in the Abrahamic religions.

RELIGION AND GENDER IDENTITY

The Abrahamic Religions: Judaism, Christianity, Islam

Judaism Upon awakening each morning, the observant male Jew thanks God "that You did not make me a woman," while the Jewish female prays, "Thank you for having made me according to Your will" (Schneider, 1984, p. 34). Judaism is among the oldest patriarchal religions, tracing its formal history back to Abraham. Jewish law, however, is traced to Moses, who is believed to have received the Torah (the first five books of the Bible) from Yahweh, the god of the Hebrews, on a mountaintop in Sinai around 1250 BCE.

Although the Torah included the 613 laws which address virtually all aspects of Jewish life, practical interpretation of implementing the laws in daily life required the collective wisdom of the Talmud (the oral tradition), which is the basis for Halachah (The Way) as discussed in a previous chapter. Imbedded in the Halachah are the rules governing a woman's roles in the religious community as well as in her personal and family life. Commitment to these rules depends, of course, on the individual's level of observance, which tracks a continuum from ultra-Orthodox to Reform to non-observant. It is important to note that a Jew does have a choice in these levels and may decide at any point in her life that she prefers Conservative or Reform Judaism to Orthodox, or vice versa. However, insofar as she is a committed member of the community, her life will be regulated by laws which she has had no role in creating.

Halachic law is in many ways considerate of women, particularly in the area of female sexuality. Schneider (1984) reports that sex within marriage is a sacred act and the woman's willingness and satisfaction is paramount. She has a right to orgasm, and it is the man's obligation to bring this about (p. 203). On the other hand, the husband may not press his desires on his wife if she resists, and marital rape is both "a crime and a sin" (p. 203), as is intercourse while either partner is angry, unconscious, sleeping, or drunk (ibid.). Schneider reports the rabbis' claim that "women have a greater capacity and need for sex" [than men] and the husband whose work keeps him away from the marriage bed or fatigues him too much to perform once there, should change jobs (ibid).

Jewishness as such is traced through the mother, not the father; thus, her role as guarantor of the survival of the faith keeps her reproductive capacity in focus at all times. This focus is reinforced in the laws concerning adultery. If a married woman commits adultery, her husband must divorce her and can never remarry her (she has sinned against God). However, a man who has sex outside of marriage has committed adultery only if he has had sex with a married woman (Schneider, pp. 201–202).

Birth control is strictly the woman's responsibility, but she cannot choose
to stop having children without a rabbinical decision. "This is a far cry from
one of the nonnegotiable points of feminists: women have the right to full
control over the reproductive powers of their own bodies" (Schneider, 1994,
p. 227). Such paternalism is predictable, however, when one learns that in a
court of (Jewish) law, *bet din,* women are helpless dependents, "with hardly
more rights or status than a child" (p. 38).

As reported in a previous chapter, Jewish laws concerning abortion also
safeguard the woman, as opposed to the fetus. Here again, however, one won-
ders whether the potential for the mother's further pregnancies guides this
preference at some level.

In religious practice, women are not enjoined to pray at any particular
time, given that such a schedule might interfere with their childcare and
household responsibilities. This leniency sounds thoughtful; but, as Schneider
(1984) points out, in Halachic tradition, that which is necessary is placed
above that which is voluntary. Effectively, the nonobligatory nature of her
participation in communal religious activity marginalizes the woman while
sanctifying the "necessary" role of men (p. 60). Women have achieved considerable success in the Reform tradition, which now has more than one
hundred female rabbis. However, although the Reform tradition officially
agreed to accept women as rabbis in the 1840s, the first woman was actually
ordained in 1972—"when the host culture offered feminism," according to
anthropologist Riv-Ellen Prell (Schneider, p. 53).

While female cantors are quite common now in Reform congregations,
they still are not accepted in Orthodox and Conservative traditions. The
reasoning here reflects, again, concern with female sexuality—or perhaps
more to the point, men's lack of control over theirs. According to Talmud, a
woman's singing voice is sexually arousing to men, "as is her hair and leg," not
to mention her actual touch (which is forbidden to Orthodox men except
for women in his family). Again, woman is a sexual being from whose
enticements men cannot defend themselves.

Such sensitivity also guides women's attire among the Orthodox and more
strictly observant Jews of other traditions. She must wear long sleeved dresses,
opaque stockings, and (if married) a covering that conceals her hair in public
("because exposed hair equals nudity"). Schneider (1984) points out the irony
of women who cover their own hair with "gorgeous wigs" (p. 236).

Empowerment for Jewish women must come through the doors of
academia, according to Judith Hauptman, the first woman Ph.D. in Talmud,
cited in Schneider:

> Hauptman . . . who teaches Talmud at the Conservative movement's
> Jewish Theological Seminary, believes that learned women could look at the

sources and investigate issues of concern to women which have not until now attracted serious rabbinic attention. According to Hauptman, a decision about a religious issue is not based only on Halachah but also involves some personal bias . . . Therefore, she says, it is important for women to be involved in such decision-making, as scholars if not as rabbis (pp. 44–45).

Some movement in this direction is already apparent. A group of young educated Conservative women successfully lobbied the legislative branch of the Rabbinical Assembly to count women in the *minyan* (the ten adult Jews required for communal prayer or services), and to be called to the Torah (Schneider, 1984, pp. 46–47).

As Jewish women continue to excel in every profession, they may become less likely to accept reproduction as their primary responsibility. Many young Jewish women are deferring marriage and childbearing to later years, or are deciding against having children. Of major concern to Jews today is the tremendous rate of out-marrying. Men who marry non-Jewish women must convince them to convert lest their children be born outside the religion. Despite a fledgling initiative among Reform Jews to consider the patrimony of the child sufficient to consider the child Jewish, this is not acceptable to Orthodox and Conservative branches of Judaism. With memories of the Holocaust still vivid, the loss of even more Jews through non-Jewish matrilineage is an ominous threat to the future of the religion.

Christianity All Christians have in common a foundation in the New Testament, which adds twenty-seven books to the Jewish canon that is also accepted as the Old Testament. The Christian creed posits the Trinitarian nature of godhead (three persons in one god), the crucifixion, death, and resurrection of Jesus Christ who is believed to be the Son of God, and his role as judge at the end of time.

The status of women in Christianity is variously interpreted along the lines of literalness of interpretation. Two primary New Testament resources determine women's status (Old Testament sources are rarely cited as precedents for Christians). The four Gospels themselves recount activities and alleged sayings of Jesus during his three-year ministry. In these scriptures Jesus accepts women as disciples and followers, some (such as Mary Magdalene) having special significance. He also fosters their spiritual interests, as is most evident in his one-to-one conversation with Mary, sister of Martha and Lazarus, despite Martha's objections that she needed Mary's help in the kitchen (Luke 10:38–42). Hurley (1981) remarks on this interchange that, "Jesus was clearly not of the rabbis' opinion that women should hear but could not learn or that their only wisdom was with the spindle" (p. 89). Jesus accepts the concern and support of women throughout his ministry, and it is women who come to anoint his body in the tomb from which he had recently arisen following the crucifixion.

The other resource, which seems to be even more frequently used than the Gospels by fundamentalist Christians, is the considerable opus of Paul that makes up much of the New Testament. His letters to fledgling churches throughout the Mediterranean area are the documents to which many denominations return to anchor their gender definitions and behaviors. Paul never met Jesus, who was crucified before Paul had ever heard of him. In fact, Paul (originally Saul) was a rabbinical student who was intensely intolerant of The Way (as the first Christians called their movement) as a blasphemous Jewish anomaly.

Paul was a devout Jew, a rabbinical student, and had no opportunity to observe Jesus in his ministry as he interacted with women. Moreover, none of the Gospels had yet been written. Thus, it is no surprise that Paul's letters contain instructions for women that mirror Jewish attitudes and laws about the status of women. The "headship/submission" relationship of husband and wife is based on Paul's letter to the Ephesians (5:21–33), in which he advises wives to submit to their husbands as to the Lord, "For the husband is the head of the wife as Christ is the head of the church, his body, of which he is the Savior." Husbands are instructed to "love your wives just as Christ loved the church."

The issue of "headship" does not end with authority within marriage, but continues in 1 Corinthians (11:2–16) with the rationale for women's veiling of their own heads while praying. In a bald statement of woman's status and role in a fledgling Christianity, Paul insists:

> But I wish for you to understand that, while every man has Christ for his Head, woman's head is man, as Christ's Head is God. A man who keeps his head covered when he prays or prophesies brings shame on his head; a woman, on the contrary, brings shame on her head if she prays or prophesies bare-headed; it is as bad as if her head were shaved. If a woman is not to wear a veil she might as well have her hair cut off; but if it is a disgrace for her to be cropped and shaved, then she should wear a veil. A man has no need to cover his head, because man is the image of God, and the mirror of his glory, whereas woman reflects the glory of man. *For man did not originally spring from woman, but woman was made out of man; and man was not created for woman's sake, but woman for the sake of man; and therefore it is woman's duty to have a sign of authority on her head, out of regard for the angels* (1 Corinthians, 11:2–10; italics added).

Paul also forbids women to speak in meetings of the faithful, instructing them to take their questions to their husbands (their "heads") later on:

As in all congregations of God's people, women should not address the meeting. They have no license to speak, but should keep their place as the law directs. If there is something they want to know, they can ask their own husbands at home. It is a shocking thing that a woman should address the congregation (1 Corinthians, 14:33–35).

At no point in the Gospels does Jesus refer to a legal code for his followers; therefore, these notions had to have been imported from Paul's own Jewish underpinnings. Nonetheless, literalist-fundamentalist Christians follow these texts to the letter, in essence deferring Gospel Christianity to Pauline Christianity.

Groups which are most in line with strict obedience to Pauline injunctions are the Anabaptists (Amish, Mennonites, Hutterites), the Southern Baptists, Pentecostals, and Church of God. In Billson's (1995) study of several ethnic groups in her native Canada, she captured the spirit of Old Order Mennonite women's ready acceptance of the "headship" of men in the family and the church, as well as head coverings for women:

This culture highly values women's unique qualities and contributions. Although in terms of gender stratification women clearly rank below God and men, the religious principle of "headship" that defines a hierarchical order of God–Christ–Man–Woman also mandates men to consult their wives on important decisions (p. 207).

One woman explains to Billson:

I guess that's what our coverings are all about. Our veils are a sign that we believe in headship—first God, then man, then woman. Headship does not involve superiority. It's a line of authority that God has established for order in his family. You have to have some sort of line (p. 208).

Billson's (1995) study clearly suggests that Old Order Mennonite women distinguish between "authority" (which is male-oriented) and "influence" (which is the province of women). While at the end of the day any final decision is the province of the Mennonite male, his wife will have been brought into the discussion, her ideas weighed, and her perspective taken seriously. With the distribution of labor in communities that are primarily farm-based, equality in role evaluation is self-evident. Especially among more urban and less conservative Mennonites, women and men are considered virtual equals.

Not all women reared in Mennonite homes stay the course. A major advantage of adult baptism (which is what "Anabaptist" signifies), is that children are not asked to commit to the religion or the lifestyle until they are at least adolescents. Usually by 18 or 19 years of age (though sometimes later), the young person has had enough life experience in the tradition to make a conscious decision about her or his future. If they choose to opt out, there is sadness in the community, but the youth is not "shunned" or cast out. Given that this decision is freely made, Mennonite women resent the "outsider" definition of them as "oppressed women" (Billson,1995, p. 212).

Another woman, Judith, held back from full belief in the literalist version of scripture: "Those passages had a certain relevance in their time, and they still hold some truth—we have to respect them for what they were—but we still have to keep our cultural situation in mind. You can't bury your head in the sand" (Billson, 1995, p. 226–227). In the least conservative General Conference of Mennonites, women are taking positions at all levels in the church, including ordination. Billson remarks, "Old attitudes are changing, but slowly . . . "(p. 219).

Roman Catholicism dominates most of Europe and the southern Americas (including Mexico, Central America, and South America), as well as many of the Caribbean islands. As Burgos reports in her chapter on Hispanics, women's roles are centered in the home and in the church. The advent of menarche is the beginning of identity and true female status, for now the young woman has motherhood potential. As one Chicana (a Mexican American female) explained to Zavella:

> I was taught that it is very important to have a family and sacrifice for your family. You should get married because the husband will take care of you; he has to be the provider. You need to learn how to cook, sew, clean up the house and do all the chores, and especially make good food because that will give happiness to your husband. You've got to have children because that's your role in life, as a woman, is to have children. If you don't have children, nothing in life that you may do will be meaningful (Zavella, in Lancaster & di Leonardo, 1997, p. 398).

The sanctification of sacrifice and suffering is burned deeply into the socialization of Roman Catholic girls, who are constantly reminded of the suffering of the Mother of Christ. In fact, Mariology, or the extreme reverence (but not worship, as Protestants sometimes believe) for Mary is especially entrenched in Latina females, who are expected to emulate the Holy Virgin.

The Catholic Church's long-standing prohibition of all birth control measures except the rhythm method and abstinence virtually assures large families. In a previous chapter Burgos cites statistics indicating that the fertility rate for Hispanics in the United States is 50% higher than that of non-Hispanic women (1.8 births per woman). This is not necessarily a problem for men (whose sexual prowess is thereby documented) or for women (who are duly performing their social role). However, feeding, clothing, and educating many children is a hardship for families who may be subsisting at or below the poverty line.

Chicana Mirella Hernandez, one of Zavella's informants, may represent a new tone in Hispanic thinking as a younger generation sifts through and selects the elements of its traditional Mexican upbringing that it will keep:

> She has incorporated some of the teachings of her mother and the Catholic Church as guides for her behavior so that she would not be considered "easy"; this is one source of her self respect. But she also resisted her family's preoccupation with virginity and her mother's model of a traditional role within marriage. Now closer to economic stability herself, Mirella prefers a relationship with a man working towards a career, and she claims the right to her own sexual pleasure outside of marriage (Zavella, in Lancaster & di Leonardo, 1997, p. 398).

Christianity as a contributor to the construction of gender identity draws heavily on its Jewish roots in many cases, especially as it follows Pauline teachings. In the Gospels themselves, Roman Catholics are drawn to the archetypal icon of Mary as the appropriate model for women, Hispanic or non-Hispanic. Frequent alleged "visitations" and "apparitions" from Mexico to the former Yugoslavia, not to mention the ubiquitous "weeping Virgins" from statues, paintings, and even bank windows, draw thousands, evidence of the lasting impact of the Mother of God on Catholic and non-Catholic populations alike. There is, perhaps, a wistfulness in this, a nostalgic glance back to a simpler time in which one's intellect was more easily subordinated to one's faith.

Islam The very word "Islam" means "submission" (the root word in Arabic means "peace"), and a Muslim is "one who submits." Not only women, then, but men, too, are accustomed to the term, which refers to humankind's primal and rightful submission to the will of God. The youngest of the Abrahamic religions, Islam traces its roots to Ishmael, the son of Abraham through his wife's handmaiden, Hagar.

The revelator Muhammad, "God's Messenger," received the entire text of the Qur'an, or "Recitation," over a period of twenty-two years, beginning in 610 CE and ending at his death in 632 CE. Prior to and during Muhammad's life, the "period of ignorance" or *Jahiliyyah,* was marked in the Arabian peninsula by the isolation of desert tribal groups who led their flocks from one grazing area to another throughout the year. Each tribe had its own patron deity and was led by a headman who was selected for his ability to care for the extended family that comprised his clan. It was his responsibility to divide raided spoils equitably, to provide for widows and orphans, and to adjudicate disputations among the clan members. Girls were often considered a liability and were sometimes buried alive in the sand at birth. Women were male property and could be sold, abandoned, divorced, or neglected at the whim of their husbands.

As these bands of nomads (Bedouins) began to settle more permanently in the booming trade route nexus of Mecca, the values which helped them survive cohesively in the desert failed them. Mecca itself had no internal law, and the comparative anonymity achievable in the hectic streets of the city allowed tribal headmen to forget their responsibilities. Widows and orphans were neglected and abandoned. Cheating, stealing, drunken brawls, and "marriages" that did not last the night were common. It was to these issues that the Qur'an speaks dramatically and unconditionally, effectively creating a moral code in the place of chaos.

An orphan himself, Muhammad was keenly aware of the hardship and insecurity of such bereft children. His mother having been widowed while pregnant with him, the Prophet was also especially sensitive to the plight of women without male support. Much of the Qur'an, then, is in support of women and their protection. When engaged in warfare, many of Muhammad's comrades lost their lives, leaving widows with no kinship support. The Prophet himself married many of these women after the death of his first wife (and dearest friend) Khadija, in order to protect them from the devastation lone women faced in such a harsh and lawless environment. Far from being "oppressive" to women, the initial impulse of Islam was to elevate them to the status of full human beings with rights and obligations commensurate with those of men, but with additional protection *from* men. So it is with disbelief that many contemporary Arab women would observe their religion as portrayed by Western media, particularly as it addresses the alleged plight of Muslim females.

This is not to suggest in any way that Islam is not patriarchal, male dominant, and biased against full adult status for women. Nor is it the case that women have equal rights under the Shari'a (the Islamic law code) in marriage, child custody, or divorce. The Muslim woman may be strictly constrained in those areas. Nonetheless, these constraints are not epitomized by the *hijab,* the head-to-toe garment that many Muslim women wear in public, a symbol that draws the fire of Western feminists much more frequently than do the serious issues defined by Muslim women themselves.

Further, the "Arab World" is not monolithic. A wide range of application of Shari'a and concomitant opportunities exists. Tunisia, Syria, and Jordan exemplify the liberal end of the spectrum, which contrasts with the conservatism of Saudi Arabia. Other Arab countries occupy the mid-range as women's issues are advanced, then buried, then advanced again. While this restlessness frustrates the women of these countries, they and they alone know the pace at which they must move and the appropriate mechanisms to employ. The conflation of Western cultural (and often political) hegemony with Muslim women's rights has contaminated the entire topic for the Arab world, as Haddad and Smith explain:

Absolutely basic to the Islamist discourse is the rejection of the West and the conviction that "freedoms" enjoyed by Western women are among the key factors in the moral and ethical disintegration of Western societies . . . . Islamist women are deeply convinced that Western women are not only used and misled, but that they have lost their sense of pride and dignity and despite their feminist protestations are not happy in their circumstances. From their perspective, even the highly touted Western freedoms for women render them not free at all but deprived of healthy familial relationships and subject to sexual and other forms of exploitation. These freedoms have not liberated Western women who are still subject to the chauvinism of the males in Western society. They have in fact turned them into sexual objects (Haddad & Smith, in Sabbagh, 1996, p. 138). ["Islamist" is the term used to identify the contemporary trend toward more conservative Islamic behaviors.]

Further, Muslim women who appear to seek the same kinds of freedom as those apparently enjoyed in the West are considered outside their culture, "misguided or even traitorous," and a source of shame for their families (Haddad & Smith, in Sabbagh, 1996, p. 139).

Although the Qur'an demands equal accountability to God for both men and women (ontologically, at least, their souls are at the same level), and the Shari'a provides for legal equality for Muslim men and women, the reality is that Muslim women (like those most everywhere) are considered primarily in their role as mothers and wives. As women, they are subject to the successive authorities of father, husband, and adult sons. In courts of law, the testimony of two women is equivalent to that of one man. (In Judaism, by contrast, women are not allowed to testify or be witnesses at all.) They receive only half of the inheritance portion allotted to their brothers, can divorce only with the greatest difficulty, and lose custody of their children to their father in any divorce action (which is relatively simple for men in most Arab countries). These prerogatives are grounded in Shari'a law.

Traditionally, Muslim women gained power only through motherhood, which followed close on the heels of a very early marriage. The legal age for marriage in most Muslim countries is 15, with the legal age in Iran at 13 for girls. Yet the current trend toward much later marriages throughout the area is creating a different picture of the Muslim woman, as Mernissi (1996) reports:

The idea of an adolescent unmarried woman is a completely new idea in the Muslim world, where previously you had only a female child and a menstruating woman who had to be married off immediately so as to prevent dishonorable engagement in premarital sex. The whole concept of patriarchal honor was built around the idea of virginity, which reduced a woman's role to its sexual dimension: to reproduction within early marriage. The concept of an adolescent woman, menstruating and unmarried, is so alien to the entire Muslim family system that it is either unimaginable or necessarily linked to *fitna* (social disorder). The Arab countries are a good example of this demographic revolution in sex roles (Mernissi, in Sabbagh, 1996, p. 166).

Even as some Islamic countries are turning toward more conservative interpretations of shari'a or are trading secular governments for national Islamic law (as Pakistan is doing at this writing), others are embracing universal education for all children and opening doors to unprecedented employment opportunities for women. With hundreds of thousands of Muslim women now attending universities throughout the region and earning degrees in medicine, law, engineering, architecture, education, and the social sciences, their economic options are no longer automatically tied to men. Just as importantly, their prestige as women is no longer tied exclusively to their wombs. On the reverse side, men find that they, too, need longer periods of higher education and are having to defer marriage until they can successfully support a family. As women are increasingly involved in the shaping of the new Arab world, the net result is marriage at older ages, female financial emancipation, less assurance that men can effectively dominate their wives (or sisters or mothers), and a move toward political parity.

So, why the *hijab*? Why are some of the most economically and educationally advantaged women in the Arab world freely burying their bodies in yards of dusky cloth? On their own report, it to preserve their own right to the privacy of their bodies, and to be able to move with relative freedom in the meandering mainstream of Arab culture:

> It is a feminism true to its society's traditions; these are women who choose to identify in Islamic terms and developed a consciousness that is Islamic in character. Their Islamic dress, so mystifying and misunderstood in the West, is in fact an anti-consumer claim for their right to modesty, to control of their own bodies, to sexual space and moral privacy (El Guindi, in Sabbagh, 1996, p. 161).

The conceptualization of women in the Muslim world is changing dramatically at all levels of society. Despite desperate attempts to reverse the wheels and halt women's transformation, there is a sense of inevitability in it all. Mernissi says it best:

> [W]henever one has to define oneself to others, whenever one has to define one's identity, one is on the shaky ground of self-indulging justifications. For example, the need for Muslims to claim so vehemently that they are traditional, and that their women miraculously escape social

change and the erosion of time, has to be understood in terms of their need for self-representation and must be classified not as a statement about daily behavioral practices, but rather as a psychological need to maintain a minimal sense of identity in a confusing and shifting reality (Mernissi, in Sabbagh, 1996 p. 162).

Despite locally successful attempts to revoke women's rights (note the Taliban movement in Afghanistan), the weight of education leans heavily on the side of ultimate gender redefinition for and by women in the Arab world. But it will be accomplished their way, within the context of their religion, their families, their political structures, and their own reconstruction of sexual identity.

The Asian Religions: The Hindu, Buddhist, and Confucian Traditions

The Hindu Traditions of India It is said that when boys are born to Hindu families, there are great celebrations. When a girl is born, the family claims "Nothing has happened." While that has been true for a great many centuries of the long history of civilization on the Indian subcontinent, it was not always true, and not ever true in some parts of this enormous land mass. The south of India, Kerala for example, has been dominated for as long as anyone knows by matriarchal peoples. The Aryan invaders who insinuated themselves into the Indus region and had become culturally dominant by 1500 BCE brought with them their pantheon of male sky gods as well as an incipient social structure that ultimately resulted in a caste system.

As the Aryan hegemony congealed into an organized political structure, the caste (varna) system developed, with the Brahmin (priest, landowner) at the top, followed by the Kshatriya (warrior, landowner, administrator), Vaishya (merchant, land owner) and Shudra (laborers). The latter were primarily the indigenous peoples who were conquered and economically displaced by the invaders.

The caste system became increasingly top-heavy with power and wealth, with Brahmins and Kshatriyas amassing most of the land and its productivity, albeit on the backs of the Shudra laborers. Loath to relinquish these perquisites, a marriage system was devised to assure the perpetuation of wealth in the same caste. In this patriarchal, patrilocal society, sons inherited land, while daughters, who moved to their husbands' families, were given dowries. To guarantee that the caste bloodline had not been sullied by any indiscretion on the part of the woman, she was married off well before attaining puberty, sometimes as an infant, usually to a much older male whom she had never seen.

Reinforcing the fact that she belonged utterly to her husband, the woman was forbidden to remarry after his death (which, given the age difference, could have occurred while she was still a child) (Kinsley, 1993, p. 144) and was encouraged to immolate herself on his funeral pyre as a sign of her utter devotion. This was the phenomenon of *sati,* the final definitive act of a woman brought up to value "husband worship," which, along with producing male offspring, was her entire reason for being.

Over the centuries the higher castes, especially the Brahmin, reacted to any threat to their power (read "wealth") with increasingly restrictive constraints on their women, ultimately imposing complete seclusion within the household. (Notably, these restrictions applied only to the uppermost caste because the lower castes needed their women to help in the daily drudgery of field work and cottage industries such as basket-making. Nor were their bloodlines so vulnerable to "contamination" that they needed to impose the safeguards that were required for upper-caste women.)

Upper caste women have long been able to receive some sort of education at home or in private convent schools. While the young women themselves wanted education for its own sake, their fathers saw it pragmatically, as enhancing her marriage opportunity—higher prestige for the groom and his family. However, in this sex-segregated society, women professionals were also needed to provide education and health care to other women in strictly female environments. Since these occupations were seen to be "natural" for women, teaching and medicine soon became logical disciplines for them to pursue, which in turn opened the doors to other positions such as highly prestigious government service.

As Liddle and Joshi (1986) point out, "caste" concerns massive groups of people *as* groups. Over many decades, it is possible for a subcaste to raise itself to a higher level within the caste, taking all individuals within it along. "Class," on the other hand, is an individual phenomenon, based on personal merit as indicated by high-status occupations and accompanying compensation. While "caste" carries its own prestige for the group, "class" has come to provide individual families with prestige when one of their own, son or daughter, is recognized (socially and financially) as outstanding in a high-status professional arena. As more women are educated abroad, bringing Ph.Ds and impeccable credentials back home, they achieve their long awaited independence from patriarchal rule at both the familial and the bureaucratic levels.

As long as women were fettered by the dual chains of economic dependency on fathers and husbands and by absolute control over their sexuality, they lived at the mercy of ancient and often brutal systems over which they had no control. They were defined exclusively as instruments of reproduction for the benefit of male power and prestige. Again we see the direct path from consciousness to education, to meaningful employment, to financial independence, to power, and to final autonomy. Now, a tiny fraction of the women of India are able to participate personally in this redefinition of gender. Nonetheless, the consciousness is wakeful and watchful.

Buddhism   When Buddhism arose in India in the sixth century BCE, Brahmanic power was at its height. While the Hindu legal codes prohibited women and shudras from learning the scriptures, prevented "polluting" women from ritual participation, and restricted the activities of all castes to severely circumscribed roles, Buddhism and Jainism (which predates even Buddhism) offered antidotes to these exclusions.

Even as it carried much of the patriarchal baggage from Hinduism with it, Buddhism rejected many of its tenets, including the Vedas, the gods (who are inferior to the enlightened Buddhas), the caste system, and the exclusion of women. It is said that the Buddha's own wife came to him after his enlightenment and he accepted her as the first Buddhist nun. Indeed, alongside many centuries of Buddhist monks, there has been a strong tradition of women who dedicated themselves to the Buddhist spiritual life, especially if they were widowed or chose not to marry. There were more rules for nuns than for monks in their respective orders, but at least women were included in the religious community as such.

Women's ideal demeanor, however, is clearly articulated in a story in which the Buddha instructs an "unruly" young wife from a wealthy family on the seven types of wives.

> The executioner wife was pitiless and corrupt, a prostitute. The thief robbed her husband of his gains. The lazy gossip and shrew with loud voice was a mistress. The mother-wife cared for her husband and his possessions as she would for an only son. The sister-wife behaved like a younger sister to an elder. The companion-wife behaved as the term would indicate, as a companion. The slave-wife endured all things, remaining calm and pure in heart, and obedient. The last four kinds of wife would, at death, wander in a heavenly world. Sujata said that she would be the seventh kind. . . .   The Buddha did not refuse her request to be taught (Saddhatissa, 1987, p. 122).

The Three Vehicles of Buddhism represent the three paths, or denominations, that a Buddhist can track. Theravada Buddhism, or the Wisdom of the Elders, was the first and considers itself the most orthodox. Nearly all males become monks for some period of their lives.

Mahayanists, followers of the "Great Vehicle," arose approximately one hundred years before the common era and interpreted the Buddha's life itself as one enormous act of compassion, as evidenced by his remaining in physical form for 45 years to teach after he achieved enlightenment, the point at which he could have released the body and gone into utter extinction, which is the state of paranirvana.

Vajrayana Buddhism was exported from India to Tibet in the tenth century and built upon the Mahayana and the Theravadin traditions. Its key embellishment is the emphasis on visualization of deities who can facilitate the enlightenment process.

Wherever Buddhism was accepted, it melded with the culture of the people. Thus, it is not wise to generalize about the status of women from the purely religious (supercultural) perspective to the parochial realities of their lives as lived. Even though the status of women in Buddhism is nearly as high as that of men from an ideal perspective (since being human at all indicates great merit from past lives), the male form implies even better karma than the female human. In the countries where Buddhism has been and continues to be practiced, it is clear that women are subject to the same patriarchal dominance and sexual management as they tend to be everywhere, religion notwithstanding.

When an interest in Buddhism surfaced in the United States in the 1960s, American women would have little of the second-class status often accepted by women in the East. Zen Buddhism, which is officially in the Mahayana tradition but is radically austere in comparison to the more popular temple-based denominations, was open to women as well as men from its earliest days on the West coast. At this time, many Asian-American as well as Anglo women have assumed high leadership roles in Mahayana organizations across the country; further, the Vajrayana tradition attracts as many women as men to its teaching posts, requiring an intense three-year, uninterrupted retreat. Women are being ordained and are opening their own retreat and teaching centers in the United States and in Canada. While the most esteemed teachers in this tradition are still Tibetan natives, they treat women with the same high regard and respect as they do men. Whether this egalitarian posture translates back to the Eastern cultures from whence Buddhism was launched to the West remains to be seen.

Confucianism and the Yin/Yang Dyad Confucius (Kung Fu-Tze) set out in sixth century BCE China to design a system which would assure civility and harmony in human society. The period in which he lived was fraught with the barbarism and brute force of local rulers whose lordship over feudal lands was based on hereditary power, unjust laws, and fierce punishments. They were unguided by principle and unratified by merit. Reflecting on an earlier age when rulership was based on morality and values, Confucius sought to redirect society toward a foundation grounded in virtue.

Confucianism is not a religion, then, but a philosophy of social relations, although temples to the great teacher abound and Japanese school children salute his teachings each day. The philosophy is humanistic and utterly grounded in the natural world. (According to his students, Confucius refused to speculate on the supernatural.) (Chan, 1963, p. 36). The reason this thought system is included in a section on religion and gender identity lies in the overwhelming impact Confucianism has had on the relative statuses of and interactions between the sexes for literally billions of people throughout East and Southeast Asia over 2500 years.

There are five relationships requiring particular order, or ritual: those between husband and wife, between father and son, between older friend and younger friend, between teacher and pupil, and between ruler and subject. The latter term in each dyad is by definition positioned in a deferential mode to the former. Through the ultimate standardization of terms of address and appropriate behaviors in each of these dyads, relationships were assured of maximum civility, harmony, and predictability. But in any relationship, deference (even servility in many cases) to one's superior became routine. The bowing we observe among most East Asian peoples is a demonstration of deference, as is the wife's soft-spoken manner with her husband.

Confucianism is not the sole support for East Asian thought. Although males are clearly superior to females in the Confucian model, deeper currents run through the supernatural presuppositions of pre-Confucian times. These are based on the primordial female/male dyad of Yin/Yang, whose dynamic equilibrium lies at the core of cosmic harmony and permeates both the natural and supernatural realms. Yin is all things female, dark, moist, passive, regressive. Yang is the antithesis—male, light, dry, active, aggressive. We note that these characteristics are neither "evil" nor "good." Rather, each has its place in the eternal equation. The implications for family life are poignantly expressed by the great-aunt of Pang-Mei Natasha Chang, an American of Chinese descent who interviewed her great-aunt during her eighth decade.

> I already told you that a woman is nothing in China. Now I will tell you why. People pass from the Light World to the Shadow World when they die. The Shadow World is female, Yin, the negative essence, the moon, and all things passive and deep. The Light World is male, yang, Positive Essence, the sun, and all things strong and high.

> You might think it unfair, but only males—sons, grandsons, great-grandsons and all in unending succession—have the proper elements of the Light World in order to care for ancestors in the Shadow World. Caring correctly for the ancestors and maintaining the balance between the two worlds is very important. Otherwise, the dead will leave the Shadow World and invade the Light World as lonely ghosts. We women can only assure our places in both the Light World and the Shadow World by providing male descendants for our husbands' families (Chang, 1996, p. 91).

This goes far in explaining both the inferiority of females and the necessity for males in a culture that believes ancestors are at the mercy of their living male heirs for their sustenance. Maxine Hong Kingston (1994) reports that her grandfather would glare at her and her sister and female cousins and spit, "Maggots! Where are my grandsons? I want grandsons! Give me grandsons! Maggots!" (p. 191). She also recalls her parents' shame when walking with her and her sister in the streets of China Town in San Francisco, when passing Chinese couples would say, "Oh, a girl . . . and then another girl," shaking their heads (p. 46). Other "proverbs" concerning girls that Kingston remembers include: "Feeding girls is feeding cowbirds." "There is no profit in raising girls. Better to raise geese than girls." "When you raise girls, you're raising children for strangers" (p. 46). This level of social pressure for male children may be based not only on the obvious benefits of wealth consolidation in the natural world, but *also* on the long, long, sojourn in the world beyond.

In Hinduism women can overcome their status through education and successful employment. By contrast, Chinese women have historically been unable to compensate for their essential Yin nature.

EDUCATION AND EMPLOYMENT:
TICKETS TO AUTONOMY

In many of the cultures examined above, women have overcome, or are in the process of overcoming, the economic and sexual constraints which have prevented them from exercising critical choices about their lives. They are learning to name and actualize their own goals, transcending the valid but not always consummate yearnings of motherhood and domesticity. The issue is not whether women are dedicating their lives to their homes and families (which has become a source of apologetic embarrassment for women who feel criticized about this role), but whether they have had the opportunity to make this choice freely. The long road from second-class gender status, wherever and in whatever mode it exists, to autonomy and self-definition would seem to begin with education.

Jewish women are encouraged to become Talmudic or Halachic scholars in order to influence decisions that impact women. Arabic and Indian women are using their respective religious systems, which often require separate educational and health care facilities for males and females, to justify their entry into high-status, high-salary professions, which assure them role equivalency to men. They are creating a new paradigm within which they are redefining what it "means" to be a woman. The most interesting aspect of this development is that they are creating this paradigm within the very framework that would exclude them!

A CLOSING THOUGHT

Fifty years ago Simone de Beauvoir came close to apologizing for bringing up the tired issue of "woman": "Enough ink has been spilled in the quarreling over feminism, *now practically over,* and perhaps we should say no more about it" (de Beauvoir, p. xiii; italics added). Half a century later, peering across the threshold of a new millennium, it is clear that she need not have defended *The Second Sex,* her seminal and exhaustive work on the female condition.

Situated in the very heart of the early-to-mid-twentieth century French literati (who included her own consort, existentialist Jean-Paul Sartre, as well as phenomenologist Merleau-Ponty and anthropologist Levi-Strauss), Ms. de Beauvoir's formidable intellect was nourished by the most innovative philosophical and anthropological theories of post-modern Europe. As such, she could not escape confrontation with the purported ontological "necessity" of woman's subjugation to man, nor with the obligatory sociopolitical-anthropological question, "Why?".

The same foundational questions continue to exercise feminists today. However, as the preceding chapters attest (and as this chapter has advanced), the issues surrounding women are no longer strictly the province of the intelligentsia of either sex. The streets and paths of the world have become conscious, perhaps self-conscious, of the sociocultural construction of gender identity.

Perhaps at no time in history has this dynamic ambiguity been more pronounced than it is now. Radical innovations in global information gathering and dissemination assure education to virtually anyone on the planet — even developing countries have fax machines and access to the Internet in their larger cities. Technological advances often obviate the need for labor-intensive subsistence and maintenance, calling into question both the need for large families and for home-bound wives. Biological discoveries could eventually reduce males to supernumeraries in species reproduction (herds of identical cattle have already been produced through genetic engineering). The notion of "family" itself is increasingly challenged as "blended" step-configurations, same-sex couples with their biological or adopted children, single-parent households, multigenerational kin groups, and polygamous co-wife models assert their ability to nurture just as competently as the so-called "nuclear" family paradigm in the West. With our traditional "identities," our statuses and roles, unraveling before our eyes, we do not face this new world bravely, but with hesitation, confusion, even fear. The Chinese character for "change" combines the ideographs "danger" and "opportunity," apt symbols for our contemporary historical nexus. There *are* dangers. One lies in clutching desperately to dysfunctional but familiar constructs, which may be defended fiercely and oppressively by their major stakeholders. Another danger lies in discarding traditional elements through infatuation with a premature reconceptualization of gender identity—elements that are, in fact, intrinsically or extrinsically valuable. Yet another danger is the peremptory imposition of "acceptable" models of gender identity and roles by the currently dominant feminists of the United States. As we have noted, such unsolicited models are neither meaningful nor welcome to millions of women around the world who choose to create their own agendas to meet their self-identified needs and aspirations.

Even with such caveats in mind, the opportunities implicit in the contemporary situation are manifold. To define oneself is the ultimate perquisite of autonomy. Yet, paradoxically, autonomy does not occur in a vacuum. It dances with the ineluctable "Other" in shaping the contours of life-as-lived and would-be-lived. Freedom manifests in the *choice* one has in selecting one's role in relationship to Other, and in setting goals and boundaries for one's life that cannot be abridged by Other. Painful though it may be for some feminists to conclude that their sisters are making poor choices about these relationships, goals, and boundaries (inasmuch as some of these may appear to be restrictive, oppressive, or self-abnegating), the operative condition is *choice*. If such decisions appear to be thinly-veiled capitulations to dominant constructs, it behooves us to remember that the most radical among us pick our battles, and that our battles themselves have been fought in open fields for a modest fragment of time. And it may even be that, for these women, the choice is indeed freely made. As a psychological concept, autonomy itself is a uniquely Western one.

Change itself takes on different values in various cultural settings. Some, such as the Amish and to some extent Appalachians, tend to be past-oriented, accepting change only slowly and carefully after weighing the possible gain against the definite loss. In mainstream American culture, change is seen as a constant to be enfolded into our lives with enthusiasm. We expect it, generally welcome it, and track it through time as a measure of our progress. We often assume that newcomers to our country or cities, or established ethnic groups within them, should have the same readiness to embrace the novel. Having returned to the roots of a few different cultural and religious systems around the world, perhaps we can more readily appreciate the embeddedness of resistance to change and applaud the women who in their own way and within their own social structures are "pushing the envelope."

As social science professionals, it is important to recognize the multiple barriers often confronting women from cultural and ethnic subsystems. What are the circumstances of their home lives? What are the expectations that surround them in their nuclear and extended families? What is their status relative to men? What have been their opportunities for education and financial independence? Who gets blamed when women are abused? What are their *real* options in such cases? Are women in these cultures and ethnicities allowed to have personal goals above and beyond those set for them by their religions, their families, and their social systems? Awareness of difference is the first step in the program of cultural competence. The successful professional will have learned to discover, acknowledge, validate, honor, and work within the context of those differences.

REFERENCES

Billson, J. M. (1995). *Keepers of culture: the power of tradition in women's lives.* New York: Lexington Books.

Bouvoir, S., de (1952). *The second sex.* (trans. H.M. Parshley). New York: Alfred A. Knopf.

Chan, W-T. (1963). *A sourcebook in Chinese philosophy.* Princeton, NJ: Princeton University Press.

Chang, P-M. N. (1996). *Bound feet and western dress.* New York: Doubleday.

Guindi, F., el (1996). Feminism Comes of Age in Islam. In S. Sabbagh (Ed.), *Arab women, between defiance and restraint* (pp. 159–161). New York: Olive Branch Press.

Hurley, J. B. (1981). *Man and woman in Biblical perspective.* Grand Rapids, MI: Zondervan Publishing House.

Kingston, M. H. (1994). *The woman warrior: Memoirs of a girlhood among ghosts.* New York: Alfred A. Knopf.

Kinsley, D. R. (1993). *Hinduism, a cultural perspective* (2nd ed.). Englewood Cliffs, NJ: Prentice-Hall.

Lancaster, R. N., & di Leonardo, M. (Eds.) (1997). *The gender/sexuality reader: culture, history, political economy.* New York: Routledge.

Liddle, J., & Joshi, R. (1986). *Daughters of independence: gender, caste and class in India.* London: Zed Books.

Mernissi, F. (1996). Muslim women and fundamentalism. In S. Sabbagh (Ed.), *Arab women, between defiance and restraint* (pp. 162–168). New York: Olive Branch Press.

Sandmel, S. (Ed.). (1976). *New English Bible with the Apocrypha.* London: Oxford University Press.

Sabbagh, S. (Ed.). (1996). *Arab women, between defiance and restraint.* New York: Olive Branch Press.

Saddhatissa, H. (1987). *Buddhist ethics: the path to nirvana.* London: Wisdom Publications.

Schneider, S. W. (1984). *Jewish and female: choices and changes in our lives today.* New York: Simon and Schuster.

Zavella, P. (1997). Playing with fire: the gendered construction of Chicana/Mexicana sexuality. In R. N. Lancaster & M. di Leonardo (Eds.), *The gender/sexuality reader: culture, history, political economy* (pp. 392–408). New York: Routledge.

Index